MATHEMATICAL CRYPTOLOGY
FOR COMPUTER SCIENTISTS
AND MATHEMATICIANS

Mathematical Cryptology

for
Computer Scientists and Mathematicians

WAYNE PATTERSON

Department of Computer Science
University of New Orleans

ROWMAN & LITTLEFIELD
Publishers

ROWMAN & LITTLEFIELD

Published in the United States of America in 1987
by Rowman & Littlefield, Publishers
(a division of Littlefield, Adams & Company)
81 Adams Drive, Totowa, New Jersey 07512

Library of Congress Cataloging-in-Publication Data

Patterson, Wayne, 1945–
   Mathematical cryptology.

   Bibliography: p. 287
   Includes index.
   1. Cryptography.   I. Title.
   Z103.P35   1987   652'.8   86-13117
   ISBN 0-8476-7438-X

   American Mathematical Society categories:
   94A60 (Cryptography); 11T71 (Coding Theory)

87   89   91   90   88

1   3   5   4   2

Printed in the United States of America

Contents

Chapter 8   **Other Security Problems, 115**

Tables

Figures

Acknowledgments

I would like to thank Rowman & Littlefield for their assistance in publishing this work. In particular, I thank Paul Lee for his work as editor, and Martyn Hitchcock for assistance in production design. Thanks also are due to my colleague Rod Cooper for his valuable comments, and to my students at the University of New Orleans for comments made in Computer Science 4990. John Vassilopoulos aided in the translation from the Greek. Clara Jaramillo provided one of the Pascal programs. Figure 1.4 was adapted from a digitization of a photograph originally published in *The Enigma War*, by Josef Garlinski, for Scribner's.

This book was prepared in camera-ready fashion on an Apple LaserWriter printer. The text and graphics were prepared on an Apple Macintosh computer using Microsoft Word text processing software, and (Apple) MacDraw and MacPaint, (Enabling Technologies) Easy3D, and (Microsoft) Chart for graphics.

All of the programs have been run using the Apple Macintosh Pascal interpreter, and in very slightly modified form using the Digital Equipent Corporation VAX Pascal compiler. Since all of the programs were written in ISO Standard Pascal, they should run as well under any standard Pascal compiler.

This book is perhaps the first computer science text to use this remarkable "desktop publishing" concept developed by the Apple Corporation.

*   *   *

I would like to dedicate this work to my parents, Ralph and Mary Patterson, and also to my friend Savanah Williams.

Wayne Patterson
New Orleans, Louisiana, USA

Symbols

«K, M, C, T»	Cryptosystem
M	Message space
M_n	Message space of n-bit strings
K	Key space
C	Ciphertext space
T	Family of encryption transformations
Σ	Alphabet
$\sum$	Summation
$\subseteq$	Set inclusion
$\subset$	Proper subset
$\times$	Cartesian product
$\rightarrow$	Mapping
$\mapsto$	Is mapped to
$\leftrightarrow$	Is interchanged with
$\circ$	Composition of functions
$\forall$	Universal quantifier ("for every")
$\exists$	Existential quantifier ("there exists")
.ꓱ.	Such that
$\in$	Set membership
$\notin$	Set non-membership
$\equiv$	Congruence
$\prod$	Repeated product
!	Factorial
$\approx$	Is approximately equal to
|	(a) Such that (set notation)
	(b) Divides (integers)
$\nmid$	Does not divide
$\oplus$	(a) Exclusive-or (of booleans)

	(b) Direct sum (of groups or vector spaces)
A^c	(a) Set complement of A
	(b) Boolean complement of A
S_M or $S(M)$	Symmetric group of M
A_M or $A(M)$	Alternating group of M
$O(f)$	Big-Oh of the function f
$\cup$	Union
$\cap$	Intersection
$[x]$	Smallest integer greater than x
$[[x]]$	Greatest integer smaller than x
$\mathbb{Z}$	The set of integers
$\mathbb{Q}$	The set of rational numbers
$\mathbb{N}$	The set of natural numbers
$\mathbb{R}$	The set of real numbers
$\mathbb{R}^n$	n-dimensional real vector space
$\mathbb{C}$	The set of complex numbers
$\mathbb{Z}_n$	The set of integers (modulo n)
$\cdot$	Multiplication
GCD or gcd	Greatest common divisor
ϕ	Euler ϕ-function or totient
$\varnothing$	Empty set
$\begin{pmatrix} a \\ b \end{pmatrix}$	Jacobi symbol of the pair a, b
$C(m,n)$	Combinations of m things n at a time
det	Determinant
$\cdot$	Dot product (of vectors)
$\Leftrightarrow$	If and only if
$\Rightarrow$	Implies
$\Leftarrow$	Is implied by
Q.E.D.	Quod erat demonstrandum (end of proof)
abs	Absolute value
$|v|$	Length of the vector v
$|x|$	Absolute value of the number x
$|G|$	Order of the group G
$\log_n$	Logarithm to the base n
$\sqrt{\ }$	Square root
$d_H(X,Y)$	Hamming distance between X and Y
Z_n	Set of n-bit strings

C	Coset
GF(p,n)	Galois field of order p^n
$\mu(n)$	Möbius function of n
A^T	Transpose of the matrix A
♠	Spades
♣	Clubs
♦	Diamonds
♥	Hearts
~	Is equivalent to
<G, ·>	Group G with operation ·
≤	(a) Is a subgroup of (in group theory)
	(b) Less than or equal to (real numbers)
«g»	Group generated by g
index(G:H)	Index of subgroup G in H
QR(n)	Quadratic residue set of n
QNR(n)	Quadratic non-residue set of n
«R, + , ·»	Ring R with operations + and ·
«F, + , ·»	Field F with operations + and ·
R[x]	Ring of polynomials over ring R
F[x]	Integral domain of polynomials over field F
dim[A:B]	Dimension of the vector space A over B
≅	Is equivalent to or is isomorphic to

Introduction

The subject of cryptology, although in one form or another an area of interest throughout much of recorded history, has been given a new impetus with the explosion of high-speed communications over computer networks of varying complexity.

Whereas at one time the uses of "secret writing" were principally in aid of military communications, today the sheer volume of information being transmitted and processed demands that better and better methods of making information secure be researched and developed.

Two of the most noticeable applications in this field are unnoticed by the average person, but present nonetheless: the encryption of cable television signals (such as HBO's) being sent to and received from a satellite, and the encryption of messages in the new international banking networks such as Cirrus.

As an academic subject, cryptology has tended to fall between the cracks. Although it is a subject necessary for the overall study of computer communications and computer security, it usually makes only a brief appearance in the computer science curriculum. And further, it does not often find its way into the mathematics curriculum.

My purpose in writing this book has been twofold: First, I wish to encourage the systematic study of cryptology, in either the context of computer science or of mathematics, and by producing one reference book that both introduces and specializes on the topic, rather than discussing other aspects of computer security, I hope to provide such encouragement.

Second, for persons already having a working knowledge of cryptology, I wanted to provide a source for the discussion of many contemporary results, essentially up to the beginning of 1986. Most of the other works now available seem to have been written prior to some very interesting developments of the last three to four years.

Why have I chosen *Mathematical Cryptology* as the title of this book? There is a point to be made, in that in order to achieve a contemporary understanding of the field, it is surely necessary to pass comfortably from one branch of mathematics to another: abstract algebra, number theory, logic, and complexity theory are all useful now in cryptology; and combinatorial group theory, finite fields, coding theory, projective geometry, or topology may all come into play in the near future.

Consequently, for the computer scientist, this is an indication of subjects which may be necessary to develop. I have attempted to address this need by providing five appendices as introductions (of varying degrees of difficulty) on separate mathematical topics: Modular Arithmetic, Group Theory, Number Theory, Computational Complexity, and Galois Field Theory.

The mathematicians studying cryptology should also become familiar with a number of subjects in computer science: structured programming in a high-level language (I have used *Pascal* throughout this book, to the chagrin of several of my colleagues, who feel, as I do, that Pascal is now outdated for many purposes - nevertheless, it remains as almost a universal language for anyone studying computer science); data structures; data communications and computer networks. I have not addressed any of these subjects in this book, but interested readers will undoubtedly be able to find many references on these subjects in any computer science section of a good library or bookstore.

It should perhaps be noted here that I have collected all of the Pascal code in a single appendix at the end of the book.

The arrangement of the chapters follows this plan of attack:

In the first chapter, I try to give a brief summary of some of the important cryptologic methods throughout history. Historical interest provides one justification; another is that some of these methods have become components of modern-day methods. A common factor in all these methods is that communications took place primarily using "paper-and-pencil"; and cryptanalytic attacks likewise.

The second chapter develops the Data Encryption Standard, or DES. DES is undoubtedly the most widely used computer-based encryption system in the world today, at least among those systems of which there is any public knowledge. Recent announcements by the United States Government, however, along with recent developments in the cryptanalysis of the DES, have cast doubts on its viability beyond 1987.

The third chapter discusses a fundamental difficulty in the use of the DES, namely the problem of exchanging keys, or *key management;* and describes a paradigm for the development of cryptosystems which eliminates the problem of key management. This is the model for the so-called *public-key cryptosystem*, or PKC.

In the fourth chapter, we begin the quest to find satisfactory PKCs. We are first led to a problem known as the *knapsack problem,* which in its most prosaic form reads: Suppose I have n objects of differing weights, w_i, and suppose I have a knapsack that can carry W pounds. What subset(s) of the n objects can I load into the knapsack for a trip?

The solutions to this problem indeed lead to the development of a PKC, as we shall see. Chapter four discusses numerous variations on the original Merkle-Hellman, or *knapsack,* PKC.

Chapter five introduces another mathematical problem which turns out to be suitable for the development of PKCs, namely the difficulty of factoring large (i.e. $\approx$ 200-digit) integers.

This approach has led to the best-known, and to date most secure, PKC, namely the Rivest-Shamir-Adelman, or *RSA,* public-key cryptosystem.

The sequence of the chapters, to a great extent, models the chronological development of the subject. This it was that in 1983, both the knapsack and RSA cryptosystems were being analyzed. In a series of papers, first Shamir, then Lagarias and Odlyzko, then Brickell, showed how, under various assumptions, knapsack cryptosystems could be "broken" or cryptanalyzed. Consequently, chapter six is devoted to discussing these efforts and is entitled "Breaking Knapsacks".

After the work of Merkle-Hellman and Rivest-Shamir-Adelman in proposing PKCs, a number of other researchers were led to different models for public-key cryptosystems. The seventh chapter provides a survey of several other of these methods. Among these are one due to McEliece, using error-correcting codes; further knapsack methods by Cooper-Patterson and Chor-Rivest; and a method using combinatorial group theory by Wagner.

With the exception of the Chor-Rivest PKC, these have been found to be either impractical or insecure.

In the eighth chapter, a number of problems are presented involving information security, that are related to the standard problem of cryptography. Perhaps the most important of these problems is the *authentication problem:* can a system be devised to enable the verification that a message alleged to come from a given sender, actually came from that person.

Of course, throughout the history of communication, authentication has usually been achieved by the analysis of handwritten signatures. In a digital computer network, however, only bits will be transmitted; a handwritten signature would not be feasible.

Other problems discussed in this chapter are: the "oblivious transfer" problem; protocols for conducting a coin flip by telephone; a protocol for playing "mental poker"; a method for sharing a secret among any k of a set of n people; one-way encryption functions; and a protocol for multiple-key encryption in data base systems.

The ninth chapter deals with the current attempt, by the International Standards Organization (Working Group on Public Key Cryptosystems and Applications), to define standards for PKCs. I have quoted extensively from the first Annual Report (1985) of this Working Group.

The final chapter of the book discusses renewed efforts in 1985 to cryptanalyze the DES. Although, at the time of this writing, no one has announced a cryptanalysis of the DES, nevertheless there seems to be momentum gathering in the attempt to provide such a result.

It should be noted that the contents of this book and its organization very much reflect the author's own observations about important developments in this field. There are many, many more important results which, by the author's own decision, were left out of this book. Recall that in part this work was meant to be an introduction to the field. Consequently, the absence of certain results means that these are less important for an introduction to the field of cryptology, and not that they are any less significant as research contributions.

MATHEMATICAL CRYPTOLOGY
FOR COMPUTER SCIENTISTS
AND MATHEMATICIANS

— 1 —
Cryptography Before 1970

Cryptography is the science, or art, of secret writing. The word itself is derived from the Greek, κρυπτο (kripto), for *hidden*, and γραφια (grafia), *something which is written*.

The need to send messages secretly undoubtedly arose before history began to record such acts. And the desire for secrecy or privacy in communications resides in all of us. One would guess that most children have devised some method of sending coded messages to special friends.

One of the earliest recorded techniques for sending messages secretly is attributed to Julius Caesar. It is not surprising that a great deal of the history of cryptography arises from the battleground. Where else is the secrecy of a message so directly related to the potential loss of life, or of a kingdom or empire?

The Caesar Shift

The **Caesar shift**, attributed to Julius Caesar, encodes messages in the following way:

Suppose the message to be sent is:

HANNIBAL IS COMING AND HE HAS ELEPHANTS

A table is made of the letters in the message, grouped in blocks of, perhaps five; then the line is repeated several times, each time incrementing each letter by one. If the code for the day is 7, say, the process is repeated seven times, as demonstrated in Figure 1.1. The last line is the message sent.

Several points should be mentioned here. First of all, by examining the coded message, or *cipher text,* one notes that the alphabet is considered as *cyclic,* that is, that "A" follows "Z" as in Figure 1.2 below. Next, if this

Mathematical Cryptology

HANNI	BALIS	COMIN	GANDH	EHASE	LEPHA	NTS
IBOOJ	CBMJT	DPNJO	HBOEI	FIBTF	MFQIB	OUT
JCPPK	DCNKU	EQOKP	ICPFJ	GJCUG	NGRJC	PVU
KDQQL	EDOLV	FRPLQ	JDQGK	HKDVH	OHSKD	QWV
LERRM	FEPMW	GSQMR	KERHL	ILEWI	PITLE	RXW
MFSSN	GFQNX	HTRNS	LFSIM	JMFXJ	QJUMF	SYX
NGTTO	HGROY	IUSOT	MGTJN	KNGYK	RKVNG	TZY
OHUUP	IHSPZ	JVTPU	NHUKO	LOHZL	SLWOH	UAZ

Figure 1.1
A Caesar Shift

table were continued, one would notice that there are only 26 different ways of coding this message (and one of the 26 is the identity coding, that is, the message is not transformed at all). Finally, one assumes that breaking ordinary text into blocks of some fixed length does not impede ones ability to read a message. Isthi sreal lythe case?

The Caesar shift is not a very secure method of message transmission. But it will serve to illustrate some points and to define some terms.

The Model for a Cryptographic System

A general cryptographic system, or **cryptosystem**, can be defined as an ordered quadruple, or 4-tuple, χ = « K, M, C, T », where the elements of the 4-tuple are defined as follows.

Let Σ be a finite set of symbols, to be called an **alphabet**. For example, one might use { A, B, ..., Z }, or { a, b, g, d, ..., w }, or { 0, 1 }. Σ^* is the set of all strings over the alphabet S. We will say that a **space** is some subset $\Sigma \subseteq \Sigma^*$.

K, the **key space** of a cryptosystem, is a space over some alphabet Σ. M, the **message space**, is a space over another alphabet, Σ'. C, the **ciphertext space**, is a space over a third alphabet, Σ''. Finally, T is a transformation T : K × M → C, such that each restriction, t_k : M → C, defined by $t_k(m)$ = T(k,m), is **invertible** (that is, there exists a transformation t_k^{-1} : C → M such that $t_k^{-1} \circ t_k(m)$ = m, $\forall$ m ∈ M, and $t_k \circ t_k^{-1}(c)$ = c, $\forall c \in$ C).

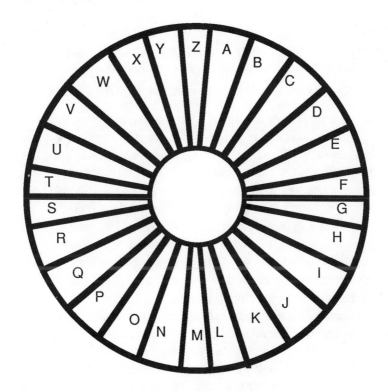

Figure 1.2
The Cyclic Alphabet

Of course, in the above definition, it is possible that the alphabets may be the same ($\Sigma = \Sigma' = \Sigma''$); indeed, that the message space and the ciphertext space may be the same ($M = C$).

In the case of the Caesar shift, the 4-tuple is:

$$\chi_{Caesar} = \text{« } K_{26}, M_{Roman}, M_{Roman}, T_{26} \text{ ».}$$

The key space, $K_{26} = \{ 0, 1, 2, ..., 25 \}$, represents the number of increments to the message before coding; the message space and ciphertext space consist of arbitrary strings over the Roman alphabet (or strings of length 5 if each block is considered a single message). Finally, the transformation t_i, for each letter $m \in M_{Roman}$ is defined as

$$t_i(m) = \phi((\phi^{-1}(m) + i) \bmod 26)$$

where ϕ is the isomorphism between the integers mod 26 and characters of the Roman alphabet given by $0 \leftrightarrow A$, $1 \leftrightarrow B$, ..., $25 \leftrightarrow Z$.

It needs to be shown that each transformation t_i has an inverse, but:

EXERCISE 1.1: *Show that* $t_j = t_{i-1}$ *where* $i + j \equiv 0$ *(mod 26).*

Part of the assumption about a cryptosystem is that the sender of a message, the receiver of a message, *and a potential interceptor of a message as well*, know what system is being used. In addition, after the sender **encrypts** a message (i.e. chooses a value $k \in K$ and applies t_k to the message m) and sends it; the receiver must know how to compute the inverse t_k^{-1}, and apply it to $t_k(m)$ to recover $m = t_k^{-1} \circ t_k(m)$.

The assumption is made that the *only* pieces of information *not* available to any interceptor or **attacker** are the message text, and the specific choice of key, k, from within the set K. In other words, one always assumes that the attacker knows the method being used, what the key space is, and that the attacker is able to obtain the ciphertext.

The classical methods of cryptography all assume that the method by which the receiver decodes or **decrypts** the method is by knowing the specific value of k, upon which the sender and receiver have previously agreed. However, as will be seen in most of this monograph, "knowing how to compute the inverse t_k^{-1}" and "knowing the specific value of k" are two separate and *inequivalent* conditions. And therein lies the renewed interest in the field of cryptography in recent years. But this subject will be discussed in greater detail in later chapters.

Cryptography is a two-way street. For every ingenious attempt to discover ways of *hiding* information, usually equally ingenious solutions are found to uncover this hidden information. Indeed, usually the same scientists are concerned both with devising cryptosystems and **cryptanalytic attacks**.

Indeed, the current use of terminology has come to distinguish between **cryptography** and **cryptographers**, on the one hand (encryption and those who devise encryption systems); **cryptanalysis** and **cryptanalysts** on the other hand (the breaking of codes and those who do it); and, generally, **cryptology** and **cryptologists** (the study of the entire field).

The title of this monograph is chosen as it is because we will be discussing in the monograph both the development of encryption algorithms, and the cryptanalysis of certain cryptosystems.

The first cryptanalytic attack we will describe is the obvious one:

```
OHUUP IHSPZ JUTPU NHUKO LOHZL SLWOH UAZ
PIVVQ JITQA KVUQV OIVLP MPIAM TMXPI VBA
QJWWR KLURB LWVRW PJWMQ NQJBN UNYQJ WCB
RKXXS LMVSC MXWSX QKXNR ORKCO VOZRK XDC
SLYYT MNWTD NYXTY RLYOS PSLDP WPASL YED
TMZZU NOXUE OZYUZ SMZPT QTMEQ XQBTM ZFE
UNAAV OPYVF PAZVZ TNAQU RUNFR YRCUN AGF
VOBBW PQZWG QBAWB UOBRV SVOGS ZSDVO BHG
WPCCX QRAXH RCBXC VPCSW TWPHT ATEWP CIH
XQDDY RSBYI SDCYD WQDTX UXQIU BUFXQ DJI
YREEZ STCZJ TEDZE XREUY VYRJV CVGYR EKJ
ZSFFA TUDAK UFEAF YSFVZ WZSKW DWHZS FLK
ATGGB UVEBL VGFBG ZTGWA XATLX EXIAT GML
BUHHC VWFCM WHGCH AUHXB YBUMY FYJBU HNM
CVIID WXGDN XIHDI BVIYC ZCVNZ GZKCV ION
DWJJE XYHEO YJIEJ CWJZD ADWOA HALDW JPO
EXKKF YZIFP ZKJFK DXKAE BEXPB IBMEX KQP
FYLLG ZAJGQ ALKGL EYLBF CFYQC JCNFY LRQ
GZMMH ABKHR BMLHM FZMCG DGZRD KDOGA MSR
HANNI BALIS COMIN GANDH EHASE LEPHA NTS
```

Figure 1.3
Exhaustive Key Search to Decrypt a Caesar Shift

Attack No. 1: Exhaustive Key Search

Again using the same example as above, suppose the message "OHUUP IHSPZ JUTPU NHUKO LOHZL SLWOH VAZ" had been intercepted. Exhaustive key search applied to this ciphertext means that every possible inverse is tested until one is found that produces a meaningful message, as in Figure 1.3.

An implementation of the Caesar Shift algorithm for both encryption and decryption can be found in Appendix VI, program P1 (The Caesar Shift).

One might ask the question, just because we intercept some text, and through exhaustive search, discover a message, how do we know whether this is the proper decryption? In other words, how do we know that we have computed $t_k^{-1} \circ t_k(m) = m$, rather than $t_{k'}^{-1} \circ t_k(m) = m'$?

The answer is, we don't. However, the set of strings of Roman characters that make up English words and English sentences is very *sparse* in the set of all strings in M_{Roman}.

EXERCISE 1.2: Find two strings of the greatest length which make sense in English and which are related by a Caesar shift. (Example: $t_4(CAP)$ = GET. Thus, $t_1(BZO)$ = CAP and $t_5(BZO)$ = GET. Ignore blanks.)[1]

Consequently, the Caesar shift example is instructive in that it establishes a necessary condition for a successful cryptosystem:

FOR A CRYPTOSYSTEM TO BE SUCCESSFUL, THE KEY SPACE MUST HAVE CARDINALITY LARGE ENOUGH FOR AN EXHAUSTIVE KEY SEARCH ATTACK TO BE COMPUTATIONALLY INFEASIBLE.

What is computational infeasibility? Certainly in the days of Caesar, and indeed until very recent years, computationally infeasible meant being too difficult to compute with paper and pencil. Thus, even with only paper and pencil, breaking a Caesar cipher is a simple task.

Many of the other early cryptosystems used as key spaces a set of permutations either on a subset of the integers, or on the underlying alphabet of the message space. (QUESTION: Are individual permutations always invertible?)

In all the cryptosystems discussed in the rest of this chapter, the message space M will be M_{Roman} as defined above; further, to simplify matters, we will ignore blanks and consider that all characters in the message are upper case characters.

Transposition Cryptosystems

A **transposition** cryptosystem, χ_{trans} = « K_{Π}, M_{Roman}, M_{Roman}, T » is based on the following. Let N be a set of n objects, perhaps the first n natural numbers. Let K_{Π} be the set of all **permutations**, Π, on N; therefore a key value will be some permutation of the first n numbers.

---

[1] *Ars gratia artis.* In the August 1985 issue, shortly after this had been given as a homework assignment, the same problem appeared, with prizes offered for the best solutions, in GAMES magazine.

The encryption will map blocks of n letters to blocks of n letters. The ith character of the message text will be written to the $\pi(i)$-th position in the cipher text, where $\pi \in \Pi$ is some permutation. As an example, if n=6, and the permutation is $\pi(1\ 2\ 3\ 4\ 5\ 6) = (5\ 3\ 2\ 4\ 6\ 1)$, then the message "MODULA" is encrypted as "ADOUML".

In this case, the size of the key space is n!, the number of permutations of n things. n does not have to be very large for n! searches to be infeasible, even with the fastest computers and the highest degree of parallelism.

EXERCISE 1.3: Suppose that we can perform one search every microsecond, of a key space based on the permutations of 100 objects. How many minutes of computing time will an exhaustive search take?

In point of fact, the actual transposition cryptosystems used in early times did not use arbitrary permutation sets, but rather highly simplified subsets. For example, one method known as **columnar transposition** essentially used a permutation generated by matrix transposition followed by column permutation. If the key is the permutation $\pi(1\ 2\ 3\ 4) = (2\ 4\ 3\ 1)$, then 16-character blocks are written, in row-major order, into a 4-by-4 matrix:

PLAY IT AGAIN, SAMMY

$\Rightarrow$

P	L	A	Y
I	T	A	G
A	I	N	S
A	M	M	Y

and then sent, using column-major order, with the permutation of columns, to give ciphertext:

$$\Rightarrow\ \text{YGSY PIAA AANM LTIM}$$

Consequently, a cryptanalyst, knowing that this method was being used, would not have to search through the $16! \approx 2 \times 10^{13}$ permutations of 16 letters, but rather the $4! = 24$ permutations of four things (columns).

Substitution Cryptosystems

The other type of cryptosystem, the **substitution cryptosystem**, is based on permutations of the underlying alphabet of M. The Caesar shift is essentially a simple version of this approach.

The **keyword mixed alphabet** cryptosystem uses as the key space $K_{keyword}$, the set of all words, with duplicate letters removed, in the English language. Indeed, the requirement for words to be English words (in addition to being Xenophobic) is imposed only because the distribution of the keyword is made simpler if it is a word rather than an arbitrary character string.

*The messenger, having ridden from Lexington to Valley Forge in half a day, was exhausted, out of breath, and indeed near death as he approached General Washington to tell him the secret key for the cipher system: "XRUTGDKWQFP", he panted, then expired. Did he say "XRUTGDKWQF**P**" or "XRUTGDKWQF**T**" ? puzzled General Washington.*

The method itself uses the keyword to define a mapping or permutation of the message space alphabet, S. The alphabet is written in normal order; and under it is written a permuted alphabet: the letters of the keyword followed by the remaining letters of the alphabet.

Keyword: FACETIOUSLY

```
                   ABCDE FGHIJ KLMNO PQRST UVWXY Z
Permuted Alphabet:  FACET IOUSL YBDGH JKMNP QRVWX Z
```

The encryption maps each letter of the message text to a letter of cipher text according to the permutation defined above. Thus, "MAY THE FORCE BE WITH YOU" becomes "DFX PUT IHMCT AT VSPU XHQ", or more likely, "DFXPU TIHMC TATVS PUXHQ".

The **Vigenère cipher** was a widely-used cryptosystem dating back to the 16th century, using a keyword combined with a Caesar shift. If the keyword is "FACETIOUSLY", as before, the encryption will use 11 different Caesar shifts periodically. (Each letter determines a Caesar shift, or modular addition. Suppose that $0 \leftrightarrow A$, $1 \leftrightarrow B$, ..., $25 \leftrightarrow Z$, as usual. Then, the first letter to be encoded uses the shift corresponding to F, the second to A, the third to C, and so on until the cycle repeats:

```
ALGORITHMS PLUS DATA STRUCTURES EQUAL PROGRAMS
```

ALGOR ITHMS PLUSD ATAST RUCTU RESEQ UALPR OGRAM S

FACET IOUSL YFACE TIOUS LYFAC ETIOU SLYFA CETIO U

⇓

FLISK QHBED NQUUH TBOML CSHTW VXASK MLJUR QKKIA M

None of the above systems, if well-designed, is vulnerable to an exhaustive key search attack. However, they are certainly vulnerable to a very simple attack using a knowledge of the frequency of occurrence of characters in the message space alphabet.

There are certainly situations that could be conceived wherein the probability of the occurrence of any given character in the message space alphabet was 1/n, where n is the size of the alphabet. However, in most practical systems of communication, be they human languages, programs in a high-level computer language, or symbol strings in propositional calculus, symbols do *not* occur with equal probabilities.

It is possible, in the English language, to make some estimates about the relative frequency of occurrence of letters. Is there an absolute relationship?

There can be no deterministic relationship of letter frequencies because one must compute these frequencies with respect to some *sample* of English text; e.g. the text in this book, or the text in all the books in the Library of Congress, or the text in all the books in your bookcase, and so on.

Armed with this knowledge about the frequency of occurrence of symbols in the message alphabet, we can develop the following:

Attack No. 2: Frequency Analysis

For a sufficiently large sample of the cipher text, do a frequency analysis. That is, examine the frequency of occurrence of each character in the cipher text. A program to accomplish this analysis is found in Appendix VI, program P2 (Letter Frequency Analysis). Further, the results of running this program on the text of this chapter are contained in the accompanying Table 1.1.

If it is known that the method is based on a 1-1 mapping of elements of the message alphabet to elements of the cipher text alphabet, then a trial substitution should be made whereby the letter most frequently occurring in the cipher text is replaced by "E"; the second most frequently occurring by "T", and so on.

Letter Occurrences in Chapter 1

Letter	Count	Freq	Letter	Count	Freq	Letter	Count	Freq
a	1592	0.0740	b	375	0.0174	c	837	0.0389
d	642	0.0299	e	2811	0.1307	f	562	0.0261
g	409	0.0190	h	1122	0.0522	i	1396	0.0649
j	61	0.0028	k	226	0.0105	l	744	0.0346
m	611	0.0284	n	1288	0.0599	o	1416	0.0659
p	613	0.0285	q	114	0.0053	r	1318	0.0613
s	1541	0.0717	t	2097	0.0975	u	531	0.0247
v	211	0.0098	w	310	0.0144	x	139	0.0065
y	472	0.0220	z	62	0.0029			

TOTAL   21500

The letters in decreasing frequency of occurrence are:

e t a s o i r n h c l d p m f u y g b w k v x q z j

Table 1.1
Frequency of Letters Occurring in This Chapter
(Output from Program P2)

This process will be iterative. Furthermore, it is not deterministic. One must decide at some point that "E" really transforms to "Q" and not "R", for example. But the law of large numbers indicates that if we have enough cipher text, that we will be able to reconstruct the initial alphabet.

EXERCISE 1.4: Can the results shown in Table 1.1 be used as a general guideline for letter frequencies? Is there anything about the contents of Chapter 1 that might tend to skew the values in the table?

Both the keyword mixed alphabet and the Vigenère cipher can be broken using this approach. In using this attack on the Vigenère cipher, one needs to find additionally the period of the Vigenère cipher; but since this is no longer than one word, it is reasonable to attempt a frequency analysis attack iteratively using incremental expected values for the period.

The frequency attack as described above will not succeed on the transposition cipher, since the mapping does not change letters, but only their position.

EXERCISE 1.5: *Suggest a method of attacking the transposition cipher.* (Hint: *Question the quirks of language which organize certain sequences of letters in certain patterns.*)

Thus one principle that can be established about cryptosystems is the following:

THEOREM: For a cryptosystem χ = « K, M, C, T », if the transformations t_π are all extensions of a mapping π, of the underlying alphabets $\pi: \Sigma \rightarrow \Sigma'$, and if the occurrences of symbols of Σ is not uniform, then the cryptosystem can be broken.

PROOF: Apply the frequency analysis attack.

Q.E.D.

Consequently, as these systems evolved historically, methods were sought which would avoid detection by the frequency analysis method. One approach taken was the **homophonic substitution cipher**. Again in this cryptosystem the transformations t_π are extensions of transformations of the alphabets Σ and Σ', $t_\pi: \Sigma \rightarrow \Sigma'$; however, a careful definition of the ciphertext alphabet, Σ', is made, to nullify the effects of frequency distribution.

To simplify an example, suppose the message alphabet Σ = { A,B,C,D,E,F,G,H } and that, empirically, it was determined that, on average, for 100 characters of message text, that the occurrences of the elements of Σ are:

A	21	E	23
B	9	F	7
C	14	G	6
D	15	H	5

Then, for the ciphertext alphabet, Σ', choose Σ' = { 00, 01, 02, ..., 99 }. Partition Σ' into subsets, first choosing 21 elements of Σ' randomly. This subset, Σ_A', will correspond to the character A. From $\Sigma' - \Sigma_A'$, choose 9 elements at random to form Σ_B', and so on.

The key space, K, will consist of all possible choices of subsets Σ_A' ... Σ_H'. (How large is the key space?) To encrypt a letter of message text, for a given key value, choose one element of the subset corresponding to that letter at random.

The frequency analysis attack will be defeated, because, on average, every letter of the ciphertext alphabet will occur with the same frequency.

The first recorded occurrence of this method was in correspondence between the Duchy of Mantua and Simeone de Crema in 1401 [KAHN 67]. For paper and pencil attacks, homophonic ciphers may be indeed very secure. However, if we have modern electronic detection methods (i.e. we can pass the ciphertext through a computer), the precision of the frequency occurrences may serve to defeat the method. In other words, it is highly unlikely that the relative frequency occurrences of characters would be related by integers, and therefore, after a large enough sample of ciphertext, discrepancies in the relative frequencies would show up in the cipher text.

Suppose that the actual frequency of occurrence of the letter A was actually 14.4 and not 14. Then, after a sufficiently large amount of ciphertext, the 14 numbers corresponding to the letter A would show up more than expected. Then, they would be candidates for the encryptions of the letter A. And so on.

A second approach to avoid frequency analysis attacks is called the **polygram substitution cipher**. In terms of our notation, the enciphering transformations t_π are not extensions of a mapping between the underlying alphabets, but rather a mapping of the Cartesian products of these alphabets. An n-gram substitution would be defined from a mapping

$$\pi : \Sigma \times \Sigma \times \ldots \times \Sigma \rightarrow \Sigma \times \Sigma \times \ldots \times \Sigma$$

$$\underbrace{\qquad}_{n \text{ times}} \qquad \underbrace{\qquad}_{n \text{ times}}$$

One widely used 2-gram or **digram** substition is the **Playfair square**. It was named after Lyon Playfair in 1854, although actually invented by Charles Wheatstone [KAHN 67]. It was used by England during World War I, and can still be found today in occasional crossword puzzles.

We use the Roman alphabet for both messages and ciphertext, $M = M_{Roman}$, and $C = M_{Roman}$. However, we consider a pre- (and post-) processing that will map Js into Is. Thus, we are left with a 25-letter alphabet. To form an enciphering transformation, choose a word with no duplicated letters from the key space of all such words (as in the Vigenère cipher). Now write the twenty-five letters of the alphabet into a five-by-five square, in row-major order, beginning with the key word, and then following with all the other letters of the alphabet. For example, if the key word is "AUTOMATION", one would form the square:

```
A   U   T   O   M
I   N   B   C   D
E   F   G   H   K
L   P   Q   R   S
V   W   X   Y   Z
```

To encrypt a message, first eliminate the possibility of repeated letters by introducing between those letters a redundant character, perhaps Q; then divide it into digrams (or strings of length 2 over the message alphabet). Encrypt each digram according to these three rules:

1. If the two letters of a digram do not fall in the same row or the same column, transmit the two characters forming the other two corners of the rectangle defined by the two characters.

As a convention, choose as the first "corner" the one in the same row as the first letter of the diagram.

2. If the two letters are in the same row, transmit the *succeeding* two characters in the row (thinking of it as cyclic, in other words if the last character of the row appears, replace it by the first).

3. If the two letters are in the same column, transmit the *succeeding* two characters in the column, again thinking of it as cyclic.

Decryption involves knowing the secret key, and simply unraveling the digrams of the ciphertext using the same square.

Example: If the message text is "GEORGE LUCAS SAYS, MAY THE FORCE BE WITH YOU" then one first writes (note the appropriate insertion of Qs) :

GE OR GE LU CA SQ SA YS MA YT HE FO RC EB EW IT HY OU

and then encodes:

HF CY HF PA IO LR LM ZR AU XO KF HU YH GI FV BA RO MT

The Playfair square cipher is not vulnerable to frequency analysis of letters, since, for example, "O" is encoded as a "C", "U", and "M" respectively. Single letters are not mapped to single letters.

However, digrams are mapped to digrams, and another type of frequency attack will succeed.

Attack No. 3: Frequency Analysis of Digrams

For a sufficiently large sample of the cipher text, do a frequency analysis of the $26^2 = 676$ digrams. That is, examine the frequency of occurrence of each digram in the cipher text.

This attack might be difficult to perform on a paper and pencil basis. That is, enough ciphertext must be analyzed for the 676 digrams to appear with the frequencies that one might expect in a random sample of normal English text. Consequently, the Playfair square cipher, although relatively impenetrable to paper and pencil attacks, could not survive in an electronic environment.

Cryptographers of earlier days looked for other ways to evade frequency attacks. One method, often used in mystery novels, is the **running key cipher**. This is a method similar to the Vigenère cipher with the exception that the key space, $K=K_{library}$, can be approximately described as "all the letter positions in all the books in the library". The transformation $t_{(Gone\ With\ the\ Wind,\ 197,\ 100)}$ might represent a transformation of the message text by a sequence of Caesar shifts determined by the sequence of letters that begin with the one hundredth character on page 197 of a certain edition of "Gone With the Wind".

Then the periodicity inherent in the Vigenère is eliminated. However, other frequency attacks can be developed based on the frequency of characters in the key text (i.e. the library).

A much more secure cipher is the **one-time pad**. Indeed, the security of this approach has never been breached. The key space is simply the set of all arbitrary strings over the Roman alphabet.

Each character of the key is used to encrypt precisely one character of the message, using a Caesar shift. Then it is discarded, hence the name "one-time pad". Thus, if the message is:

```
MESSAGE:        THE RAIN IN SPAIN FALLS MAINLY
BLOCKED:        THERA ININS PAINF ALLSM AINLY
PAD:            XJWLR SJFOW DHALR IDJNG MSFDG
                _____
CIPHERTEXT:     QQACR AWNBO SHIYW IOUFS MASOE
```

The method is secure because the pad provides no periodicity or frequency in order to give a handle to the attacker. However, it is difficult to use. For every character of a message to be sent, a letter of the key pad must be sent --- of course, by another channel, since if the attacker were to intercept the pad, then the system would be useless.

Rotor Machines

To mechanize the production of ciphertext, various devices were invented which speed the process. One important family of such devices were the **rotor machines**, invented in the 1920's, to implement Vigenère-type ciphers with very long periods.

A rotor machine has a keyboard, and a series of rotors. A rotor is a rotating wheel with 26 positions. Each position completes an electric contact, and depending on the position, determines a different Caesar shift. When a key on the keyboard is depressed, a letter is generated depending upon the position of the rotors.

Two of the best-known of these devices are the **Hagelin** and the **Enigma** machines. Both were invented in the 1920's; the Enigma machine, the German code machine, was actually patented in the United States by Arthur Scherbius in 1923.

In general, the period of a rotor machine with k rotors is 26^k. (Think of the odometer in your automobile.) Consequently, the rotor machine is a simple way to implement a Vigenère cipher with very long period.

The Enigma machine consisted of a **plugboard** or *Steckerboard*, which simply permutes the message text, thence a sequence of rotors (usually 3 or 5), and a **reflecting rotor**; it connects letters of the alphabet in pairs.

The Enigma cryptosystem is $\chi_{Enigma} = \ll K, M_{Roman}, M_{Roman}, T \gg$, where K is a space parametrized by the Steckerboard permutation, by the initial positions of the rotors, and by the reflecting rotor. The transformation t_π is a composition of the following transformations:

$$t_\pi = \text{STECKER}^{-1} \circ R_{C(k)}^{-1} \circ T_i^{-1} \circ R_{C(k)} \circ$$
$$R_{B(j)}^{-1} \circ T_j^{-1} \circ R_{B(j)} \circ$$
$$R_{A(i)}^{-1} \circ T_k^{-1} \circ R_{C(k)} \circ \text{REFL} \circ$$
$$R_{C(k)}^{-1} \circ T_k \circ R_{C(k)} \circ$$
$$R_{B(j)}^{-1} \circ T_j \circ R_{B(j)} \circ$$
$$R_{A(i)}^{-1} \circ T_i \circ R_{A(i)} \circ \text{STECKER}$$

The breaking of the German Enigma machine is probably the most important contribution of cryptanalysis to history. There is little doubt that the efforts of the British team at Bletchley Park, led to a great degree by

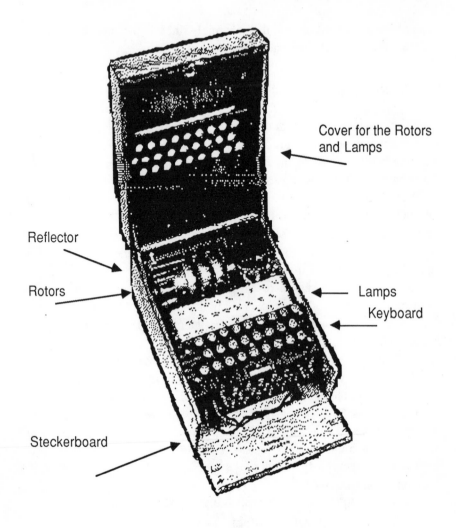

Cover for the Rotors
and Lamps

Reflector

Rotors

Lamps

Keyboard

Steckerboard

Figure 1.4
The Enigma Machine

Alan Turing, resulted in the saving of thousands of allied lives and the
shortening of the war. [DEAV 80], [HODG 83], [KAHN 67], [WELC 82].

However, based on all published material on the efforts at Bletchley
Park, it would have required only a very simple modification of the Enigma
machine to have defeated the best efforts of the British cryptographers.

Indeed, the subject of the techniques developed by this group, and the devices they invented, could be the subject of a course by itself. And still to this day, many of the techniques developed are considered classified by the British government.

Final Comments

Cryptosystems based on the Caesar shift and the Vigenère cipher formed the basis for most of the successful cryptosystems of the early history of the subject, up through the end of the Second World War (and beyond).

Methods such as those implemented by the Enigma machine are essentially secure from paper-and-pencil attacks. It is only the development of the computer that has rendered further methods necessary.

Hints for Some Exercises

EXERCISE 1.3. The number of permutations possible is 100! A good estimate of the size of n! is given by Stirling's formula:

$$n! \approx (2\pi)^{1/2} \, e^{-n} \, n^{n+1/2}$$

There are 10^6 microseconds in a second, thus 6×10^7 microseconds in a minute.

EXERCISE 1.4. Are there any words or patterns of words which tend to appear more often in this text than they might in some other sample of English text?

EXERCISE 1.5. What happens when a "Q" shows up in the message text? What must follow it (in English)?

— 2 —

The Data Encryption Standard

Between the end of the Second World War and today, the science of cryptology underwent a fundamental change. As with many scientific advances of the last generation, this change was fueled by the development of the digital computer.

The Enigma machine and its counterparts were defeated, during the War, and since that time computers had evolved to play such an important rôle in communications that it was clear that future communications over substantial distances were going to be digital, computer to computer.

Because of their slow speeds, the Enigma devices were obsolete as machines (the original Enigma machines required an operator to encipher a message, and then a second operator to transmit the message, say by radio or over telegraph lines). Furthermore, the methods that were used at Bletchley Park were still classified, so that designers of encryption systems were loathe to consider the use of an Enigma device, lest it be the case that a successful attack was already known.

In the late 1940's, Chaude Shannon, the pioneer of information theory, suggested a number of ideas for future encryption systems [SHAN 49]. His suggestions encompassed performing multiple operations, mixing transpositions and substitutions.

These ideas were improved upon at IBM in the early 1970's and a cryptosystem was developed that was named LUCIFER [FEIS 73], again a method that involved both transpositions and substitutions.

Shortly thereafter, the United States National Bureau of Standards requested of science and industry that they develop proposals for a Data Encryption Standard, the idea being that if a single standard encryption method could be agreed upon, then it might be promulgated throughout the US government, and, in all probability, throughout the private sector and also abroad.

After consideration, such a standard was adopted in 1976 [DES 77].

The method is based on LUCIFER, and in its original form, transforms every 64 bits of the message to 64 bits of ciphertext. The key is a 56-bit string.

Unquestionably, the Data Encryption Standard (henceforth called DES) has had the greatest impact upon data encryption since its adoption almost ten years ago. However, in addition to the success in its use, the DES has drawn more than its share of critics. After the method itself is discussed, we will be in a position to discuss the reasons both for the laurels and for the brickbats.

Upon entry into the computer age, one of the first changes to impact upon the field of cryptography was the introduction of different alphabets. Two that we will constantly use will be message spaces based on the alphabet $\Sigma_2 = \{0,1\}$, in other words messages consisting of bit-strings; and Σ_{ASCII}, the alphabet of ASCII codes[1].

Thus, the definition of the DES cryptosystem is as follows. Let

$$M_n = \{ \; m_n \mid \; m_n = b_0 b_1 \ldots b_{(n-1)} \, , \, b_i \in \Sigma_2 \; \}$$

(in other words, n-bit strings). Then

$$\chi_{DES} = \text{«} \; M_{56}, M_{64}, M_{64}, T_{DES} \; \text{»}.$$

Messages are divided into 64-bit blocks (consequently, cryptosystems defined over message strings M_n are also called n-block ciphers).

The keys are 56-bit blocks. Thus, if as is normal, the text to be encrypted is electronically recorded, the message text will be broken into 8-byte or 8-character blocks. The ciphertext will have the same length. Furthermore, the individual key value will consist of 7 bytes or 7 characters.

The transformation $t_k(m_{64}) = T_{DES}(k, m_{64})$ is, in fact, a composition of 18 transformations. Summarized, t_k becomes:

---

[1]ASCII = American Standard Committee for Information Interchange. ASCII codes are standard mappings for the sequences of bits generated by a key-stroke or otherwise that mark the correspondence between bytes and characters. Strictly speaking, the usual ASCII code is defined between 7-bit strings and characters; although in many computers today, the 8th or "high bit" is always zero, thus giving a correspondence between 8-bit strings, or bytes, and characters.

$$IP = \begin{array}{cccccccc} 58 & 50 & 42 & 34 & 26 & 18 & 10 & 2 \\ 60 & 52 & 44 & 36 & 28 & 20 & 12 & 4 \\ 62 & 54 & 46 & 38 & 30 & 22 & 14 & 6 \\ 64 & 56 & 48 & 40 & 32 & 24 & 16 & 8 \\ 57 & 49 & 41 & 33 & 25 & 17 & 9 & 1 \\ 59 & 51 & 43 & 35 & 27 & 19 & 11 & 3 \\ 61 & 53 & 45 & 37 & 29 & 21 & 13 & 5 \\ 63 & 55 & 47 & 39 & 31 & 23 & 15 & 7 \end{array}$$

Table 2.1

The Initial Permutation IP

$$t_k = IP^{-1} \circ T_{16} \circ T_{15} \circ T_{14} \circ \dots \circ T_2 \circ T_1 \circ IP$$

where IP is an initial permutation of the 64 bits, and each of the T_j's is a variation on a theme to be described.

IP interchanges the 64 bits in the fashion described by table 2.1. We assuming the bits are written from 1 to 64 row-wise, or in row major order. In other words, if the message string is $M = m_1 m_2 \dots m_{64}$, the result of the initial permutation, IP(M), is $m_{58} m_{50} m_{42} \dots m_7$.

The transposition T_j is defined in two parts. First, define the 64-bit string, which is its domain, as the (Cartesian) product of two 32-bit strings, the left half and the right half, L_{j-1} and R_{j-1}. Then, the result is the product of L_j and R_j.

$$L_j = R_{j-1}$$
$$R_j = L_{j-1} \oplus f(R_{j-1}, K_j)$$

The operation $\oplus$ is the exclusive-or operation[2], and K_j is a 48-bit key defined from the 56-bit key, k.

The function f, mentioned above, which maps 32-bit strings into 32-bit strings, is computed from this key and the afore-mentioned R_{j-1}.

First, the "right half" R_{j-1} is expanded to 48 bits using the bit-selection table E. Then, the exclusive-or of this new 48-bit string and the key K_j is calculated. The resulting 48-bit string is compressed to 32 bits using the S-boxes.

---

[2] $\oplus : \Sigma_2 \to \Sigma_2$, $0 \oplus 0 = 0$, $1 \oplus 0 = 1$, $0 \oplus 1 = 1$, $1 \oplus 1 = 0$.

$$
E = \begin{array}{cccccc}
32 & 1 & 2 & 3 & 4 & 5 \\
4 & 5 & 6 & 7 & 8 & 9 \\
8 & 9 & 10 & 11 & 12 & 13 \\
12 & 13 & 14 & 15 & 16 & 17 \\
16 & 17 & 18 & 19 & 20 & 21 \\
20 & 21 & 22 & 23 & 24 & 25 \\
24 & 25 & 26 & 27 & 28 & 29 \\
28 & 29 & 30 & 31 & 32 & 1
\end{array}
$$

Table 2.2

The Expansion Function E

$$
P = \begin{array}{cccc}
16 & 7 & 20 & 21 \\
29 & 12 & 28 & 17 \\
1 & 15 & 23 & 26 \\
5 & 18 & 31 & 10 \\
2 & 8 & 24 & 14 \\
32 & 27 & 3 & 9 \\
19 & 13 & 30 & 6 \\
22 & 11 & 4 & 25
\end{array}
$$

Table 2.3

The Permutation P

The eight S-boxes are designed to map 6-bit strings to 4-bit strings. Consider a 6-bit string as the address in a 4×16 matrix [0..3, 0..15]. (The first and the sixth bits are interpreted as a 2-bit string to give the row [0..3]; the second through the fifth bits are interpreted as a 4-bit string to give the column [0..15].)

For example, a 6-bit string 101011 would be interpreted as the array position [3,5].

The element at that address is in binary form a 4-bit string. Thus, the 48-bit string is considered as 8 6-bit blocks; each is subjected to the transformation described by one of the S-boxes; the result is thus 8 4-bit blocks, i.e. a 32-bit block.

Using the same example, the 6-bit string 101011 input to the S2 - box gives the output of 15, or 1111.

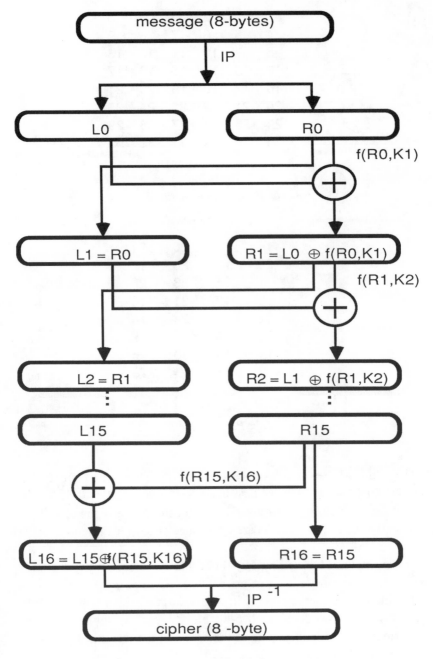

Figure 2.1
Sketch of the DES Transformation

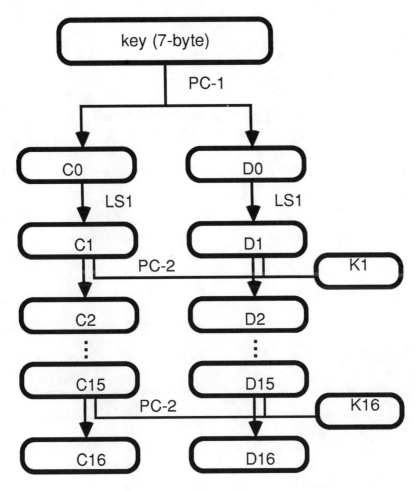

Figure 2.2
Sketch of the Key Calculations in DES

Column

S1:

Row	0	1	2	3	4	5	6	7	8	9	10	11	12	13	14	15
0	14	4	13	1	2	15	11	8	3	10	6	12	5	9	0	7
1	0	15	7	4	14	2	13	1	10	6	12	11	9	5	3	8
2	4	1	14	8	13	6	2	11	15	12	9	7	3	10	5	0
3	15	12	8	2	4	9	1	7	5	11	3	14	10	0	6	13

****

S2:

Row	0	1	2	3	4	5	6	7	8	9	10	11	12	13	14	15
0	15	1	8	14	6	11	3	4	9	7	2	13	12	0	5	10
1	3	13	4	7	15	2	8	14	12	0	1	10	6	9	11	5
2	0	14	7	11	10	4	13	1	5	8	12	6	9	3	2	15
3	13	8	10	1	3	15	4	2	11	6	7	12	0	5	14	9

****

S3:

Row	0	1	2	3	4	5	6	7	8	9	10	11	12	13	14	15
0	10	0	9	14	6	3	15	5	1	13	12	7	11	4	2	8
1	13	7	0	9	3	4	6	10	2	8	5	14	12	11	15	1
2	3	6	4	9	8	15	3	0	11	1	2	12	5	10	14	7
3	1	10	13	0	6	9	8	7	4	15	14	3	11	5	2	12

****

S4:

Row	0	1	2	3	4	5	6	7	8	9	10	11	12	13	14	15
0	7	13	14	3	0	6	9	10	1	2	8	5	11	12	4	15
1	13	8	11	5	6	15	0	3	4	7	2	12	1	10	14	9
2	10	6	9	0	12	11	7	13	15	1	3	14	5	2	8	4
3	3	15	0	6	10	1	13	8	9	4	5	11	12	7	2	4

Table 2.4
The First Four S-Boxes

Column

S5:

Row	0	1	2	3	4	5	6	7	8	9	10	11	12	13	14	15
0	2	12	4	1	7	10	11	6	8	5	3	15	13	0	14	9
1	14	11	2	12	4	7	13	1	5	0	15	10	3	9	8	6
2	4	2	1	11	10	13	7	8	15	9	12	5	6	3	0	14
3	11	8	12	7	1	14	2	13	6	15	0	9	10	4	5	3

****

S6:

Row	0	1	2	3	4	5	6	7	8	9	10	11	12	13	14	15
0	12	1	10	15	9	2	6	8	0	13	3	4	14	7	5	11
1	10	15	4	2	7	12	9	5	6	1	13	14	0	11	3	8
2	9	14	15	5	2	8	12	3	7	0	4	10	1	13	11	6
3	4	3	2	12	9	5	15	10	11	14	1	7	6	0	8	13

****

S7:

Row	0	1	2	3	4	5	6	7	8	9	10	11	12	13	14	15
0	4	11	2	14	15	0	8	13	3	12	9	7	5	10	6	1
1	13	0	11	7	4	9	1	10	14	3	5	12	2	15	8	6
2	1	4	11	13	12	3	7	14	10	15	6	8	0	5	9	2
3	6	11	13	8	1	4	10	7	9	5	0	15	14	2	3	12

****

S8:

Row	0	1	2	3	4	5	6	7	8	9	10	11	12	13	14	15
0	13	2	8	4	6	15	11	1	10	9	3	14	5	0	12	7
1	1	15	13	8	10	3	7	4	12	5	6	11	0	14	9	2
2	7	11	4	1	9	12	14	2	0	6	10	13	15	3	5	8
3	2	1	14	7	4	10	8	13	15	12	9	0	3	5	6	11

Table 2.5
The Last Four S-Boxes

	57	49	41	33	25	17	9
	1	58	50	42	34	26	18
	10	2	59	51	43	35	27
PC-1 =	19	11	3	60	52	44	36
	63	55	47	39	31	23	15
	7	62	54	46	38	30	22
	14	6	61	53	45	37	29
	21	13	5	28	20	12	4

Table 2.6
The Key Permutation PC-1

	14	17	11	24	1	5
	3	28	15	6	21	10
	23	19	12	4	26	8
PC-2 =	16	7	27	20	13	2
	41	52	31	37	47	55
	30	40	51	45	33	48
	44	49	39	56	34	53
	46	42	50	36	29	32

Table 2.7
The Key Permutation PC-2

Iteration i:

1	2	3	4	5	6	7	8	9	10	11	12	13	14	15	16

# of Left Shifts LS_i:

1	1	2	2	2	2	2	2	1	2	2	2	2	2	2	1

Table 2.8
The Key Schedule of Left Shifts LS

Finally, this 32-bit block is permuted by the permutation P, and XORed with L_{j-1} to give R_j.

In summary, then, the function f can be written as:

$$f(R_{j-1}, K_j) = P(S(E(R_{j-1}) \oplus K_j)) \qquad j = 1, 1, ..., 16$$

where S is a function from M_{48} to M_{32} computed by applying the 8 S-boxes.

This entire process is repeated 16 times to give the entire encryption. However, the *sixteenth* round, does *not* perform the switch of the halves. Therefore, T_{16} is written as:

$$(L_{16}, R_{16}) = T_{16}(L_{15}, R_{15}) = (L_{15} \oplus f(R_{15}, K_{16}), R_{15}).$$

This composition of transformations is also depicted in Figure 2.1.

How are the 48-bit keys in each of the 16 rounds defined? We need to consult the tables 2.6, 2.7, and 2.8 for PC-1, PC-2, and LS.

At each stage, the original 56-bit key is used to generate a 48-bit key K_j, $j=1,...,16$. In the first round of the 16, the entire key is injected into a 64-bit string, with the 8th, 16th, and so on being parity bits; then the result is subjected to a 64-bit permutation, PC-1, which also discards the parity bits. Then, at each stage, the 56-bit key is split into a left half and a right half, C_{j-1} and D_{j-1} (28 bits each). These 28-bit pieces are subjected to one or two left shifts, corresponding to the iteration and the key schedule of left shifts, above. The concatenation of C_{j-1} and D_{j-1} then has 48 bits selected from it by PC-2. (See the diagram in Figure 2.2.)

The Decryption Process

By the nature of the construction of the encryption function, it is not difficult to see that the transformation is in fact invertible, and that the inverse, or decryption transformation consists of performing IP, then T_1 through T_{16}, then IP^{-1}, except that derived keys are used in *reverse* order: $K_{16}, K_{15}, ..., K_1$. The proof of this statement is obtained by solving the following exercise:

EXERCISE 2.1: Show that the composition of $T_{16}(L_{15}, R_{15}) = (L_{15} \oplus f(R_{15}, K_{16}), R_{15})$ and $T_1^D(L_{16}, R_{16}) = (R_{16}, L_{16} \oplus f(R_{16}, K_{16}))$ is equivalent to the transformation which interchanges the 32-bit halves, L_{15} and R_{15}. (The notation T_1^D refers to the first round of the decryption step.)

EXERCISE 2.2: Use the results of exercise 2.1 to compute the inverse of the DES encryption transformation.

An example follows (Figures 2.3 and 2.4) giving each round of the DES for the message 'computer' with key 'program' (using ASCII code).

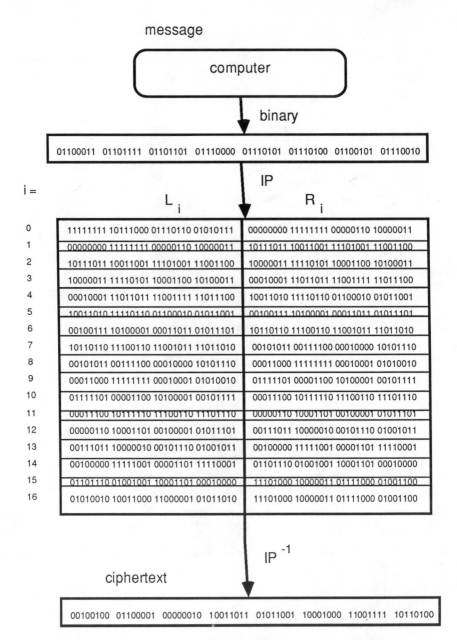

Figure 2.3
Computation of the Rounds and the Ciphertext for DES Example

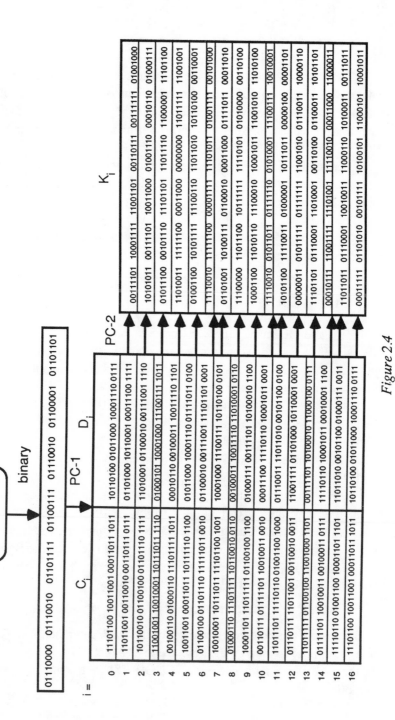

Figure 2.4

Key Calculations for DES Encryption

Comments

1. There are no known intuitive ways to see how the DES function is generated. Indeed, one of the main criticisms of the method is that the design criteria have never been made public. It is possible that they have been chosen because of some powerful but undescribed properties of the group of transformations of Σ_{64}.

2. The method is very fast to implement, at the machine level, since all of the transformations are either XORs or table-lookups; both of these are usually very fast.

EXERCISE 2.3: Write a program to implement DES for the encryption and decryption of arbitrary text files.

Potential Attacks on the DES

Diffie and Hellman [DIFF 77] propose an attack on the DES using exhaustive key search. There are 2^{56} keys, and it is reasonable to consider, with today's technology, that each key could be checked in a microsecond, or **μsecond**, using a special chip.

Since $2^{56} \approx 7 \cdot 10^{16}$, and since there are $8 \cdot 10^{10}$ μseconds in a day, a special-purpose machine with one million ($= 10^6$) chips in parallel could check all of the keys in one day.

At an estimated cost of $20 per chip, such a machine could be built for $20,000,000. It is not known if anyone has built such a device.

One easily demonstrated identity shows that the size of the search for an exhaustive key attack can be effectively halved. This involves the demonstration of a relationship of DES encrypted messages and their Boolean complements. Suppose that m^c is used to denoted the Boolean or bitwise or two's complement of the bit-string m. Then, for the DES transformation T_{DES}, show:

EXERCISE 2.4: Prove that $(T_{DES}(m,k))^c = T_{DES}(m^c,k^c)$.

Because of this potential weakness of the DES, a number of suggestions have been made to enlarge the key size to 112 bits. Principal among these are the suggestions of Tuchman [TUCH 78] and sequential multiple encryption.

Tuchman's approach consists of choosing independent keys, k_i and k_j, and then performing the sequence of transformations:

$$T_{Tuchman} (k_i k_j , m) = T_{DES} (k_i, t_{j-1}(t_i(m)))$$

Or, writing only the invertible transformations, one can write the Tuchman transformation as:

$$t_{ij} = t_i \circ t_{j-1} \circ t_i$$

Sequential multiple transformation, by contrast, can be written as:

$$t_{ij} = t_i \circ t_j.$$

Since there are now 2^{112} keys, the possibility of cryptanalyzing the DES by exhaustive search is eliminated. However, no extension to 112-bit keys has been adopted as part of the standard.

Commercial and Government Use of the DES

Since the adoption of the DES, it has received considerable acceptance by industry and government. However, the adoption has not been complete.

Only certain branches of the United States Government have adopted DES as a standard for encryption. The most notable, perhaps, is the recent adoption by the Department of Commerce for all EFT (electronic funds transfer) transactions of the United States Government. However, the most notable absence in the government from adoption is the Department of Defense.

In the private sector, the American Banking Association has been working on adopting a cryptographic standard but has not yet accepted DES as a standard.

DES Devices

A number of special-purpose cryptographic devices have been put on the market which use the DES. The maximum speed obtained to date is on the order of 10,000 bits per second. Consequently, on-line encryption is feasible for many forms of communication. For example, communication to remote devices over public networks is usually at 300 or 1200 baud; that is, approximately 300 or 1200 bits per second. Some networks are beginning now to provide service at 2400 baud.

In addition, many computer systems permit communication via serial ports to terminal devices at 9600 baud, still within the range of DES encryption. Thus it is possible in these sorts of configurations to envision an encryption device at the host computer encrypting and sending encrypted messages, which would be decrypted by other devices at the terminal, without giving the appearance to the user of a slowdown in performance.

Group Properties of the DES

One of the more interesting questions about the DES is, what are the characteristics of the subgroup of the group of all permutations of 64-bit strings, generated by the set of DES transformations?

A related question is, is the *set* of all DES transformations, Ω_{DES}, a group in and of itself? If the answer were to be yes, then the composition of two DES transformations would also be a DES transformation; thus both the sequential multiple transformation and the Tuchman extension would reduce to single 56-bit encryption; and the Hellman and Diffie attack could defeat either.

Furthermore, if the DES is a group, Kaliski, Rivest and Sherman demonstrate an algorithm (the "meet in the middle" algorithm) [KALI 85a] to cryptanalyze the DES in $2^{28} \approx 250,000,000$ steps.

Let G_{DES} be the *group* generated by the DES transformations. We say that a cryptosystem is faithful if distinct keys always give distinct transformations. (Another way of saying this is that the mapping from 56-bit keys to transformations is 1-1.)

For readers unfamiliar with the concept of a group, it is suggested that your next reading in the text be the first two appendices, on Modular Arithmetic and Group Theory.

If the DES is faithful, then the order of G_{DES} is at least 2^{56}. However, G_{DES} is a subgroup of the symmetric group on the message space, S_M. (Note: $| S_M | = (2^{64})!$)

It has been noted [COPP 75] that actually $G_{DES} \leq A_M$, the alternating subgroup (or group of even permutations), since every round of the DES is an even permutation.

Thus the security of the DES would be further enhanced if it were known that the set of DES transformations was not a group, in other words, that $\Omega_{DES} \neq G_{DES}$.

Kaliski, Rivest, and Sherman, in a very recent announcement, have performed a number of statistical tests which give strong statistical evidence that DES is not a group.

Hint for Exercise 2.4

Begin by showing that for any two bit-strings of equal length, a and b, $(a \oplus b)^c = a^c \oplus b$.

— 3 —
The Public-Key Paradigm

For any number of reasons, the modern view of cryptology has indicated that the model that we have been using for cryptography has numerous weaknesses.

In the systems we have discussed to date, we have ignored the problem of exchanging keys --- both the sender and the receiver of a message must agree upon a key in some way.

The Key Management Problem

Envision the development of a computer network consisting of one thousand subscribers where each pair of users requires a separate key for private communication. (It might be instructive to think of the complete graph on n vertices, representing the users; with the $n(n+1)/2$ edges corresponding to the need for key exchanges. Thus in the 1000-user network, approximately 500,000 keys must be exchanged in some way, other than by the network!)

In considering this problem, Diffie and Hellman [DIFF 76] asked the following question: Is it possible to consider that a key might be broken into two parts, $k = (kp, ks)$, such that only kp is necessary for encryption, while the entire key $k = (kp, ks)$ would be necessary for decryption?

If it were possible to devise such a cryptosystem, then the following benefits would accrue. First of all, since the information necessary for encryption does not, *a priori,* provide an attacker with enough information to decrypt, then there is no longer any reason to keep it secret. Consequently kp can be made public to all users of the network. A cryptosystem devised in this way is called a **public-key cryptosystem** (or **PKC**).

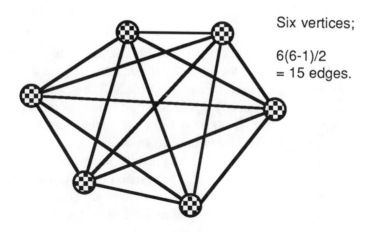

Six vertices;

6(6-1)/2
= 15 edges.

Figure 3.1
The Complete (Undirected) Graph on Six Vertices

Furthermore, the key distribution problem becomes much more manageable. Consider the hypothetical network of 1000 users, as before.

The PKC Model

For each user, choose a key $k_i = (kp_i, ks_i)$, i=1, ..., 1000. In a system-wide public directory, list all of the "public" keys kp_i, i=1, ..., 1000. Then, to send a message m to user j, select the public key, kp_i, and apply the *encryption* transformation

$$c = T(kp_i, m).$$

Send the ciphertext, c.
Only user j has the rest of the key necessary to compute:

$$T((kp_i, ks_i), c) = m.$$

Thus, rather than having to manage the *secret* distribution of $O(n^2)$ keys in a network of n users, only n keys are required, and they need not be distributed secretly.

Furthermore, the public-key concept could also be used for the **authentication** of messages in a way that a "secret-key" system could not address.

Authentication

Consider a cryptosystem based on the traditional "secret-key" approach. Consider also that it is used for funds transfer in a banking network. One day the system manager receives a message from X. The manager decrypts the message using the secret key agreed upon by X and the manager. The message reads, "transfer $1,000,000 from my account to the system manager's account". The manager dutifully does so.

X complains to the authorities, saying that the message was a forgery, sent by the manager himself(herself). The system manager, when reached for comment by long distance telephone from Tahiti, says that the message was authentic and that X had recanted his desire to make the transfer.

Since both X and the manager had to know the secret key, there is no way, using the cryptosystem, to resolve the dispute.

However, a public-key cryptosystem could have resolved the issue. Suppose that, in addition to the message, every transmission in the network is required to be "signed", that is, to contain a trailer encrypted using X's public key. Then, this requirement would carry with it the ability to authenticate X's message, since only X, knowing the rest of the key, would be able to decrypt the trailer.

Therefore, if we could devise a PKC, it would certainly have most desirable features. But many questions remain to be asked. First of all, can we devise a PKC? What should we look for? Second, if we can find one, will it be secure? Will it be efficient?

These questions will, of course, be addressed in the succeeding chapters. For now, we will consider only the general parameters of *finding* PKCs.

From the earlier description, we need to find functions that are "one-way", that is, that enable an efficient computation sufficient for encryption, but whose inverses are cryptanalytically very difficult to find.

It is interesting that the two examples we will study next are analogous in some sense: one involves the ease of adding numbers together combined with the difficulty (or impossibility) of determining the original addends, given a sum; the other involves the ease of multiplying numbers together combined with the difficulty of finding the original factors, given a product.

— 4 —
The Knapsack Approach
to Public-Key Cryptography

The first approach developed to the model of public-key encryption, as described in the previous chapter, drew its inspiration from a classic combinatorial mathematics problem known as the **knapsack problem**.

To state the problem in the form from which it drew its name, suppose that we have a knapsack that can hold exactly S pounds. Further, suppose that we have a number of objects that weigh w_1, w_2, ... , w_k pounds respectively.

What objects can we choose to take on a trip that will most nearly fill the knapsack, or fill it exactly, without exceeding the weight limit?

Phrased more generally, the knapsack problem, in one form, asks:

Given a finite set of natural numbers, $W = \{w_1, w_2, ..., w_k\}$, and a natural number S, is there a subset $W' \subseteq W$, $W' = \{w_{i1}, w_{i2}, ... , w_{im}\}$ such that $\sum w_{ij} = S$?

In general, the solution of the knapsack problem is very difficult indeed. Consider the approach of simply trying to exhaust all of the possibilities. If there are k elements in the set W, as described, then there are 2^k possible subsets, and therefore, for k any larger than, say, 100, the compute time to check all possibilities becomes hopeless.

In fact, it can be shown [GARE 76] that the knapsack problem falls into the category of **NP-complete problems**. For now, we will simply say that this is a class of problems that are believed to be, by their nature, incapable of being solved with an algorithm that can run in polynomial time.

Furthermore, with the "usual" set of numbers in a knapsack set, there would be so much over-determination that, if a certain solution to the knapsack problem were being sought, the attempt to find it would be hopeless.

EXERCISE 4.1: Suppose that W ={1,2,...,50} is a knapsack set. How many subsets of W sum to 625?

"Easy" Knapsack Sets

There are certain sets, however, for which both the *existence* and *uniqueness* problems as described above are easily solved. These are often referred to as **"easy" knapsack sets**, or more properly, as **super-increasing knapsack sets**.

An ordered set of natural numbers $W=\{w_1, w_2, ... , w_k\}$ is said to be **super-increasing** if, for every $j > 1$,

$$w_j > \sum_{i<j} w_i.$$

An example of a super-increasing set is $W=\{1,2,4,8, ..., 2^k\}$.

For the example given above, the algorithm to decide whether or not there exists a subset of W which sums to a given S is $O(|W|)$ --- simply put, it is a variation on the binary decomposition algorithm:

Super-increasing Subset Decomposition Algorithm

1. Let S be the sum, and $W = \{w_i\}$ the super-increasing set. Set n=i. Let $W' = \{ \}$ be the (initially empty) sum subset.

2. While $n \geq 1$, if $S \geq w_k$, then add w_k to W' ($W' = W' \cup \{w_i\}$), replace S by $S - \{w_i\}$. In any case, decrement i by 1.

3. Sum the elements of W'. If they add to S, then the subset W' is the (unique) subset sum. If they do not sum to S, then there is no subset which can sum to S.

In general, super-increasing sets are very rare amongst all possible knapsack sets. The super-increasing sets also have the interesting property that the ratio of the number of elements in the knapsack set, divided by the length of the bit-string required to represent the sum of the elements in the knapsack set, is not greater than 1.

To demonstrate this last statement, consider the example of the powers-of-2 knapsack set described above. If the number of elements of the knapsack set is n, the last element will be 2^{n-1}; and the sum of all the elements will be $2^n - 1$. The length of the bit-string required to represent the sum $2^n - 1$ is:

$$[\log_2 (2^n - 1)] = n.$$

(The notation [x] means the smallest integer greater than x.)

The ratio described in the above paragraph will henceforth be called D, for **density**. As a rough indication, the more "spread-out" the knapsack set, the lower the density. As we will see much later on, techniques have been developed to break most cryptosystems that have been devised using "low-density" knapsacks.

The First Public-Key Cryptosystem Proposed

About a year after the description of the "public-key" concept appeared, Merkle and Hellman [MERK 78] were able to describe a cryptosystem based on the public-key concept that seemed to have very desirable features indeed.

The Basic Merkle-Hellman Transformation

Suppose that $W=\{w_1, w_2, \ldots , w_k\}$ is a super-increasing knapsack set, as before. Suppose that it is possible to find a prime number p, larger than Σw_i; then choose, at random, a number m in the interval [1,p-1].

Because p is a prime, m must have an inverse modulo m (see Exercise A1 in Appendix A) in the multiplicative group $<\mathbb{Z}_p - \{0\}, \cdot >$. Call this element, as usual, m^{-1}.

Define E_{MH} to be a transformation *between knapsack sets* as $E_{MH}(w_i) = m \cdot w_i = w_j'$ (modulo n), $j = 1,\ldots,k$. In general, the transformed knapsack set in this way will *not* be an "easy" knapsack set.

Now we have enough development to describe the Merkle-Hellman cryptosystem. Let $\chi_{MH} = \ll K_{MH}, M_n, M_n, T_{MH} \gg$, where:

$$K_{MH} \subseteq \mathbb{N} \times \mathbb{N} \times \{W \mid W \text{ is an "easy" knapsack set }\}$$

In other words, we have two natural numbers, m and p, chosen as described above, along with an easy knapsack set.

The message space and the ciphertext space each consist of n-block ciphers, where n is the size of the knapsack set. Finally, the transformations that make up T_{MH} can be described as follows:

The easy knapsack set is chosen and transformed into a "hard" knapsack set $\{w_i\} \rightarrow \{w_i'\}$ by E_{MH}. The hard knapsack set $\{w_i'\}$ is placed in a public directory with access given to every user of the system. Similar public key sets are generated, as well, for every user. In other words, using the notation of the previous chapter, $kp = \{ w_i' \}$, and $ks = (m, p, \{ w_i \})$.

When user A wishes to send a message to user B, A encrypts his(her) message text, n bits at a time. Suppose the message is $b_1 b_2 ... b_n$. Then A looks up B's table of public keys, $\{ w'_{B,i} \}$, and forms a weighted sum

$$\sum_{i=0}^{n} b_i \cdot w'_{B,i}$$

This can also be interpreted as forming a subset sum based on a subset of the $\{ w_{B,m}' \}$ corresponding to the values of b_m which are 1.

Then this weighted sum is sent to B. When B receives the message, B proceeds to decrypt by applying the inverse transformation E_{MH}^{-1}. (Only B can apply this inverse, since only B knows the values of m and p.)

The inverse transformation is:

$$
\begin{aligned}
E^{-1}_{MH}(\sum b_i \cdot w'_{B,i}) \quad &\equiv\; m^{-1} \cdot \sum (b_i \cdot w'_{B,i}) &&(\bmod\ p) \\
&\equiv\; \sum b_i \cdot (m^{-1} \cdot w'_{B,i}) &&(\bmod\ p) \\
&\equiv\; \sum b_i \cdot w_{B,i} &&(\bmod\ p)
\end{aligned}
$$

This now is a subset sum in the easy knapsack set and can be deciphered using the super-increasing subset decomposition algorithm, giving the values of the b_i's.

An attacker would have difficulty proceeding directly with an attack on this problem, since the attacker would have only the "hard" knapsack sum; in general, trying to decompose such a sum is an NP-complete problem.

EXAMPLE:

We begin with a super-increasing knapsack set of 8 numbers:

$$\{ w_i \} = \{ 1, 3, 7, 13, 26, 65, 119, 267 \}.$$

Next, a prime number is sought which is greater than $\sum w_i = 501$. $p = 523$ is selected. Then, a number m is randomly chosen from the interval $[1, 522]$. Suppose the choice is $m = 467$.

Now the public keys are constructed, by multiplying each w_i by 467 and reducing mod 523, giving:

$$
\begin{aligned}
1 \cdot 467 &\equiv 467 \quad (\bmod\ 523) \\
3 \cdot 467 &\equiv 355 \quad (\bmod\ 523)
\end{aligned}
$$

$$
\begin{array}{rcccl}
7 \cdot & 467 & \equiv & 131 & (\text{mod } 523) \\
13 \cdot & 467 & \equiv & 318 & (\text{mod } 523) \\
26 \cdot & 467 & \equiv & 113 & (\text{mod } 523) \\
65 \cdot & 467 & \equiv & 21 & (\text{mod } 523) \\
119 \cdot & 467 & \equiv & 135 & (\text{mod } 523) \\
267 \cdot & 467 & \equiv & 215 & (\text{mod } 523)
\end{array}
$$

These numbers are published. To complete the secret key, we must compute $m^{-1} \equiv 28$ (mod 523). Thus the PKC is generated.

Suppose now that we wish to encrypt a message. Messages will be encrypted in blocks of 8 bits (since the size of the knapsack set is 8). We will illustrate only with the bitstring '01001011'.

Forming the sum:

$$
\begin{aligned}
\sum_{i=0}^{n} b_i \cdot w_i' \; = \; & 0 \cdot 467 + 1 \cdot 355 + 0 \cdot 131 + 0 \cdot 318 + \\
& 1 \cdot 113 + 0 \cdot 21 \; + 1 \cdot 135 + 1 \cdot 215 \\
= \; & 818.
\end{aligned}
$$

This number, 818, is sent.

To decrypt, we first multiply 818 by $m^{-1} \equiv 28$ and reduce mod 523, giving 415 mod 523. Now we decompose:

$$
\begin{array}{r}
415 \\
-\;\underline{267} \\
148 \\
-\;\underline{119} \\
29 \\
-\;\underline{26} \\
3 \\
-\;\underline{3} \\
0
\end{array}
$$

$$
\begin{aligned}
\Rightarrow \; \Sigma\, w_i \; = \; & 3 + 26 + 119 + 267 \\
= \; & 0 \cdot 1 + 1 \cdot 3 + 0 \cdot 7 + 0 \cdot 13 + \\
& 1 \cdot 26 + 0 \cdot 65 + 1 \cdot 119 + 1 \cdot 267
\end{aligned}
$$

yielding the decryption '01001011'.

In this example, the message could be intercepted and decoded by an attacker because the numbers used were too small, and there were too few of them. However, in the original Merkle-Hellman proposal, it was suggested that n be chosen to be 100; and that the easy knapsack numbers be chosen to be large to avoid an attack based on guessing their value. In particular, the ith knapsack number, w_i, was to be chosen at random from the interval

$$[2^{100+i-1} , 2^{100+i} - 1].$$

Since these knapsack numbers are so large, they could not possibly be guessed. Then a prime number $p > 2^{201}$ must be chosen, and then m chosen at random in the interval $[1,p-1]$.

One might ask whether or not this is computationally feasible. Can one find easily a prime number $> 2^{201}$? The answer is yes, using the Solovay-Strassen or Peralta methods as we will see in the next chapter.

However, it should be noted that a prime number is not really necessary here. All that is needed is that m have an inverse in the modular system $<Z_p - \{0\}, \cdot >$; that is (see Exercise I.1 in Appendix I), that m and p are relatively prime (GCD(m,p)=1).

Thus, the most efficient way of finding a usable m and p is to choose p at random in the interval $[2^{201}, 2^{202}]$ --- p may not be prime --- and then choose m at random as before. Apply the Euclidean algorithm (see Appendix III on Number Theory) to compute the GCD of m and p. If the GCD is greater than 1, choose another m until the condition is satisfied. The probability that m is relatively prime to p is so great that a successful candidate should be found after a few tries. In fact, the probability that two numbers chosen at random are relatively prime is $6/\pi^2$, a result known as Cesàro's Theorem.

Graham-Shamir Knapsacks

Independently, and almost at the same time as the development of the Merkle-Hellman public-key cryptosystem, Graham and Shamir [SHAM 80] proposed a slightly different approach to the use of knapsacks for public-key encryption.

In the Graham-Shamir cryptosystem, $\chi_{GS} = \ll K_{GS}, M_n, M_n, T_{GS} \gg$, the message space, ciphertext space, and the transformations are the same as in the Merkle-Hellman cryptosystem, $T_{GS} = T_{MH}$. The difference is that the easy knapsack set is constructed differently (and consequently decryption proceeds differently).

Each easy knapsack number comes from a bit-string that can be decomposed into three parts,

$$w_i = (L_i, I_i, R_i).$$

Each L_i and R_i is a random bit string of l bits and r bits, respectively. The I_i bit-string consists of n bits (where n is the size of the knapsack set), and it is:

$$I_i = (0, 0, ..., 0, 1, 0, ..., 0)$$
$$\uparrow \text{ } i^{th} \text{ place}$$

Generation of the public keys proceeds as before; that is, an appropriate m and p must be chosen, and a modular multiplication performed. Encryption also proceeds as with the Merkle-Hellman approach.

Decryption first applies E_{GS}^{-1}, that is, multiplication by m^{-1} and reduction modulo p. However, at this stage, the message text can be read directly by reading the $(l+1)^{st}$ to $(l+n)^{th}$ bits after applying E_{GS}^{-1}. This is true since the decryption of the term corresponding to a bit in the ith position of the message, leads to the use of the ith easy knapsack number, which is the only easy knapsack number with a 1-bit in the $(l+i)^{th}$ position.

Iterated Knapsacks

Another variant on both the Merkle-Hellman and the Graham-Shamir knapsack cryptosystem is the iterated version of each of these.

Instead of choosing one easy knapsack set, and one pair (m,p), one performs iterated transformations on each of r such knapsack sets.

In other words, at the jth stage, one transforms

$$\{ w_i^{j-1} \} \rightarrow \{ w_i^j \}$$

by a modular multiplication,

$$w_i^j = m_j \cdot w_i^{j-1} \quad (\text{modulo } p_j).$$

Encryption proceeds as in the basic Merkle-Hellman and Graham-Shamir methods; decryption consists of multipying by r inverses m_j^{-1} and reducing mod p_j.

Comparisons of the Knapsack Approaches and DES

The knapsack approaches all have the advantage over the DES in that they eliminate the problem of key distribution. However, these knapsack methods can been shown to be less computationally efficient than the DES.

Key storage in the DES requires 7 bytes per key. In the basic Merkle-Hellman knapsack scheme, there are 100 public keys, each containing between 100 and 200 bits. In addition, there are two private keys of 200 bits each. This gives a total of approximately 15,400 bits for key storage, or approximately 1,925 bytes per key.

Encryption and decryption in the DES both use the same algorithm. The computational cost is approximately 500 table lookups. Encryption in the knapsack method consists of 100 additions; decryption consists of 100 comparisons and 100 subtractions.

Key generation also has little overhead in the DES --- it consists of generating a 7-byte string at random. The key generation in the knapsack schemes is more complicated; at the very least it involves choosing 100 integers at random (from selected intervals), and m and p; which involve at best several applications of the Euclidean algorithm.

Final Comments

As will be seen in later chapters, the knapsack approach is vulnerable to various kinds of attack. However, the concept is important fundamentally because it led the way to further development of public-key cryptosystems; and, as we will see much later on, survives today in an altered, but as yet secure, variation.

EXERCISE 4.2: Write a program to implement either the Merkle-Hellman or the Graham-Shamir knapsack PKC.

— 5 —
The RSA Algorithm

About a year after the first description of a public-key cryptosystem using the knapsack problem, Rivest, Shamir, and Adelman [RIVE 78] described another cryptosystem using as an inherently difficult problem, the problem of factoring large numbers.

(Prior to reading this chapter, it is suggested that the reader be familiar with the contents of Appendix III on Elementary Number Theory.)

Factoring

How hard is factoring numbers in any case? The method most often encountered in elementary courses relies upon generating all the prime numbers up to the square root of the number to be factored, using, for example, the Sieve of Eratosthenes.

If the number we sought to factor contained, let us say, 200 digits, then we would need to be able to generate all the prime numbers of ≤ 100 digits.

Then we would have to test each of these prime numbers for factorization. The direct approach will be $O(n)$, which is infeasible to compute when n is a 200-digit number.

The current state of factoring algorithms would be a subject worthy of a chapter (or a book) by itself. A great deal of research is being done currently on this problem.

For now, suffice it to say that the best results, as of mid-1986, have been obtained by the research group at the Sandia National Laboratories, who are able to factor numbers of the size of 10^{70} in a few dozen hours, using a Cray XMP supercomputer; and at the Mitre Corporation, using a network of Sun-3 scientific workstations, who have factored numbers around 10^{80} in a *total* CPU time (for all Suns in the network) of 1200 hours. As a general principle, it order to factor numbers of any size effectively, an algorithm of O(log n) would be required.

All of the current algorithms being used for factoring have running time $L^{1+O(1)}$, where $L = \exp((\log n \, \log\log n)^{1/2})$. However, this algorithm is still not of the order of O(log n), nor is it polynomial in log n. *Six* algorithms share this theoretical result for complexity: they are the Lenstra elliptic curve algorithm [LENS 85], the Schnorr-Lenstra class-group algorithm [SCHN 84], the Schroeppel linear sieve algorithm [COPP 86], the Pomerance quadratic sieve algorithm [POME 85],the Coppersmith-Odlyzko-Schroeppel residue list sieve algorithm [COPP 86], and the Morrison-Brillhart continued fraction algorithm [MORR 75].

A common starting point of all these algorithms is that they convert the problem of factoring an integer, n, into the problem of finding non-trivial solutions to the equation:

$$x^2 \equiv y^2 \qquad (\bmod\ n)$$

By *non-trivial* is meant that $x \neq y$ and $x \neq (n-y)$.

Finding a non-trivial solution to this (mod n) equation immediately results in a factorization of n, since $x^2 \equiv y^2 \pmod{n} \Rightarrow (x^2 - y^2) \equiv 0 \pmod{n} \Rightarrow (x+y)(x-y) \equiv 0 \pmod{n} \Rightarrow (x+y)(x-y) = kn$ for some k. Thus, since it was assumed that x+y and x−y are not multiples of n, then either (x+y) or (x−y) must factor n. Thus the GCD(x+y,n) or GCD(x−y,n) is a non-trivial factor of n.

Rivest-Shamir-Adleman Algorithm

The basic idea of Rivest, Shamir and Adelman was to take two (100-digit) prime numbers, p and q, and multiply them together to obtain n = pq. n is published. Furthermore, two other numbers, d and e, are generated, where d is chosen randomly, but relatively prime to $\emptyset(n)$, in the interval [max(p,q)+1, n-1].

(Here $\emptyset(n)$ is the **Euler $\emptyset$-function**, or **totient**, which is the number of integers in the range [1, n-1] relatively prime to n. If n = p·q, p and q being primes, then $\emptyset(n) = (p-1)(q-1)$. See the discussion in Appendix III.)

KEY GENERATION:

1. Choose two 100-digit prime numbers randomly from the set of all 100-digit prime numbers. Call these p and q.

2. Compute the product $n = pq$.

3. Choose d randomly in the interval $[\max(p,q)+1, n-1]$, such that $GCD(d, \emptyset(n)) = 1$.

4. Compute $e \equiv d^{-1}$ (modulo $\emptyset(n)$).

5. Publish n and e. Keep p, q and d secret.

ENCRYPTION:

1. Divide the message into blocks such that the bit-string of the message can be viewed as a 200-digit number. Call each block, m.

2. Compute and send $c \equiv m^e$ (modulo n).

DECRYPTION:

1. Compute $c^d \equiv (m^e)^d \equiv m^{ed} \equiv m^{k\emptyset(n) + 1} \equiv$

$$m^{k\emptyset(n)} \cdot m \equiv 1 \cdot m \equiv m \quad \text{(modulo n)}.$$

Note that the result $m^{k\emptyset(n)} \equiv 1$ used in the preceding line is Theorem III.5 from Appendix III.

It may seem that some of these steps are not easily computed. But, first of all, the generation of 100-digit prime numbers is reasonable to compute using the methods of Solovay and Strassen, or Lehmann and Peralta, to be discussed below.

Additionally, we need to be able to determine numbers that are relatively prime to one another in a modular system, compute inverses in a modular system, and compute large exponents.

Reasonably fast algorithms for all of these steps are given in the aforementioned Appendix III.

EXAMPLE: (RSA ALGORITHM)

KEY GENERATION:

Choose p and q to be 2-digit primes, $p = 41$, $q = 53$.
Then $n = pq = 41 \cdot 53 = 2173$.
By Theorem III.2, $\emptyset(n) = (p-1) \cdot (q-1) = 40 \cdot 52 = 2080$.

Now d is chosen to be between 54 and 2079; such that $GCD(d, \emptyset(n)) = 1$. Say, $d = 623$.

Now we need to compute $e \equiv d^{-1}$. A convenient algorithm for computing the inverse is described both in Appendix III, and in the Pascal program to generate RSA keys.

One begins by writing a (3×2)- array (called A) where the first row of A consists of the modulus and the number to invert; the second and third rows consist of the rows of the (2×2) identity matrix.

The following steps are performed until the last element of the top row is zero:

1. The greatest integer multiplier (m) of the [1,2]- element of the array is found, such that the product is less than the [1,1] element of the array. Then $A[1,1] - m \cdot A[1,2]$ is computed.

2. It is only necessary to carry two columns' worth of information. Thus $A[1,1]$ can be replaced by $A[1,2]$, and $A[1,2]$ by the quantity computed in 1 above.

3. The same process is carried out for the second and third rows: computing $A[j,1] - m \cdot A[j,2]$, replacing $A[j,1]$ by $A[j,2]$, and $A[j,2]$ by the previous computation $(j = 2, 3)$.

4. Once $A[1,2]$ becomes zero, the desired inverse is the value of $A[3,1]$. The calculation for 623^{-1} (mod 2080) is as follows:

m			3	2	1	20	10
A[1,·]	2080	623	211	201	10	1	0
A[2,·]	1	0	1	-2	3	-62	
A[3,·]	0	1	-3	7	-10	207	

Thus the required inverse is $e \equiv 207$ (mod 2080).

Now, publish n = 2173 and e = 207.

ENCRYPTION:

We need a method for the division of the message text into blocks. Consequently, choose the highest power of 2 less than the value of n. Since n = 2173, we need $2^{11} = 2048$. This will guarantee that 11-bit blocks will have a unique representation when viewed as integers modulo n (=2173).

Thus, if we want to encrypt the message "JABBERWOCKY":

JABBERWOCKY

(ASCII) $\Rightarrow$	4A 41 42 42 45 52 57 4F 43 4B 59 hexadecimal
(binary) $\Rightarrow$	0101 1010 0100 0001 0100 0010
	0100 0010 0100 0101 0101 0010
	0101 0111 0100 1111 0100 0011
	0100 1011 0101 1001

(11-bit blocks)

$\Rightarrow$ 01011010010

$$00001010000$$
$$10010000100$$
$$10001010101$$
$$00100101011$$
$$10100111101$$
$$00001101001$$
$$01101011001$$

(reinterpret as decimal numbers)

$$\Rightarrow \qquad 722$$
$$80$$
$$1156$$
$$1109$$
$$299$$
$$1341$$
$$105$$
$$857$$

Call these messages m_1 through m_8. The respective ciphertexts will be c_1 through c_8. Then, for $i = 1, ..., 8$, compute m_i^e (mod n).

722^{207}	$\equiv$ 1794	$= c_1$	(mod 2173)
80^{207}	$\equiv$ 1963	$= c_2$	(mod 2173)
1156^{207}	$\equiv$ 1150	$= c_3$	(mod 2173)
1109^{207}	$\equiv$ 702	$= c_4$	(mod 2173)
299^{207}	$\equiv$ 145	$= c_5$	(mod 2173)
1341^{207}	$\equiv$ 593	$= c_6$	(mod 2173)
105^{207}	$\equiv$ 2013	$= c_7$	(mod 2173)
857^{207}	$\equiv$ 1861	$= c_8$	(mod 2173).

The ciphertext $c_1, ..., c_8$ is transmitted.

DECRYPTION:

When the ciphered messages $c_1, ..., c_8$ are received, each is raised to the (secret) d power (d = 623) and reduced mod 2173 (also secret):

$c_1 = 1794,$	$1794^{623} \equiv$	722 $= m_1$	(mod 2173)
$c_2 = 1963,$	$1963^{623} \equiv$	80 $= m_2$	(mod 2173)
$c_3 = 1150,$	$1150^{623} \equiv$	1156 $= m_3$	(mod 2173)
$c_4 = 702,$	$702^{623} \equiv$	1109 $= m_4$	(mod 2173)
$c_5 = 145,$	$145^{623} \equiv$	299 $= m_5$	(mod 2173)

$$c_6 = 593, \quad 593^{623} \equiv \quad 1341 \; = m_6 \qquad (\bmod\ 2173)$$
$$c_7 = 2013, \quad 2013^{623} \equiv \quad 105 \; = m_7 \qquad (\bmod\ 2173)$$
$$c_8 = 1861, \quad 1861^{623} \equiv \quad 857 \; = m_8 \qquad (\bmod\ 2173)$$

Then the 11-block bit-strings can be reconstructed from their binary forms, and thence back to ASCII and finally to text.

In a practical version of the algorithm, it is recommended by Rivest, Shamir, and Adelman that the primes p and q be chosen to be approximately of the same size, and each containing about one hundred digits.

The other calculations necessary in the development of an RSA cryptosystem have been shown to be relatively rapid. Except for finding the primes, the key generation consists of two multiplications, two additions, one selection of a random number, and the computation of one inverse modulo another number.

The encryption and decryption each require at most $2 \cdot \log_2 n$ multiplications (in other words, one application of the Fast Exponentiation algorithm) for each message block.

The Solovay-Strassen Test

A technique developed by Solovay and Strassen to determine, to a high degree of probability, that a number is prime [SOLO 77], is useful in choosing our secret primes p and q.

Suppose that a 100-digit number, p, is chosen randomly and that it is a candidate for primality. In other words, one might determine through the usual simple digit analysis tests that the number was not divisible by a small prime factor —— (for example) the number should be odd, digits not divisible by 3, last digit not 5, and the sum of the even and odd digits not equal modulo 11 (which is the test for divisibility by 11).

Having determined such a p, one then performs the **Solovay-Strassen primality test**:

1. Choose one hundred numbers a_i, $i = 1, 2, ..., 100$, randomly in the interval $[1, p-1]$.

2. If, for each number a_i, $GCD(p, a_i) = 1$ and

$$\left(\frac{a}{p} \right) \bmod p \; = a^{(p-1)/2} \bmod p$$

where $\begin{pmatrix} a \\ b \end{pmatrix}$ is the **Jacobi symbol** for the pair a, b defined as

the **Legendre symbol** (same notation) if b is a prime:

$$\begin{pmatrix} a \\ b \end{pmatrix} = \begin{array}{l} + 1, \quad \text{if a is a quadratic residue of b} \\ - 1, \quad \text{otherwise.} \end{array}$$

And, if b is not a prime, but has prime factorization $b = p_1 p_2 p_3 \cdots p_k$, then

$$\begin{pmatrix} a \\ b \end{pmatrix} = \begin{pmatrix} a \\ p_1 \end{pmatrix} \begin{pmatrix} a \\ p_2 \end{pmatrix} \begin{pmatrix} a \\ p_3 \end{pmatrix} \cdots \begin{pmatrix} a \\ p_k \end{pmatrix}$$

A recursive function which evaluates the Jacobi symbol is given in the attached program, P3 in Appendix III.

A number p which passes the Solovay-Strassen test will have a probability of *not* being prime of approximately 1 in 2^{100}. This is so because, if p is prime, the values of the Jacobi symbol for p and a_i will always coincide with $p^{(a_i - 1)/2}$, by definition of quadratic residues and of the Jacobi symbol. On the other hand, if p is not a prime, the probability that the Jacobi symbol and the exponential expression coincide is $\frac{1}{2}$. (This is essentially because the quadratic residue set and the quadratic non-residue set for a prime are of the same cardinality - Theorem III.10.)

Consequently, the probability that a number p is *not* prime and yet passes the test is $\frac{1}{2}$; the probability that a number which is not prime could pass all the tests is $(\frac{1}{2})^{100}$.

The Lehmann and Peralta Test

A test simpler to implement than the Solovay-Strassen was developed by Lehmann [LEHM 82] and later, independently, by Peralta [PERA 85].

As with the Solovay-Strassen test, one chooses 100 numbers a_i, i = 1,2,...,100 at random from the interval [1,..,p-1].

Then the test is as follows:

1. If $a_i^{(p-1)/2} \equiv 1$ for *all* i = 1,.., 100 then p is composite.
2. If $a_i^{(p-1)/2} \not\equiv 1$ or -1 for *some* i = 1,.., 100 then p is composite.
3. If $a_i^{(p-1)/2} \equiv 1$ or -1 for *all* i = 1,.., 100, *and* $a_i^{(p-1)/2} \equiv -1$ for *some* i = 1,.., 100 then p is prime.

Clearly this test is simpler to implement since it only involves raising each a_i to a power and looking at the result.

Final Comments

As we will see, most of the other proposed public-key cryptosystems have been shown to be either inefficient or insecure, except for the RSA. Consequently, the RSA algorithm is beginning to appear in many commercial applications.

RSA chips have been designed and implemented. However, the limitation even in hardware devices is that no more than a few thousand baud can be processed.

This means, for example, that an attempt to use RSA on-line inside a computer system where the transmission rates are, say, 9600 baud, would result in lag times that would probably result in dissatisfaction from a terminal user.

This problem could, in theory, be remedied by passing message text through RSA devices in parallel. However, in modern networks, where message rates are described in megabits per second or gigabits per second, rather than a few thousand bits per second, the parallel approach could be simply infeasible.

No successful attempts to cryptanalyze the RSA algorithm have been made to date. Clearly, if an efficient factoring algorithm were known, then the RSA method could be cryptanalyzed: since n's factors, p and q, would then be known, $\phi(n)$ could be computed and thus $e = d^{-1}$ could be computed.

However, what is not known is whether or not there is another algorithm to cryptanalyze the RSA which might be more efficient than attempts to factor.

Furthermore, unlike with the DES, the RSA algorithm is *flexible* in the sense that, if there was a successful approach to factoring 200-digit numbers, the algorithm could be altered to use, say, 400-digit numbers.

EXERCISE 5.1: Find an example to illustrate why, in the RSA algorithm, it is necessary to begin with two primes p and q rather than with two composites.

EXERCISE 5.2: Find primes p and q (p, q > 100, and n = p·q < 100000), which will minimize the "excess capacity" of the RSA algorithm, *that is will be such that (n-1) is greater than and yet as close to a power of 2 as possible.*

EXERCISE 5.3: *Compute the Jacobi symbols for all residue classes in mod 210 arithmetic.*

— 6 —

Breaking Knapsacks

It has been said earlier in the text that now, most knapsack methods are considered insecure. The purpose of this chapter will be to examine the techniques used in breaking knapsack methods.

Three approaches to breaking knapsacks have been published: One due to Shamir [SHAM 82], one to Lagarias and Odlyzko [LAGA 85] and one due to Brickell [BRIC 83].

Each of these is sufficient to break the basic Merkle-Hellman knapsack cryptosystem; but the latter two are successful with any knapsack cryptosystem using a *super-increasing* easy knapsack set.

As we will also see, the latter condition is found, implicitly or explicitly, in almost all knapsack cryptosystems yet proposed. However, there is one notable exception, which will also be discussed in a later chapter.

Each of the three methods that we will discuss relies on an important algorithm known commonly as the L^3 algorithm. It has been developed by Lenstra, Lenstra, and Lovász [LENS 83], and in various versions gives:

- a polynomial time solution for some integer programming problems;
- a method for finding "short" vectors in integer lattices;
- a method for factoring polynomials with rational coefficients.

The Shamir Attack

Let us recall the format of the basic Merkle-Hellman knapsack cryptosystem. In the public directory is a list of "hard" knapsack numbers $\{ w_1', w_2', \dots, w_n' \}$. A message $\mu = b_1 b_2 \dots b_n$ is encrypted by computing $C = \Sigma\, b_i w_i'$, and C is sent. Thus we assume that an attacker knows, of course, the w_i', and intercepts C.

Recall that it is an NP-complete problem, in general, to determine the b_i knowing only the w_i' and C.

The Shamir attack will proceed by analyzing the numbers w_1', w_2', ... , w_n' and attempt to find a **trapdoor pair** N and M such that the set { Mw_i' (mod N) } is a superincreasing sequence, whose sum is < N. We will define the "approximate proportionality" (representing the growth rate of the knapsack numbers) of w_{i+1}' to w_i' to be d, d = average ratio, over all i, of w_{i+1}' to w_i'. (For example, in the Merkle-Hellman algorithm, $d \approx 2$.)

Were we to find such a pair (M,N), even if they were not the original secret pair (m,p), the pair (M,N) would suffice since all knapsack instances could be solved in linear time, using the binary decomposition algorithm.

Since the w_i' arise from a superincreasing sequence by modular multiplication, we know that there exists *at least one* such trapdoor pair.

Breaking a Small Knapsack Example

Before describing Shamir's method, we will apply an approach which is a simplification of Shamir's to "break" the knapsack example given in Chapter 4.

Recall that in that example, the set of knapsack numbers $\{w_i'\}$ = { 467, 355, 131, 318, 113, 21, 135, 215 } is published.

We wish to find a pair of numbers (M,N) with the property that $\{M \cdot w_i'$ (mod n)$\}$ forms a super-increasing knapsack set.

Let us make the hypothesis that we have discovered in some way that the order of the public numbers above actually corresponds to the (increasing) order of the elements in the secret knapsack set. What this means is, that if we find the required trapdoor pair (M,N), then the number $M \cdot w_1' \equiv 467M$ (mod N) will have to be less than $2^{-7} \cdot N$.

Why? Since we have assumed in the Merkle-Hellman cryptosystem that the super-increasing knapsack numbers are each approximately *twice* as large as the preceding, and since the last in the series must be less than N, and since there are 8 such numbers, the first of these would have to be less than $2^{-7} \cdot N$.

Suppose now that we graph the (real-valued) function y = f(M) = 467M (mod N), as in Figure 6.1.

The zeroes of this function occur at M = $^N/_{467}$, $^{2N}/_{467}$, etc.

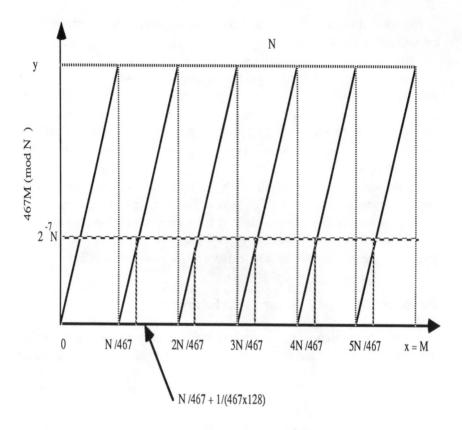

Figure 6.1
Graph of y = 467M (mod N)

Furthermore, for the value of y to be $< 2^{-7} \cdot N$, the implication is that M must lie in the interval

$$[\, p \cdot N/467, \quad p \cdot N/467 + 2^{-7} \cdot N/467 \,] \qquad p = 1, 2, \ldots, 466$$

Thus we now have a collection of 466 small intervals in [0,N] in which the value must lie.

Indeed, if instead we reparametrize the coordinates by dividing by N, then we can conclude that the ratios M/N must be in one of the 466 intervals:

$$[\, p/467, \quad p/467 + 1/(467 \cdot 128) \,] \qquad p = 1, 2, \ldots, 466.$$

Now, knowing that $w_2' = 355$, and applying the same arguments, we can conclude that $M \cdot w_2' = 355M \pmod{N}$ will be $< 2^{-6} \cdot N$. Further, the ratio M/N will be in one of the 354 intervals:

$$[\, q/355, \; q/355 + 1/(355 \cdot 64) \,] \qquad q = 1, 2, \ldots, 354.$$

With this information, we can cut down the set of intervals that we have to examine. Indeed, since the ratios M/N must lie in one each of both sets of intervals, we need to look only at:

$$(\bigcup_{p=1}^{466} [p/467, \; p/467 + 1/(467 \cdot 128) \,]) \cap (\bigcup_{q=1}^{354} [\, q/355, \; q/355 + 1/(355 \cdot 64) \,])$$

A simple program (essentially a merge sort) computed this set to be a series of nine possible intervals (the intervals were approximated by double precision reals):

[0.053533190578, 0.053565140845]
[0.107066381156, 0.107086267606]
[0.160599571734, 0.160607394366]
[0.473239436620, 0.473250133833]
[0.526766595289, 0.526804577465]
[0.580299785867, 0.580325704225]
[0.633832976445, 0.633846830986]
[0.687366167024, 0.687367957746]
[0.946478873239, 0.946483538544]

Now let's compute the effect of w_3'. We need to examine the intersection of the nine proceeding intervals with

$$[\, r/131, \; r/131 + 1/(131 \cdot 32) \,] \qquad r = 1, 2, \ldots, 130.$$

Again using merge sort, we whittle the number of possible intervals down to 4:

[0.053533190578, 0.053565140845]
[0.107066381156, 0.107086267606]
[0.526766595289, 0.526804577465]
[0.580299785867, 0.580325704225]

m	n	m/n
25	467	0.053533190578
50	467	0.107066381156
53	495	0.107070707071
28	523	0.053537284895
56	523	0.107074569790
59	551	0.107078039927
31	579	0.053540587219
62	579	0.107081174439
65	607	0.107084019769
34	635	0.053543307087
37	691	0.053545586107
40	747	0.053547523427
43	803	0.053549190535
46	859	0.053550640279
49	915	0.053551912568
50	934	0.053533190578
100	934	0.107066381156
103	962	0.107068607069
52	971	0.053553038105
53	990	0.053535353535
106	990	0.107070707071

Table 6.1

Potential Values for the Trapdoor Pair (M,N)

Finally, performing the same analysis with w_4' leads us to only two potential intervals, [0.053533190578, 0.053565140845] and [0.107066381156, 0.107086267606].

So the question to answer is, what possible values of M and N will give a fraction $M/_N$ which will lie in [0.053533190578, 0.053565140845] and [0.107066381156, 0.107086267606]? We can assume that if the public numbers are distributly randomly throughout mod N arithmetic, that N is not likely to be greater than 2·max | w_i' |. Consequently, the next step is to find rationals $M/_N$, with GCD(M,N) = 1,

		N	≤ 2·max | w_i' |
0.053533190578	≤	N/M	≤ 0.053565140845
0.107066381156	≤	N/M	≤ 0.107086267606

A simple computation shows that the pairs in Table 6.1 meet these criteria.

So, for example, transforming the public numbers by the pair (25, 467) yields:

$$0 \quad 2 \quad 6 \quad 11 \quad 23 \quad 58 \quad 106 \quad 238$$

which is not a super–increasing set.

However, transforming by (53,990) gives:

$$1 \quad 5 \quad 13 \quad 24 \quad 49 \quad 123 \quad 225 \quad 505$$

which *is* a super–increasing set.

Consequently, we would proceed as follows: Intercept a message W. Compute 53W (mod 990). Solve the subset–sum problem for the numbers { 1, 5, 13, 24, 49, 123, 225, 505 }. This will decode the message.

It is worth noting that this effort gives us, in effect, *two* knapsack pairs, (53,990) and (28,523). And, of course, for this attack, either pair will do as nicely. The second of these pairs, (28,523), is of course the original pair, as can be noted by referring again to the example in Chapter 4.

Let's examine the steps in the foregoing procedure to see what can and cannot be extended to a Merkle-Hellman PKC where the easy knapsack numbers are from 100 to 200 bits in length.

First, we made the assumption that we knew which knapsack numbers corresponded to w_1', ..., w_4'. In general, we would not know this, of course, so we might try all possible combinations, leading to a $C(n,4) = O(n^4)$ algorithm, where n is the size of the knapsack set.

This assumption would be acceptable if we knew that the search for different sets of intervals only led to a small number (e.g., 4). This will be one of the major steps demonstrated in the Shamir attack.

The computation of the intersection of the intervals in the small example was done by enumeration. This could not be extended to a 200-bit example. However, the search for such intervals leads to the search for integer solutions to a series of equations of the form (the integer programming problem):

$$q/w_j' \;\leq\; p/w_i' \;\leq\; q/w_j' \cdot (1 + 1/w_j' \cdot 2^k)$$

In this case, such solutions are possible to find in polynomial time, using the L^3 algorithm for integer programming (although the *general* integer programming problem is NP-complete).

Finally, once we have found a specific interval $[\varepsilon_1, \varepsilon_2]$, we need to find a solution to another integer programming or diophantine approximation problem

$$\varepsilon_1 \leq M/N \leq \varepsilon_2$$

with a bound on N.

A description of efficient methods to carry out this latter computation can be found in [KNUT 69] on pages 300-307.

EXERCISE 6.1: Replicate the previous attack for the Merkle-Hellman public-key cryptosystem based on the public set of knapsack numbers { 175, 238, 389, 467, 469, 1168, 1323, 1362, 1556, 1721}.

Constructing the Shamir Attack

The Shamir algorithm will find a trapdoor pair (M,N) satisfying the requirements, in many cases. (And of course, for cryptanalytic purposes, if a cryptosystem can be broken even *some of the time*, the security of the system has essentially been compromised.) The algorithm consists of two steps:

STEP ONE: Find a few small intervals in [0,1] such that a *necessary* condition for (M,N) to be a trapdoor pair is that M/N ($\in$ ℚ, the set of rational numbers) lies in such an interval.

STEP TWO: Use the fact that M/N is approximately known to divide each interval into smaller intervals such that a *sufficient* condition for (M,N) to be a trapdoor pair is that their ratio is in a subinterval. Then we will use a fast diophantine approximation algorithm based on the L^3 algorithm to find the smallest M and N.

CONSTRUCTING STEP ONE: Let N_0 be the (unknown) modulus used in the construction of the cryptosystem. Consider the real-valued function M $\longmapsto M w_i'$ (mod N_0). In other words, the function $y = f(x) = w_i' x$ (mod N_0) is as in Figure 6.1.

The slope of this sawtooth curve is (except at discontinuity points) w_i'; the number of minima is w_i'; and the distance between successive minima is N_0/w_i'.

Consider the curve associated with w_1'. The multiplier has the property that $w_1 = M w_1'$ (mod N_0) is $\leq 2^{dn-n}$, by the Merkle-Hellman algorithm.

Therefore the distance between N and the closest minimum of w_1' curve to its left is $\leq 2^{dn-n} / w_1' \cong 2^{-n}$.

The unknown N must be extremely close to some minimum of the w_1' sawtooth curve. Similarly, N must also be within

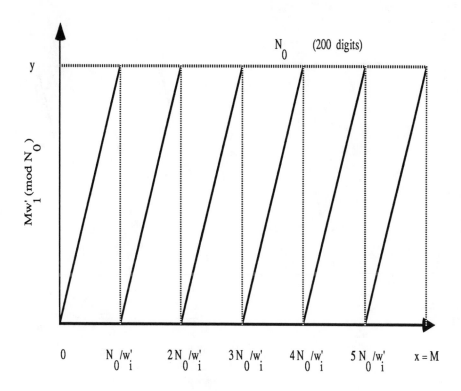

Figure 6.2
A Sample Sawtooth Curve

$$2^{dn - n + 1} / w_2' \approx 2^{-n+1}$$

from the closest w_2' curve minimum to its left.

Therefore the two minima of the w_1' and w_2' curves are very close.

Extending this argument, the required value N is an accumulation point for all of the n sawtooth curves.

How many of these sawtooth curves do we have to analyze? Suppose the number to be analyzed is λ. Consider the rth minimum of the w_1' curve, which is located at $W = rN_0/w_1'$. The closest minimum of the w_i' curve can be anywhere in the interval:

$$[rN_0/w_1' - N_0/2w_i' , rN_0/w_1' + N_0/2w_i']$$

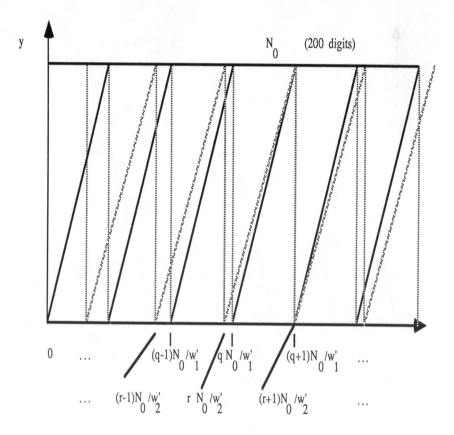

Figure 6.3
Two Superimposed Sawtooth Curves

If the assumption is made that the locations of the w_i' minima are independent random variables with uniform probability distribution over the intervals given above, the probability that the minima of the w_2', w_3', ..., w_λ' curves are close is given by:

$$2^{-n+1} \, 2^{-n+2} \, ... \, 2^{-n+\lambda-1} \; \approx 2^{-\lambda n + n + \lambda^2/2}$$

The expected number of accumulation points is

$$w_1' \cdot 2^{-\lambda n + n + \lambda^2/2} \approx 2^{dn - \lambda n + n + \lambda^2/2}$$

This value will be < 1 whenever

$$(\lambda - d - 1) \, n \; > \; \lambda^2 / 2.$$

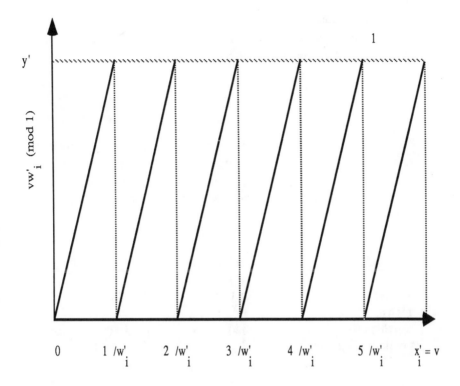

Figure 6.4
The Sawtooth Curves in the Normalized Coordinate System

Whenever n is large enough (in our case n = 100), this is satisfied by the condition $\lambda > d + 1$.

Therefore, for the case of the basic Merkle-Hellman algorithm, it will suffice to choose $\lambda = 4$, since $d \approx 2$.

The problem in determining these curves is that we don't *know* the value of N_0. However, the accumulation points depend on the *slopes*, but not on the curves themselves. Consequently, we can reparametrize by dividing both coordinates by N_0 to obtain:

$$y_i' = y_i / N_0 \; ; \quad x_i' = x_i / N_0$$
$$y_i' = f_i' (x_i') = w_i' x_i' \quad (\text{mod } 1)$$

In the new coordinate systems, the slopes remain $w_1', w_2', \ldots w_n'$. The distance between successive minima is $1/w_i'$.

The original N_0 parameter is replaced by $V_0 = M_0 / N_0$.

Clearly, if we can find the cluster point for the functions f_i', we will be able to return to the functions f_i and find the corresponding cluster point.

The location of the minima is the solution to the inequalities:

$$-\varepsilon_2 \leq p/w_1' - q/w_2' \leq \varepsilon_2' \qquad 1 \leq p \leq w_1' - 1$$
$$-\varepsilon_2 \leq p/w_1' - r/w_3' \leq \varepsilon_3' \qquad 1 \leq q \leq w_2' - 1$$
$$1 \leq r \leq w_3' - 1.$$

The preceding system can be solved in polynomial time by the L^3 algorithm as applied to integer programming. It should be noted that, in general, an algorithmic solution to the integer programming problem is an NP-complete problem. Consequently, we should proceed to discuss the L^3 algorithm.

The Lenstra-Lenstra-Lovász (L^3) Algorithm

One version of the L^3 algorithm is called the **basis reduction algorithm**.

Consider first the n-dimensional real vector space $\mathbb{R}^n$. A subset $L \subset \mathbb{R}^n$ is called a **lattice** if $\exists$ a basis $\beta_1, \beta_2, ..., \beta_n$ of $\mathbb{R}^n$.э.

$$L = \bigoplus_{i=1}^{n} \mathbb{Z}\beta_i = \{ \sum_{i=1}^{n} z_i \beta_i \mid z_i \in \mathbb{Z} \}.$$

(The vectors β_i will also be written component-wise as $(b_{i1}, b_{i2}, ..., b_{in})$.)

We say that the vectors $\{\beta_i\}$ form a **basis** for the lattice L, and n is the **rank** of L. The **determinant** $d(L)$ of L is defined by:

$$d(L) = | \det(\beta_1, \beta_2, ... , \beta_n) |.$$

EXAMPLE:

Let the lattice $L \subset \mathbb{R}^3$ be defined by

$$L = \{ z_1 \beta_1 + z_2 \beta_2 + z_3 \beta_3 \}$$
$$= \{(2z_1 + z_2, z_2, 3z_3) \mid \forall z_1, z_2, z_3 \in \mathbb{Z}\}.$$

$$d(L) = | \det (\beta_1, \beta_2, \beta_3) | = \begin{vmatrix} 2 & 0 & 0 \\ 1 & 1 & 0 \\ 0 & 0 & 3 \end{vmatrix} = 6.$$

Given two vectors β_1 and $\beta_2 \in \mathbb{R}^n$, $\beta_1 = (b_{11}, b_{12}, ..., b_{1n})$, $\beta_2 = (b_{21}, b_{22}, ..., b_{2n})$. The **inner product** (or dot product) of two vectors $\beta_1 \cdot \beta_2$ is:

$$\beta_1 \cdot \beta_2 = b_{11}b_{21} + b_{12}b_{22} + ... + b_{1n}b_{2n} = \sum_{i=1}^{n} b_{1i}b_{2i}.$$

Two vectors β_1, β_2 are said to be **orthogonal** $\Leftrightarrow \beta_1 \cdot \beta_2 = 0$.

Given n linearly independent vectors β_1, β_2, ... , $\beta_n \in \mathbb{R}^n$, a procedure called the **Gram-Schmidt orthogonalization process** produces a new set of linearly independent and pairwise orthogonal vectors β_1^*, β_2^*, ..., β_n^*. The vectors β_i^* are defined inductively as:

$$\beta_1^* = \beta_1$$

$$\beta_i^* = \beta_i - \sum_{j=1}^{i-1} \mu_{ij} \beta_j^* \qquad i = 2, ..., n$$

$$\mu_{ij} = (\beta_i \cdot \beta_j^*) \, / \, (\beta_j^* \cdot \beta_j^*) \qquad i > j.$$

(The inner product of any vector with itself, $\beta \cdot \beta$, is also the square of its length, and is written $|\beta|^2$.)

A basis $\beta_1, \beta_2, ... , \beta_n$ for a lattice L is *reduced* if:

$$|\mu_{ij}| \leq 1/2 \qquad\qquad 1 \leq j < i \leq n \qquad (1)$$

and $\quad |\beta_i^* + \mu_{i,i-1} \beta_{i-1}^*|^2 \geq (3/4)|\beta_{i-1}^*|^2 \qquad 1 < i \leq n \qquad (2)$

A good way of thinking of a reduced basis is that it consists of "relatively short" vectors in the lattice. Indeed, the search for the short vectors in a lattice is one motivation for the development of the basis reduction algorithm.

Here are two examples in $\mathbb{R}^3$ of bases for lattices that are reduced and non-reduced:

EXAMPLE 1:

$$\beta_1 = (1, 1, 1)$$
$$\beta_2 = (1, 1, -1)$$
$$\beta_3 = (-1, 1, 1)$$

This basis is not orthogonal (for example, $\beta_1 \cdot \beta_2 = 1 \neq 0$). Apply the Gram-Schmidt orthogonalization process to obtain:

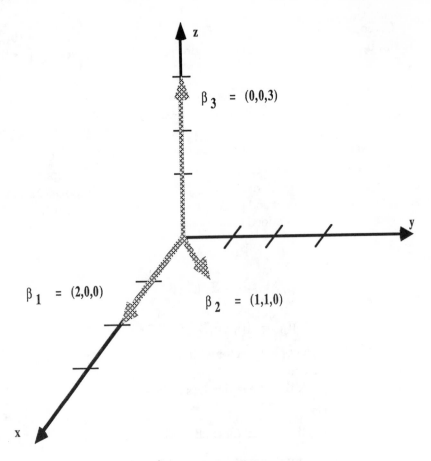

Figure 6.5
Basis for a Three-Dimensional Lattice

$$\beta_1{}^* = \beta_1 = (1, 1, 1)$$
$$\mu_{21} = (\beta_2 \cdot \beta_1{}^*) / |\beta_1{}^*|^2 = {}^1/_3$$
$$\beta_2{}^* = \beta_2 - \mu_{21}\beta_1{}^* = ({}^1/_3)(2, 2, -4)$$
$$\mu_{31} = (\beta_3 \cdot \beta_1{}^*) / |\beta_1{}^*|^2 = {}^1/_3$$
$$\mu_{32} = (\beta_3 \cdot \beta_2{}^*) / |\beta_2{}^*|^2 = (-{}^4/_3) / ({}^{24}/_9) = {}^1/_2$$
$$\beta_3{}^* = \beta_3 - \mu_{31}\beta_1{}^* - \mu_{32}\beta_2{}^*$$
$$= (-1, 1, 1) - ({}^1/_3)(1, 1, 1) + ({}^1/_2)({}^2/_3, {}^2/_3, -{}^4/_3)$$
$$= (-1, 1, 0).$$

This gives the orthogonal basis. For this basis to be *reduced*, we must have:

CONDITION (1): The quantities $|\mu_{21}|$, $|\mu_{31}|$, and $|\mu_{32}|$ are all $\leq \frac{1}{2}$.
CONDITION (2):

$$| \beta_2^* + \mu_{21}\beta_1^* |^2 = | (\frac{2}{3}, \frac{2}{3}, -\frac{4}{3}) + (1/3)(1, 1, 1) |^2$$
$$= | (1, 1, 1) |^2 = 3.$$
$$(3/4) | \beta_1^* |^2 = (\frac{3}{4}) \cdot 3 = 2.25.$$

Thus Condition 2 is satisfied for this pair. Also,

$$| \beta_3^* + \mu_{32}\beta_2^* |^2 = | (-1, 1, 0) - (\frac{1}{2})(\frac{2}{3}, \frac{2}{3}, -\frac{4}{3}) |^2$$
$$= 24/9 > 2.666.$$
$$(3/4) | \beta_2^* |^2 = (3/4) \cdot (\frac{4}{9} + \frac{4}{9} + \frac{16}{9}) = 2.$$

Thus the basis is reduced. The lengths of the reduced basis vectors are, $\sqrt{3}$, $(2\sqrt{6})/3$, and $\sqrt{2}$ respectively. The estimate of theorem 6.2 shows that no non-zero vector in the lattice can have length less than $(\sqrt{2})/4$.

EXAMPLE 2:

$$\beta_1 = (1, 1, 0)$$
$$\beta_2 = (0, 1, 1)$$
$$\beta_3 = (7, 3, 2)$$

Again, this basis is not orthogonal (for example, $\beta_1 \cdot \beta_2 = 1 \neq 0$). Apply the Gram-Schmidt orthogonalization process to obtain:

$$\beta_1^* = \beta_1 = (1, 1, 0)$$
$$\mu_{21} = (\beta_2 \cdot \beta_1^*) / |\beta_1^*|^2 = \frac{1}{2}$$
$$\beta_2^* = \beta_2 - \mu_{21}\beta_1^* = (0, 1, 1) - (\frac{1}{2})(1, 1, 0)$$
$$= (-\frac{1}{2}, \frac{1}{2}, 1)$$
$$\mu_{31} = (\beta_3 \cdot \beta_1^*) / |\beta_1^*|^2 = 5$$
$$\mu_{32} = (\beta_3 \cdot \beta_2^*) / |\beta_2^*|^2 = 0$$
$$\beta_3^* = \beta_3 - \mu_{31}\beta_1^* - \mu_{32}\beta_2^*$$
$$= (7, 3, 2) - 5(1, 1, 0) = (2, -2, 2).$$

This gives the orthogonal basis. For this basis to be *reduced*, we must have:

CONDITION (1): The quantities $|\mu_{21}|$, $|\mu_{31}|$, and $|\mu_{32}|$ all $\leq \frac{1}{2}$; clearly, the basis is *not* reduced since $|\mu_{31}| = 5 > \frac{1}{2}$.

Reduced Bases and Short Vectors

Next, we will prove two theorems that will show that the reduced basis for a lattice does consist of relatively short vectors.

THEOREM 6.1: Let $\beta_1, \beta_2, \ldots, \beta_n$ be a reduced basis for a lattice $L \subset \mathbb{R}^n$, and let $\beta_1^*, \beta_2^*, \ldots, \beta_n^*$ be defined by the Gram-Schmidt orthogonalization process. Then:

$$|\beta_j|^2 \leq 2^{i-j}|\beta_i^*|^2 \qquad\qquad 1 \leq j \leq i \leq n \qquad (3)$$

$$d(L) \leq \prod_{i=1}^{n} |\beta_i| \leq 2^{n(n-1)/4} \cdot d(L) \qquad\qquad (4)$$

$$|\beta_1| \leq 2^{(n-1)/4} \cdot d(L)^{1/n} \qquad\qquad (5).$$

PROOF: From the definition of reduced basis we have:

$$|\beta_i^*|^2 \geq (3/4 - \mu_{i,i-1}^2)\,|\beta_{i-1}^*|^2 \geq \tfrac{1}{2}\,|\beta_{i-1}^*|^2.$$

Since

$$\begin{aligned}
&|\beta_i^* + \mu_{i,i-1}\beta_{i-1}^*|^2 \\
= &\ (\beta_i^* + \mu_{i,i-1}\beta_{i-1}^*) \cdot (\beta_i^* + \mu_{i,i-1}\beta_{i-1}^*) \\
= &\ (\beta_i^*, \beta_i^*) + \mu_{i,i-1}(\beta_{i-1}^*, \beta_i^*) \\
&\ + \mu_{i,i-1}(\beta_i^*, \beta_{i-1}^*) + \mu_{i,i-1}^2(\beta_{i-1}^*, \beta_{i-1}^*) \\
= &\ |\beta_i^*|^2 + \mu_{i,i-1}^2|\beta_{i-1}^*|^2 \geq (3/4)|\beta_{i-1}^*|^2.
\end{aligned}$$

Thus

$$\begin{aligned}
|\beta_i^*|^2 &\geq 3/4\,|\beta_{i-1}^*|^2 - \mu_{i,i-1}^2|\beta_{i-1}^*|^2 \\
&= (3/4 - \mu_{i,i-1}^2)\,|\beta_{i-1}^*|^2 \geq \tfrac{1}{2}\,|\beta_{i-1}^*|^2.
\end{aligned}$$

∴, by induction:

$$|\beta_j^*|^2 \leq 2^{i-j}|\beta_i^*|^2 \qquad\qquad 1 \leq j \leq i \leq n.$$

This proves the inequality (3).
To prove (4), we have:

$$\begin{aligned}
d(L) &= |\det(\beta_1, \beta_2, \ldots, \beta_n)| \\
&= |\det(\beta_1^*, \beta_2, \ldots, \beta_n)| \\
&= |\det(\beta_1^*, \beta_2^* + \mu_{21}\beta_1^*, \ldots, \beta_n)| \\
&= |\det(\beta_1^*, \beta_2^*, \ldots, \beta_n)| + |\det(\beta_1^*, \mu_{21}\beta_1^*, \ldots, \beta_n)|
\end{aligned}$$

(since the determinant is a linear function in each row)

$$= |\det(\beta_1{}^*, \beta_2{}^*, ..., \beta_n)| = ...$$

(the second term is zero since the second row is a multiple of the first)

$$= |\det(\beta_1{}^*, \beta_2{}^*, ..., \beta_n{}^*)|.$$

Since the $\beta_i{}^*$ are pairwise orthogonal,

$$\Rightarrow \quad d(L) = \prod_{i=1}^{n} |\beta_i{}^*|.$$

Since $|\beta_i{}^*| \le |\beta_i|$, and $|\beta_i| \le 2^{(i-1)/2}|\beta_i{}^*|$, $\prod |\beta_i| \le 2^{\Sigma(i-1)/2} \cdot \prod |\beta_i{}^*|$.

And then, since $\sum_{i=1}^{n}(i-1)/2 = n(n-1)/4$:

$$\Rightarrow d(L) \le \prod |\beta_i| \le 2^{n(n-1)/4} d(L),$$

which proves (4).

Substitute $j = 1$ in (3), giving $|\beta_1|^2 \le 2^{i-1}|\beta_i{}^*|^2$

$$\Rightarrow |\beta_1|^{2n} \le 2^{n(n-1)/4} \cdot |\beta_i{}^*|^2 = 2^{n(n-1)/4} d(L)^2.$$

Taking $2n^{th}$ roots, obtain (5):

$$|\beta_1| \le 2^{(n-1)} d(L)^{1/n}.$$

Q.E.D.

THEOREM 6.2: Let $L \subset \mathbb{R}^n$ be a lattice with reduced basis $\beta_1, \beta_2, ..., \beta_n$. Then,

$$|\beta_1| \le 2^{(n-1)} |x|^2 \qquad \forall x \in L, x \ne 0. \qquad (6)$$

PROOF: Let $x \in L$. Then $x = \sum z_i \beta_i = \sum z_i{}' \beta_i{}^*$ with $z_i \in \mathbb{Z}$, $z_i{}' \in \mathbb{R}$. Let i be the largest index with z_i with $z_i \ne 0$. Then, $z_i{}' = z_i$. Then,

$$|x|^2 \ge z_i{}'^2 |\beta_i{}^*|^2 \ge |\beta_i{}^*|^2.$$

But, by theorem 6.1,

$$|\beta_1{}^*|^2 \le 2^{i-1}|\beta_i{}^*|^2 \le 2^{n-1}|\beta_i{}^*|^2 \le 2^{n-1}|x|^2.$$

Q.E.D.

These two theorems (6.1 and 6.2) taken together give an estimate on how close a vector of the reduced basis must be to the shortest (non-zero) vector in the entire lattice.

THEOREM 6.3: Let $L \subset \mathbb{R}^n$ be a lattice with reduced basis $\beta_1, \beta_2, ..., \beta_n$. Let $x_1, x_2, ..., x_n \in L$ be linearly independent vectors. Then:

$$| \beta_j |^2 \leq 2^{n-1} \cdot \max \{ |x_1|^2, |x_2|^2, ..., |x_n|^2 \}. \qquad\qquad j = 1,2,...,t$$

PROOF: Write each x_j as $x_j = \Sigma \, z_{ij} \beta_i$, with the $z_{ij} \in \mathbb{Z}$, $1 \leq i \leq n$, and $1 \leq j \leq t$. For a fixed j, let $i(j)$ denote the largest $i \ni z_{ij} \neq 0$.

Then, by Theorem 6.2,

$$| x_j |^2 \geq | \beta_{i(j)}{}^* |^2 \qquad\qquad 1 \leq j \leq t.$$

Renumber the $x_j \ni i(1) \leq i(2) \leq ... \leq i(t)$. j must be less than or equal to $i(j)$ for $1 \leq j \leq t$. Otherwise, the $x_1, x_2, ..., x_j$ would all belong to the vector space $\mathbb{R}\beta_1 \oplus \mathbb{R}\beta_2 \oplus ... \oplus \mathbb{R}\beta_{j-1}$, which would be a contradiction to the hypothesis that the $\{ x_i \}$ form an n-dimensional linearly independent set.

$$\therefore \quad | \beta_j |^2 \leq 2^{i(j)-1} \cdot | \beta_{i(j)} |^2 \leq 2^{n-1} \cdot | \beta_{i(j)} |^2 \leq 2^{n-1} \cdot | x_j |^2.$$

Q.E.D.

In other words, choosing any set of linearly independent vectors in the lattice, the reduced basis is bounded by the length of x_j (times a constant).

Combining the first conclusion of theorem 6.1 and the preceding inequality gives:

$$| \beta_i |^2 \leq 2^{n-1} \cdot | \beta_i{}^* |^2.$$

The Reduced Basis Algorithm

The central algorithm developed (and proved to run in polynomial time) by Lenstra, Lenstra, and Lovász is the **reduced basis algorithm**.

It is provided here in Appendix VI coded in Pascal, but first some explanation.

The algorithm begins with any basis $\{ \beta_i \}$ for an integer lattice, and eventually computes a reduced basis in the sense of the previous section.

The algorithm first computes a Gram-Schmidt orthogonal basis from the basis $\{ \beta_i \}$. Then the basis $\{ \beta_i \}$ is updated, each time leaving a *partial* basis satisfying conditions (1) and (2) below:

$$| \mu_{ij} | \leq 1/2 \qquad\qquad\qquad 1 \leq j < i \leq k \quad (1)$$
$$\text{and} \quad | \beta_i^* + \mu_{i,i-1} \beta_{i-1}^* |^2 \geq (3/4) | \beta_{i-1}^* |^2 \qquad 1 < i \leq k \quad (2)$$

at least up to some value k. The conditions are always trivially satisfied for $k \leq 2$. If, after some iteration, $k = n+1$, then we are finished.

There will essentially be two cases to consider at each stage in the iteration:

CASE 1. $k \geq 2$ and

$$| \beta_k^* + \mu_{k,k-1} \beta_{k-1}^* |^2 < (3/4) | \beta_{k-1}^* |^2.$$

In this case, we will proceed by interchanging the vectors $\beta_k \leftrightarrow \beta_{k-1}$, and leaving the other (k-2) β_i vectors unchanged.

CASE 2. $k = 1$ or

$$| \beta_k^* + \mu_{k,k-1} \beta_{k-1}^* |^2 \geq (3/4) | \beta_{k-1}^* |^2.$$

In this case, we check first to find a value μ_{kl} greater than $1/2$, and then replace β_k by $\beta_k - r\beta_l$, where r is the closest integer to μ_{kl}. This is repeated until all the μ_{kl}'s are of the proper size. Then k is incremented by $+1$.

It has to be shown **(a)** that the procedure terminates; and **(b)** that it terminates in **polynomial time**.

ROUGH PROOF THAT THE PROCEDURE TERMINATES:

Consider

$$d_i = abs(det \begin{bmatrix} \beta_1 \cdot \beta_1 & \beta_1 \cdot \beta_2 & \cdots & \beta_1 \cdot \beta_i \\ \beta_2 \cdot \beta_1 & \beta_2 \cdot \beta_2 & \cdots & \beta_2 \cdot \beta_i \\ & & \cdots & \\ \beta_i \cdot \beta_1 & \beta_i \cdot \beta_2 & \cdots & \beta_i \cdot \beta_i \end{bmatrix}).$$

$$d_i = \prod_{j=1}^{i} | \beta_j^* |^2 \qquad\qquad \Rightarrow \qquad d_i \text{ 's are positive reals.}$$

Further $d_0 = 1$ by definition, and $d_n = d(L)^2$. Set $D = \prod_{i=1}^{n-1} d_i$.

D changes only if some β_i^* changes (by the definition of D). This occurs only in case 1. Further, d_{k-1} is reduced by a factor $< 3/4$, $\therefore$ D is reduced by a factor $< 3/4$. But D is bounded below by 1, therefore case 1 can only be executed a finite number of times.

In case 1, k is decremented by 1, and in case 2, k is incremented by 1. Consequently, since the algorithm terminates when $k = n$, case 2 can be executed at most n-1 times more than case 1. Since case 1 can only be executed a finite number of times, this demonstrates that the algorithm terminates.

COMPLEXITY OF THE REDUCED BASIS ALGORITHM:

The running time of the algorithm is $O(n^4 \log B)$, as measured in terms of numbers of arithmetic operations, where B is a value larger than the length of any of the given basis vectors.

The crucial question is the number of times that we can pass through case 1.

Since $d_i \le B^i$, we have $D \le B^{n(n-1)/2}$. Since D is reduced by a factor of $3/4$ each time through, the number of times must be at most of the order $n^2 \log B$. The balance of the analysis giving $O(n^4 \log B)$ is omitted.

Using the L^3-Algorithm to Complete the Shamir Attack

Recall that we have to solve the following system of linear inequalities in order to complete the Shamir attack:

$$- \varepsilon_2 \le p/w_1' - q/w_2' \le \varepsilon_2' \qquad\qquad 1 \le p \le w_1' - 1$$
$$- \varepsilon_2 \le p/w_1' - r/w_3' \le \varepsilon_3' \qquad\qquad 1 \le q \le w_2' - 1$$
$$1 \le r \le w_3' - 1.$$

This problem is a form of the general *integer programming* problem, which is known to be NP-complete. However, when the size of the constants (ε's) is given a bound related to the number of variables, L^3 can be used.

In particular:

THEOREM 6.4: There exists a polynomial-time algorithm that, given a positive integer n, and rational numbers $w_1, w_2, ..., w_n, \varepsilon$ satisfying $0 < \varepsilon < 1$, will find integers $p_1, p_2, ..., p_n, q$.э.

$$| p_i - q w_i | \le \varepsilon \qquad\qquad \text{for } 1 \le i \le n$$
and
$$1 \le q \le 2^{n(n+1)/4} \varepsilon^{-n}.$$

PROOF:

Consider the lattice of rank (n+1) defined by the vectors

$$\beta_1 \qquad = \qquad (1, \quad 0, \quad ..., \quad 0, \qquad\qquad - w_1)$$
$$\beta_2 \qquad = \qquad (0, \quad 1, \quad ..., \quad 0, \qquad\qquad - w_2)$$
$$...$$

$$\beta_n \quad = \quad (\ 0,\ \ 0,\ ...,\ 1, \qquad\qquad -w_n\ )$$
$$\beta_{n+1} \quad = \quad (\ 0,\ \ 0,\ ...,\ 0, \qquad 2^{-n(n+1)/4}\,\varepsilon^{n+1}\ ).$$

Apply the basis reduction algorithm to find (in $O(n^4 \log B)$ time) a reduced basis $\beta_1^{*}, \beta_2^{*}, ..., \beta_{n+1}^{*}$. Then, by Theorem 6.3, we have

$$|\ \beta_1^{*}\ |^2 \ \le\ 2^{n/4}\ d(L)^{1/(n+1)}.$$

Recall that

$$d(L) = \quad \det \begin{bmatrix} 1 & 0 & ... & 0 & & & -w_1 \\ 0 & 1 & ... & 0 & & & -w_2 \\ & & & & ... & & \\ 0 & 0 & ... & 1 & & & -w_n \\ 0 & 0 & ... & 0 & & 2^{-n(n+1)/4}\,\varepsilon^{n+1} \end{bmatrix}$$

$$= \qquad 2^{-n(n+1)/4}\,\varepsilon^{n+1}.$$

$$\therefore\ 2^{n/4}\ d(L)^{1/(n+1)}$$
$$= \qquad 2^{n/4}\ (2^{-n(n+1)/4}\,\varepsilon^{n+1})^{1/(n+1)}$$
$$= \qquad 2^{n/4}\ \cdot\ 2^{-n/4}\ \cdot\ \varepsilon\ =\ \varepsilon.$$

$$\Rightarrow\ |\ \beta_1^{*}\ |\ \le\ \varepsilon.$$

Since the original vector $\beta_1^{*} \in L$, we can write

$$\beta_1^{*}\ =\ \sum_{i=1}^{n} p_i\,\beta_i\ +\ q\,\beta_{n+1} \qquad\qquad (p_i, q \in \mathbb{Z}\ ).$$

$$\Rightarrow\ \beta_1^{*}\ =\ (p_1 - qw_1,\ p_1 - qw_1,\ ...,\ p_1 - qw_1,\ q\cdot 2^{-n(n+1)/4}\cdot\varepsilon^{n+1}\ ).$$

Thus, by analyzing the magnitude of each coordinate, we can conclude that

$$|\,p_i - qw_i\,|\ \le\ \varepsilon \qquad\qquad \text{for } 1 \le i \le n$$
and
$$|\,q\,|\ \le\ 2^{n(n+1)/4}\,\varepsilon^{-n}.$$

There are finally two possibilities. Either q is a positive or a negative integer. If it is negative, replace β_1^{*} by $-\beta_1^{*}$ to get the desired result for q.

Q.E.D.

The Lagarias-Odlyzko Attack

As opposed to the Shamir attack, as discussed above, which is applicable only to the basic Merkle-Hellman cryptosystem, the Lagarias-Odlyzko attack can be applied to much more general subset sum cryptosystems.

First, recall the definition of *knapsack density* of a knapsack set $\{ w_1, w_2, ..., w_n \}$:

$$D = n/(\log_2 (w_n)).$$

In the basic Merkle-Hellman cryptosystem, $n=100$, $\log_2(w_n) = 200$, $\Rightarrow$ $D = 0.5$.

For "almost all" problems with $D < 0.645$, a polynomial time attack can be expected to break such cryptosystems.

The procedure for attacking arbitrary "low-density" cryptosystems consists of setting up an integer lattice, and subsequently finding, by the L^3 algorithm, a reduced basis, and consequently the "short vectors" for the lattice.

Recall that, as an attacker, we know the (public) $\{ w_i' \}$, and intercept the message C. Then we are essentially trying to solve the problem:

$$\sum_{i=1}^{n} b_i w_i' = C \tag{8}$$

for the b_i's.

In order to recast this problem as a basis reduction problem, consider the lattice L defined by the following vectors in $\mathbb{R}^{n+1}$:

$$\beta_1 = (1, 0, 0, ..., 0, -w_1')$$
$$\beta_2 = (0, 1, 0, ..., 0, -w_2')$$
$$...$$
$$\beta_n = (0, 0, 0, ..., 1, -w_n')$$
$$\beta_{n+1} = (0, 0, 0, ..., 0, \ C\ )$$

We may easily eliminate the cases $C = 0$ and $C = \sum w_i'$, so we will consider that $1 \le C < \sum w_i'$.

The solution to the problem (8) will be found by applying Lagarias and Odlyzko's **Algorithm SV**:

ALGORITHM SV (FOR SHORT VECTOR):

1. Choose a basis as above, for an (n+1)-dimensional integer lattice L = L(w,C).

2. Using the L^3 algorithm, find a reduced basis { β_i' } of L.

3. Check to see if any $\beta_j' = (b_{j,1}, b_{j,2}, ..., b_{j,n+1})$ has all $b_{j,k}$ = either 0 or some fixed B for $1 \leq k \leq n$. For any such β_j', check if $x_j = (1/B) b_{j,k}$, $1 \leq k \leq n$, is a solution to (8). If so, halt. Otherwise continue.

4. Repeat steps 1 through 3 with C replaced by $C' = \Sigma\ w_i' - C$.

If the Algorithm SV produces a solution, we say it *succeeds*, otherwise it *fails*.

The analysis of the algorithm itself is simple. It is essentially two applications of the L^3 algorithm, whose termination and running time we have analyzed.

The problem is to demonstrate that, in low-density cases, that the SV Algorithm will indeed succeed in most cases.

For the details of the proof, the reader is referred to [LAGA 85].

The value of the constant 0.645 may seem curious, and, although Lagarias and Odlyzko's proof is too detailed for inclusion here, some rationale for the aforementioned bound can be given.

First of all, let $S_n(R)$ represent the number of integer lattice points inside or on the surface of the n-dimensional sphere, centered at the origin. (This sphere is represented by all points $(x_1,...,x_n) \in \mathbb{R}^n$ such that $\Sigma\ x_i^2 \leq R$.) Lagarias and Odlyzo compute a good upper bound for this function. Their result is that

$$S_n\ (n/2)\ \leq\ 2^{1.54725n}.$$

They are also able to show that this bound does not hold if the last decimal unit is reduced by one. After noticing that $1.54725 = (0.645)^{-1}$, the main theorem shows that the SV algorithm will find a short vector almost all the time if the lattice coefficients are bounded by $2^{1.54725n}$. Furthermore, the growth of the coefficients, inverted, gives the density.

Brickell's Attack

It should be noted that Brickell [BRIC 83] has achieved approximately the same results in breaking low-density knapsacks as have Lagarias and Odlyzko, while using somewhat different techniques.

The Chor-Rivest Algorithm and Other Proposed Public-Key Cryptosystems

Since the discovery of the Merkle-Hellman and the Rivest-Shamir-Adelman public key cryptosystems, a great deal of effort has been expended to try to broaden the category of useful PKCs.

The purpose of this chapter is to describe several of the current efforts. Indeed, four other public-key cryptosystems will be described; these will be as much for the sake of disseminating new ideas about public-key encryption as for providing a practical PKC. As will be discussed, only the third of these methods is secure and (reasonably) practical.

The McEliece Method Using Algebraic Coding

Algebraic Coding Theory is the study, using algebraic structures, of methods of defining "error-correcting" codes -- which is to say, choices of character codes which permit a receiver of a transmission to determine if there have been errors in that transmission.

The subject of Algebraic Coding Theory has been treated in detail in [MacW 78], [PETE 61], [BERL 68]. We will give here a very cursory introduction to the subject.

Coding Theory

Coding, in general, is the translation of information into a form that will protect against corruption in the information, as may be introduced by noise (for example, electrical interference).

We first assume that all information to be transmitted is binary. Furthermore, we will make the working assumption that errors due to noise occur randomly and independently; and that it is just as likely for a 0 to be incorrectly received as a 1, as the reverse.

If errors occur in this fashion, say with a 1% probability, then the probability of a single error in a 3-bit string is $.01 \cdot (.99)^2 + .99 \cdot .01 \cdot .99 + (.99)^2 \cdot .01 = 0.029403 \cong 2.94\%$. The probability of all three bits being correct is $.99^3 = 0.970299 \cong 97.03\%$. The probability of all three bits being corrupted is $.01^3 = 0.000001$.

Maximum likelihood decoding assumes that when two possibilities hold for a given situation, that the most likely possibility has occurred.

For example, if we use a parity check method for the above example of a 3-bit string, the parity check may determine that an *odd* number of errors has occurred. Since the probability of a *1-bit* error is 0.0294, and the probability of a *3-bit* error is 0.000001, we assume that the single-bit error has occurred.

Thus, parity check methods are useful in enabling us to determine if a single error has occurred in a transmission. Such methods fall into the category of **single-error detecting** codes. (We will also shortly talk about **single error-correcting** codes, where not only does the coding method allow us to determine that one error has occurred, but where it has occurred so that we may fix it.)

Metrics on Bit Strings

DEFINITION: Let X and Y be binary strings of length n. The **Hamming distance** between X, and Y, $d_H(X,Y)$ is the number of components in which X and Y differ. (After Richard W. Hamming.)

$$d_H(x,y) \quad = \quad \text{\# of 1-bits in } x \oplus y \quad (\oplus = \text{XOR})$$
$$= \quad \text{number of places where the two strings} \\ \text{do not match.}$$

EXERCISE 7.1: *Show that the Hamming distance is a metric on the set of all binary n-strings (Z_n), i.e. that:*

(a) $d_H(X,Y) \geq 0$

(b) $d_H(X,Y) = 0 \iff X = Y$

(c) $d_H(X,Y) = d_H(Y,X)$

(d) $d_H(X,Z) \le d_H(X,Y) + d_H(Y,Z)$.

Suppose that we have defined a **code**, to be some subset of Z_n. (For example, ASCII is a code that is a subset of Z_7, EBCDIC of Z_8, BCD of Z_6, Baudot of Z_5, etc.)

DEFINITION: The **minimum distance** of a code is the minimum Hamming distance between all possible pairs of distinct code words.

EXERCISE 7.2: What is the minimum distance for ASCII, EBCDIC, BCD, Baudot?

Each error that occurs in the transmission of a code word adds one unit to the Hamming distance between that code word and the received word.

Using the principle of maximum-likelihood decoding, we will decode a received word as the closest code word in terms of Hamming distance.

Suppose the minimum distance of a code is $d+1$. Then suppose that a code word has been corrupted by up to d errors --- since changing d digits in a code word could not change the word into any other code word, we know for sure that errors have occurred.

Consequently a code with minimum distance $d+1$ is capable of *detecting* any combination of d or fewer errors. Such a code is called a **d-error detecting code**.

Now suppose that the minimum distance of the code is $2d+1$. If a code word X is corrupted by d or fewer errors, then the received word X' will be such that $d_H(X,X') \le d$; but for any other code word Y, $d_H(X', Y) \ge d+1$. Thus, it will be possible to correctly decode X' as X, since it is the unique code word with distance $\le d$ to the received word.

Consequently a code with minimum distance $2d+1$ is capable of *detecting and correcting* any combination of d or fewer errors. Such a code is called a **d-error correcting code**.

As a simple example of this theory, consider all 6-bit strings $Z_6 = \{ b_1 b_2 \dots b_6 \}$. The subset $C \subset Z_6$ is defined by all those strings with an even number of 1-bits (the number of 1-bits is also known as the **weight** of the string). Then, the Hamming distance between any two elements of C is ≥ 2. (Since, if two elements of C have different numbers of 1's, the distance must be at least two; and, if $x,y \in C$ have the same number of 1's, but $x \ne y$, then again at least two bits must be different.

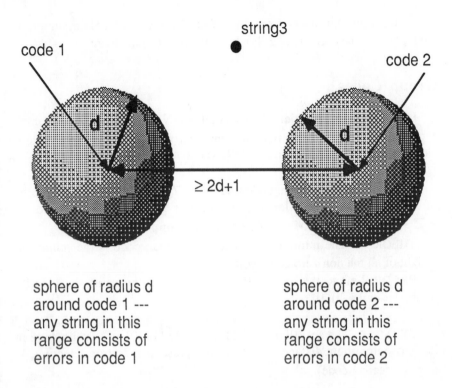

sphere of radius d
around code 1 ---
any string in this
range consists of
errors in code 1

sphere of radius d
around code 2 ---
any string in this
range consists of
errors in code 2

string3 will not decode to either code1 or code2

Figure 7.1
d-Error Correcting Codes

There are C(6,0) + C(6,2) + C(6,4) + C(6,6) = 1 + 15 + 15 + 1 = 32 elements of C. (C(m,n) is the number of combinations of m things taken n at a time.) Thus, a 32-character set can be encoded with the elements of C. Suppose such an encoding is done, and a transmission (unencrypted) is sent and received.

If the bit-string 011100 is received, the receiver would know that there had been an error in transmission, since 011100 ∉ C.

Furthermore, if the Hamming distance between any two codes is at least 3, then a code received with a *single* error can be *corrected*, since the distorted transmission would be only one bit away from one correct code and at least two bits away from any other. Thus a reasonable assumption would be that the correct code should be the one, one bit away.

Group Codes

Under modulo 2 addition, the set of all binary n-bit strings (Z_n) becomes a group. What is the identity element, and what is the inverse of any element? (Modulo 2 addition = XOR: $0 \oplus 0 = 1 \oplus 1 = 0$; $1 \oplus 0 = 0 \oplus 1 = 1$.)

We will now seek for our code a subset of Z_n that also forms a *subgroup* of Z_n under mod 2 addition (for which our group notation would be $< Z_2^n, \oplus >$). Such a code will be called a **group code**.

THEOREM. The minimum distance of a group code is the minimum weight of all the non-zero code words.

PROOF: Left to the reader. Prove the theorem by using the identity $d(a,b) = d(a \oplus (-b), 0)$.

EXAMPLE: The set {00000, 01111, 10101, 11010} is a group code in Z_5 whose minimum distance is 3 (thus it represents a 2-error detecting, 1-error correcting code).

Generating Group Codes

Let H be any $n \times r$ binary matrix with $r < n$. If $X \in Z_n$, then we can perform the matrix multiplication $X \cdot H$ (all operations are mod 2). The result will always be an element of Z_r.

Thus multiplication by H is a mapping $Z_n \to Z_r$. Furthermore, the mapping is an additive group homomorphism, by which we mean that $H(X+Y) = H(X) + H(Y)$.

The **kernel** of the mapping H is the set of all those elements X, of Z_n for which $H(X) = 0$. This kernel can be taken to be a set of code words.

The importance of this is that the minimum distance of the code can be determined by analyzing the matrix H. If H has d distinct rows that add to 0 (in Z_{n-r}), then the element X in Z_n having 1's exactly where these d rows occur will be in the kernel of H, and thus is a code word. This implies that the minimum distance will be at *most* d. However, if there is a code word with weight less than d, then the rows of H corresponding to the 1-bits of this code word will also add to zero. This shows that we can state this result as a:

THEOREM: The minimum number of rows of H adding to 0 is also the minimum distance of the code.

EXAMPLE. The matrix H is defined as:

$$
H = \begin{bmatrix}
1 & 0 & 1 \\
1 & 1 & 1 \\
1 & 0 & 0 \\
0 & 1 & 0 \\
0 & 0 & 1
\end{bmatrix}
$$

Verify that no two rows add to zero, but that 1, 2, and 4 do; thus the minimum distance of this code is 3.

In effect, in H, each column performs an even parity check of selected components of X. Thus, H is called a **parity-check matrix**.

EXERCISE 7.3: Find a group code defined by the kernel of a mapping from $Z_7 \rightarrow Z_4$ with distance 4.

Canonical Parity-Check Matrix

Given an $n \times r$ parity-check matrix H, we do not yet know what size code H generates. We can best assess this question by assuming that our parity-check matrix has a **canonical form**:

$$
H = \begin{bmatrix} B \\ I_r \end{bmatrix}
$$

where I_r is the $r \times r$ identity matrix, and B is an arbitrary $(n-r) \times r$ binary matrix.

Each of the last r components of X controls the even parity check for one of the r multiplications that are done. For X to be a code, the first $n-r$ components can be arbitrary, but the final r components will then be determined.

The maximum number of code words is the maximum number of ways to select $(n-r)$-strings, i.e 2^{n-r}. Let $m = n - r$. Then all members of Z_m can be coded as code words in Z_n by leaving the first m components alone and then choosing the last r components so that the even parity check works for each column of H. This procedure encodes members of Z_m in Z_n; such a code is called an (n,m) code. The first m components of a code word are called the **information digits,** and the last r the **check digits.**

In the example above, with n=5, r=3, H can generate 2^2 code words. Each of the words 00, 01, 10, 11 can be coded as a member of Z_5 by keeping the first two digits and adding the appropriate check digits. For example, the code for 10 is 10101.

Hamming Codes

Suppose now that we want to encode Z_m as a single error-correcting code. How big will the code words have to be?

If the code is to be 1-error correcting, the minimum distance must be 3. Thus, no two rows can be alike. Since each row has r elements, there can be no more than 2^r rows. We cannot have the zero row, however, thus the number of possible rows is $2^r - 1$. Thus, $n \le 2^r - 1$, and $m = n - r \le 2^r - r - 1$. Thus, to code the set of all binary m-tuples in a 1-error correcting code requires r check digits where r is such that $m \le 2^r - r - 1$.

If r and m are such that $m = 2^r - r - 1$, then the code is said to be a **perfect code.** In this case, the rows of the matrix consist of all the $(2^r - r - 1)$ r-tuples with at least 2 1's and the code generated by H is called a **Hamming code.** Which demonstrates the:

THEOREM. For any number $n = 2^r - 1$, there exists a perfect, single-error correcting Hamming code of length $2^r - 1$ and size $2^{2^r - r - 1}$.

The perfect code which has 3 check digits is a (7,4) code. One matrix that will generate it is:

$$
\begin{bmatrix}
1 & 1 & 0 \\
1 & 0 & 1 \\
0 & 1 & 1 \\
1 & 1 & 1 \\
\hline
1 & 0 & 0 \\
0 & 1 & 0 \\
0 & 0 & 1
\end{bmatrix}
$$

Decoding

Suppose that a code has been chosen, and we know what it is —— of course, since there is no secrecy involved here!!

Now we attempt to *decode* a given communication that is received. First of all, a direct decoding process involves simply comparing the received n-tuple X with all the code words. Then we decode X as the closest code word in terms of Hamming distance. However, there may *not* be a closest (unique) code word, and even if there is, our process may cause us to decode incorrectly, depending on the number of errors incurred in transmission and the minimum distance of the code.

If no errors have occurred, then X will be correctly decoded to itself; however, the difficulty is that if the code is of size 2^m, we will have to do 2^m comparisons in order to find the code word closest. We must have an array of all 2^m code words against which to compare. For m = 32, for example, this becomes a number so large it is unreasonable to compare.

Decoding a Group Code

However, if our code is a group code, generated by an n × r canonical parity-check matrix, then we can devise a decoding procedure requiring storage of only 2^r elements. In a 1-error correcting code, if m = 32, then r can be 6, and only $2^6 = 64$ pieces of information need to be kept available.

Recall that the set of code words is the kernel of the homomorphism defined by the matrix H from Z_n to Z_r. Thus Z_n can be partitioned into *cosets* of the form $X + C$, where C is the kernel of the homomorphism.

Since C has 2^m elements, by the index theorem for subgroups (Appendix II), the number of cosets is $2^n/2^m = 2^{n-m} = 2^r$. The cosets provide the key to decoding. Suppose a word X is received. X belongs to the coset $X + C$. Each element E of this coset can be written $X + C$, where $C \in C$.

Then, $E = X + C$, or $X + C + C = E + C \Rightarrow X = E + C$.

Thus, the 1's in E occur exactly in those components where X and C differ. Thus, the weight of E is the distance between X and C. The code word C closest to X is the one for which the corresponding E has minimum weight.

So, to decode X, we look for the element in the coset having of X having minimum weight, and, add that element to X. The result is the code word to which we decode X.

The coset element having the minimum weight is called the **coset leader**. It may or may not be unique. If two n-tuples of minimum weight occur in the same coset, one is arbitrarily chosen as the coset leader.

To summarize, suppose we use the code C = {00000, 01111, 10101, 11010} generated using the matrix:

$$H = \begin{bmatrix} 1 & 0 & 1 \\ 1 & 1 & 1 \\ 1 & 0 & 0 \\ 0 & 1 & 0 \\ 0 & 0 & 1 \end{bmatrix}$$

Suppose the message X = 11011 is received.
The members of the coset X + C are:

$$11011 + 00000 = 11011$$
$$11011 + 01111 = 10100$$
$$11011 + 10101 = 01110$$
$$11011 + 11010 = 00001$$

The coset leader is therefore 00001. Adding the coset leader to X gives us 00001 + 11011 = 11010, and we decode X to 11010.

EXERCISE 7.4: Find all the cosets of Z_5 under H as above.

Syndrome

DEFINITION. In a binary group code generated by the n × r parity-check matrix H, for any X in Z_n, the r-tuple X·H is the **syndrome** of X.

THEOREM. Let H be an n × r parity-check matrix generating a group code C; then for X, Y in Z_n, X and Y are in the same coset of C ⟺ X and Y have the same syndrome.

PROOF: X·H = Y·H   ⟺   (X-Y)·H = 0   ⟺   X and Y are in the same coset.

Q.E.D.

Galois Field Codes and Goppa Codes

Many error-correcting codes have been based on the structure of finite or Galois fields. The reader is advised to read Appendix V if he or she is not yet familiar with the elementary structure theory of Galois fields.

A **Goppa Code** is an error-correcting code defined using the elements of GF(p,n).

To construct a Goppa code, we require first, a polynomial $G(z)$ --- the **Goppa polynomial** --- whose coefficients are in GF(p,n). Further, we require a subset $L = \{ \alpha_1, \alpha_2, \ldots, \alpha_m \} \subseteq GF(p,n)$.э.

$$G(\alpha_i) \neq 0 \qquad \forall\ \alpha_i \in L.$$

Now for any vector $a = [\ a_1 \ldots a_m\ ]$ over $GF(p) = \mathbb{Z}_p$, we construct the rational function:

$$R_a(z) = \sum_{l=1}^{m} a_l / (z - \alpha_l).$$

The Goppa code $\Gamma(L,G) \subseteq GF(p,n)$ consists of all vectors $a \in GF(p,n)$.э.

$$R_a(z) \equiv 0 \qquad (\mathrm{mod}\ G(z)).$$

The properties of a Goppa code are only listed here. For a full discussion, the reader is referred to [MacW 78], [LIDL 83], or [McEL 83].

Properties of Goppa Codes

The properties of Goppa codes are:

1. $\Gamma(L,G)$ is a linear code over $\mathbb{Z}_p$. In other words, a, b $\in$ $\Gamma(L,G)$ $\Rightarrow$ $a + b \in \Gamma(L,G)$.

2. The length of a code word is $m = |\ L\ |$.

3. The dimension is $k \geq m - n \cdot r$, where $r = \deg G(z)$, the degree of the Goppa polynomial. The dimension is defined as $\log_2$ (number of code words).

4. The minimum distance is $d \geq r + 1$.

5. A parity check matrix for the code is:

$$H = \begin{bmatrix} 1/G(\alpha_1) & 1/G(\alpha_2) & \ldots & 1/G(\alpha_m) \\ \alpha_1/G(\alpha_1) & \alpha_2/G(\alpha_2) & \ldots & \alpha_m/G(\alpha_m) \end{bmatrix}$$

POLYNOMIAL NOTATION	BIT-STRING NOTATION	MULTIPLICATIVE GENERATOR (α) NOTATION
0	000	0
1	100	1
x	010	α
1+x	110	α^3
x^2	001	α^2
$1+x^2$	101	α^6
$x+x^2$	011	α^4
$1+x+x^2$	111	α^5

Table 7.1
Representations of the Field GF(2,3)

6. There exists a fast decoding algorithm due to N. J. Patterson [PATT 75].

EXAMPLE: $G(z) = z^2 + z + 1$. $L = GF(2,3) = \{0,1,\alpha,\alpha^2,...,\alpha^6\}$.
$\Rightarrow p = 2, p^n = 8$.

Suppose, for this example, that we choose the irreducible polynomial $I(x) = x^3 + x + 1 \in \mathbb{Z}_2[x]$ to construct GF(2,3).

EXERCISE 7.5: Verify that I(x) is irreducible.

We will use *three* equivalent notations for the elements of GF(2,3). On the one hand, they can be written as second-degree (or lower) *polynomials in x*. Next, by writing only the coefficients of these polynomials, written in left-to-right order of ascending powers of x, we can consider each GF(2,3) element as a *3-bit string*.

Finally, since the multiplicative group of any finite field is cyclic, all of the elements save 0 and 1 can be written as *powers of the multiplicative generator*. Table 7.1 gives these three representations.

Now, recalling that $G(z) = z^2+z+1$, we wish to construct the matrix H:

$$H = \begin{bmatrix} 1/G(\alpha_1) & 1/G(\alpha_2) & ... & 1/G(\alpha_m) \\ \alpha_1/G(\alpha_1) & \alpha_2/G(\alpha_2) & ... & \alpha_m/G(\alpha_m) \end{bmatrix}$$

For convenience, we could also consider H to be a 6×8 matrix, with $\mathbb{Z}_2$ coefficients, rather than a 2×8 matrix with GF(2,3) coefficients, by writing the bit-string notation in column vector form.

α^n	$G(\alpha^n)$		
0	1		
1	1		
α	$\alpha^2 + \alpha + 1 = 111$		$= \alpha^5$
α^2	$\alpha^4 + \alpha^2 + 1 = 011 + 001 + 100 = 110 = \alpha^3$		
α^3	$\alpha^6 + \alpha^3 + 1 = 101 + 110 + 100 = 111 = \alpha^5$		
α^4	$\alpha^1 + \alpha^4 + 1 = 010 + 011 + 100 = 101 = \alpha^6$		
α^5	$\alpha^3 + \alpha^5 + 1 = 110 + 111 + 100 = 101 = \alpha^6$		
α^6	$\alpha^5 + \alpha^6 + 1 = 111 + 101 + 100 = 110 = \alpha^3$		

Table 7.2

Computations for the function G

The computations for the function G, using multiplicative generator notation (recall that $\alpha^7 = 1$), are found in table 7.2.

And, therefore:

$$H = \begin{bmatrix} 1/1 & 1/1 & 1/\alpha^5 & 1/\alpha^3 & 1/\alpha^5 & 1/\alpha^6 & 1/\alpha^6 & 1/\alpha^3 \\ 0/1 & 1/1 & \alpha/\alpha^5 & \alpha^2/\alpha^3 & \alpha^3/\alpha^5 & \alpha^4/\alpha^6 & \alpha^5/\alpha^6 & \alpha^6/\alpha^3 \end{bmatrix}$$

$$= \begin{bmatrix} 1 & 1 & \alpha^2 & \alpha^4 & \alpha^2 & \alpha & \alpha & \alpha^4 \\ 0 & 1 & \alpha^3 & \alpha^6 & \alpha^5 & \alpha^5 & \alpha^6 & \alpha^3 \end{bmatrix}$$

or, using the bit-string notation:

$$= \left[\begin{array}{cccccccc} 1 & 1 & 0 & 0 & 0 & 0 & 0 & 0 \\ 0 & 0 & 0 & 1 & 0 & 1 & 1 & 1 \\ 0 & 0 & 1 & 1 & 1 & 0 & 0 & 1 \\ \hline 0 & 1 & 1 & 1 & 1 & 1 & 1 & 1 \\ 0 & 0 & 1 & 0 & 1 & 1 & 0 & 1 \\ 0 & 0 & 0 & 1 & 1 & 1 & 1 & 0 \end{array} \right]$$

Now, this version of H is a homomorphic mapping from $\mathbb{Z}_2{}^8 \rightarrow \mathbb{Z}_2{}^6$ (maps 8-bit strings to 6-bit strings).

By our general theory, the codes are elements of the kernel of this homomorphism.

If the homomorphism is a surjection (which we will show shortly), and the domain has $2^8 = 256$ elements, and the range has $2^6 = 64$ elements, the kernel has exactly $2^2 = 4$ elements. Thus there are four codes.

PROOF THAT H IS ONTO: The following vectors are mapped onto the natural generators of $\mathbb{Z}_6$:

$\mathbb{Z}_2{}^8$-element	Image under H
1000 0000	100 000
0001 1110	010 000
0001 0010	001 000
1100 0000	000 100
1111 0010	000 010
0010 1000	000 001

What are the four codes? Naturally, [0000 0000] is one. Another is, for example, given by adding the second, third, fourth, and fifth vectors above to [0000 0001], giving:

[0001 1110] + [0001 0010] + [1100 0000] + [1111 0010] + [0000 0001]
$$=\qquad [0011\ 1111].$$

And, as well, by adding the second, fourth, and sixth vectors to [0000 0010], giving:

$$[0001\ 1110] + [1100\ 0000] + [0010\ 1000] + [0000\ 0010]$$
$$=\ [1111\ 0100].$$

The fourth code will be the sum of these previous two, [0011 1111] + [1111 0100] = [1100 1011].

In this example, then, 8 bits are needed to code $2^2 = 4$ symbols with Hamming distance 5. In general, in a Goppa code, p^n bits are required to be transmitted in order to code $2p^h - 2n$ symbols. Thus, 2^{2n} bits are required for every bit of information.

The McEliece Public-Key Cryptosystem

The cryptosystem is designed in the following way. One chooses values of n and t as desirable, and then chooses randomly an irreducible polynomial of degree t over GF(2,n). There is about a $1/t$ probability of finding an irreducible polynomial, and a fast algorithm exists by Berlekamp for testing irreducibility. Hence this choice is reasonable.

Indeed, the exact number of monic irreducible polynomials in $\mathbb{Z}_q[x]$ (set $q = 2^n$) is given by the formula:

$$N_q(t) = 1/t \sum_{d|n} \mu(n/d)\, q^d$$

where μ is the Mœbius function,

$$\mu(n) \;=\; \begin{cases} 1 & \text{if } n = 1 \\ (-1)^k & \text{if n is the product of n distinct primes} \\ 0 & \text{if n has a square factor} > 1. \end{cases}$$

Next, generate a k × n generator matrix G for the code. A generator matrix is easily computed from the parity check matrix H by the relationship:

$$H \;=\; \begin{bmatrix} A \\ Id \end{bmatrix} \quad ; \quad G = [\, Id \mid -A^T \,].$$

The purpose of a generator matrix is to enable us to recover a codeword x from a message u by x = uG.

Then, scramble G by selecting a random, dense, k × k non-singular matrix S, and a random n × n permutation matrix P. Compute:

$$G' \;=\; S{\cdot}G{\cdot}P$$

which generates a linear code with the same information rate and minimum distance as the code generated by G. G' is made public.

Encryption

Divide the data into k-bit blocks. If υ is such a block, transmit $\xi = \upsilon{\cdot} G' + \zeta$, where ζ is a random vector of length n, weight t.

Decryption

Compute $\xi' = \xi{\cdot} P^{-1}$. Then ξ' is a codeword in the Goppa code. Several algorithms are available to "correct" the error introduced by ζ, since its weight is small enough that the error introduced is within the range of correction by the code. Then, using the aforementioned Patterson's algorithm, $\upsilon' = \upsilon \cdot S$ is computed from ξ'. Then υ is computed by $\upsilon = \upsilon'{\cdot} S^{-1}$.

Discussion

The McEliece method has not found great acceptance in the cryptographic community. One reason is that its use introduces a very large data expansion factor. That is to say, in order to encrypt one bit of information, several bits may have to be used. This is a function of the size of the Goppa code words. In addition, the scrambling of the original message by adding in noise may render the method cryptographically insecure, since this is also dependent upon the other noise introduced by the system.

Nevertheless, other researchers have continued to use algebraic coding theory and it is possible that they will arise in future PKCs.

The Cooper-Patterson Knapsack PKC Using Galois Fields

In 1983, Cooper and Patterson [COOP 84a] developed the idea of embedding the original knapsack problem in a Galois field.

The method involves defining the concept of an "easy knapsack set" for the corresponding algebraic structure to the integers in Galois field theory, namely the ring of polynomials with integer coefficients, $\mathbb{Z}[x]$, whose elements are polynomials of the form $p(x) = p_0 + p_1 x + ... + p_n x^n$.

Define an easy knapsack set $\{ w_1(x), w_2(x), ..., w_n(x) \}$ in this context to be one in which the ith coefficients of these polynomials form a super-increasing set of integers $\{ w_{1,i}, w_{2,i}, ... , w_{n,i} \}$, for all values of i.

Then the encryption method proceeds as follows:

Choose an "easy" knapsack set of polynomials as defined above. (In addition, choose all of the polynomials to be of the same degree.) Find a prime p, larger than twice the largest coefficient of all the polynomials.

Find an irreducible polynomial, $I(x)$, of degree $k+1$; then choose any other polynomial, $m(x)$, of degree $\leq k$.

Create a "hard" knapsack set of polynomials $\{ w_1'(x), w_2'(x), ..., w_n'(x) \}$ by the following transformation:

$$w_i'(x) \equiv w_i(x) \cdot m(x) \qquad (mod\ p, I(x)).$$

Publish these "hard" knapsack numbers.

Encryption

Encode a bit-string of length n by multiplying each bit by a polynomial $w_i'(x)$, and forming the sum $S'(x)$. Transmit this sum:

$$S'(x) = b_1 \cdot w_1'(x) + ... + b_n \cdot w_n'(x).$$

Decryption

To decrypt, as in the Merkle-Hellman approach, multiply the ciphertext $S'(x)$ by the polynomial which is the inverse of $m(x)$ in the Galois field $GF(p,k+1)$ defined by the irreducible polynomial $I(x)$.

The authors originally suggested that the method could be used by generating only s sets of easy knapsack numbers, each containing r elements, where $r \cdot s = n$. This approach would require that some of the sets of coefficients of the polynomials $\{ w_1(x), w_2(x), ..., w_n(x) \}$ would have easy knapsack numbers in a few rows and zeros in the other rows. Many columns that did not contain easy knapsack numbers would contain only noise.

Such a set of knapsack polynomials would still be sufficient for decryption, since the decryptor could proceed column by column, knowing which columns contained true easy knapsack sets and which did not.

The advantage of the latter approach would be a compression in the overall number of bits to be stored and transmitted.

Although the Cooper-Patterson algorithm is reasonably efficient, it is not secure. Although the algorithm may not be vulnerable to the Shamir knapsack attack, it can be shown to be broken either by the methods of Lagarias and Odlyzko or by the methods of Brickell, since it is generated from a low-density knapsack (density = 0.5).

EXAMPLE:

To construct a sample cryptosystem, suppose we choose $p = 101$, $k = 19$. For a set of "easy" knapsack polynomials, we will choose first four super-increasing sets of five numbers each, namely, $\{ 1, 4, 7, 14, 27 \}$, $\{ 1, 2, 4, 8, 16 \}$, $\{ 2, 5, 9, 18, 36 \}$, and $\{ 1, 3, 7, 12, 26 \}$. Four powers of the indeterminate x are selected at random, namely, x^2, x^7, x^{11}, and x^{14}. The numbers in each knapsack set are used as the coefficients of five of the 20 easy knapsack polynomials of the appropriate power of x. The other fifteen coefficients for the selected powers will be zero.

All other coefficients of the easy knapsack polynomials are chosen at random in the interval [0,100].

Consequently, the table (7.3) of the easy knapsack polynomials follows:

Power of x

Poly	0	1	2	3	4	5	6	7	8	9	10	11	12	13	14	15	16	17	18	19
w1	12	77	0	70	12	92	93	0	92	4	1	0	19	92	1	10	6	70	50	97
w2	21	5	0	71	80	15	55	16	45	51	58	0	97	41	0	38	1	60	85	4
w3	43	46	0	22	78	99	69	0	68	64	15	0	9	11	3	87	18	80	54	34
w4	45	67	27	76	93	26	92	0	33	0	94	0	86	9	0	1	91	33	32	81
w5	0	99	1	41	17	0	45	0	29	15	61	2	40	14	0	92	15	38	14	13
w6	7	66	0	7	22	44	70	0	54	30	16	0	98	24	0	28	30	34	55	57
w7	61	42	0	2	8	57	50	2	18	38	5	0	74	80	0	58	42	20	15	43
w8	68	69	4	68	92	62	87	0	29	68	20	0	13	66	0	20	75	34	77	53
w9	22	99	0	0	63	75	38	0	27	2	22	0	72	33	12	31	60	13	94	14
w10	98	12	0	30	17	73	42	0	0	41	95	18	3	62	0	96	91	74	37	94
w11	47	21	0	26	67	87	26	1	9	50	40	0	41	57	0	13	58	56	84	6
w12	13	7	0	89	69	44	69	0	6	29	94	5	22	97	0	89	51	7	9	68
w13	8	30	7	13	56	37	3	0	90	10	76	0	92	22	0	93	70	84	83	18
w14	48	38	0	99	12	99	91	0	52	77	56	0	81	93	7	22	19	30	15	16
w15	86	78	0	25	93	82	9	4	86	41	35	0	13	15	0	14	28	89	92	81
w16	28	26	14	37	69	13	11	0	43	44	14	0	68	29	0	50	92	21	36	76
w17	80	14	0	90	81	59	48	0	50	0	37	0	81	57	26	99	64	43	40	41
w18	79	98	0	10	26	26	59	8	52	76	91	0	3	69	0	71	64	3	91	93
w19	55	33	0	14	92	19	22	0	23	40	15	36	32	91	0	28	94	64	69	64
w20	48	46	0	38	30	72	66	0	59	75	94	9	3	75	0	85	56	36	91	95

Table 7.3
Easy Knapsack Polynomials

Now, we need to construct an irreducible polynomial of degree 20 over Z_{101}. For this, we use the following theorem found in [LIDL 83] (p. 124):

THEOREM: A binomial x^k - a is irreducible in $Z_p[x]$ $\Leftrightarrow$

(1) each prime factor of k divides the order, e, of a in Z_p but not $(p-1)/e$.

(2) $p \equiv 1$ (mod 4) if $k \equiv 0$ (mod 4).

To use this theorem, let $k = 20$, $p = 101$, and $a = 2$. Then, the prime factors of k are 2 and 5. $k = 20 \equiv 0$ (mod 4), and $p = 101 \equiv 1$ (mod 4), thus condition (2) is satisfied.

The order of 2 in Z_{101} is $e = 100$ (by direct computation), thus each prime factor of k divides e. However, $(p-1)/e = 1$, and thus 2 does not divide $(p-1)/e$. Thus, we can conclude that $I(x) = x^{20}$ - 2 is an irreducible polynomial in $Z_{101}[x]$.

Then, we need to find an m(x). For this, we choose $m(x) = x^{10} + 1$. Then it is simple to show that $m^{-1}(x) = x^{10}$ - 1.

The hard knapsack polynomials $w_i'(x)$, $i = 1, 2, ..., 20$ are determined by computing

$$w_i'(x) \equiv w_i(x) \cdot m(x) \qquad (\text{mod } p, I(x)).$$

This leads to the results of table 7.4.

Now, suppose that we wish to encrypt the 20-bit message: 10111 01100 10010 01100.

To do this, we select the polynomials corresponding to 1-bits in the message, and add them together:

$$w_1'(x) + w_3'(x) + w_4'(x) + w_5'(x) + w_6'(x)$$
$$+ w_7'(x) + w_{11}'(x) + w_{14}'(x) + w_{17}'(x) + w_{18}'(x)$$

This yields the following polynomial E(x), which is then transmitted:

$$1323 + 571x + 926x^2 + 1600x^3 + 560x^4 +$$
$$1553x^5 + 1564x^6 + 825x^7 + 1376x^8 + 1346x^9 +$$
$$903x^{10} + 571x^{11} + 479x^{12} + 1052x^{13} + 523x^{14} +$$
$$1080x^{15} + 1112x^{16} + 418x^{17} + 904x^{18} + 869x^{19}$$

To decrypt this message, we first multiply the encrypted polynomial E(x) by $m^{-1}(x) = x^{10}$ - 1, and reduce modulo I(x) and 101, yielding:

Power of x

Poly	0	1	2	3	4	5	6	7	8	9	10	11	12	13	14	15	16	17	18	19
W1'	14	77	38	254	141	12	105	140	192	198	13	77	19	162	13	102	99	70	142	101
W2'	137	5	194	153	80	91	57	136	215	59	79	5	97	112	80	53	56	76	130	55
W3'	73	46	18	44	84	273	105	160	176	132	58	46	9	33	81	186	87	80	122	98
W4'	233	67	199	94	93	28	274	66	97	162	139	67	113	85	93	27	183	33	65	81
W5'	122	99	81	69	17	184	75	76	57	41	61	99	41	55	17	92	60	38	43	28
W6'	39	70	196	55	22	100	130	68	164	144	23	68	98	31	22	72	100	34	109	87
W7'	71	42	148	162	8	173	134	42	48	124	66	42	74	82	8	115	92	22	33	81
W8'	108	69	30	200	92	102	237	68	183	174	88	69	17	134	92	82	162	34	106	121
W9'	66	99	144	66	87	137	158	26	215	30	44	99	72	33	75	106	98	13	121	16
W10'	288	48	6	154	17	265	224	148	74	229	193	30	3	92	17	169	133	74	37	135
W11'	127	21	82	140	67	113	142	113	177	62	87	21	41	83	67	100	84	57	93	56
W12'	201	17	44	283	69	222	171	14	24	165	107	12	22	186	69	133	120	7	15	97
W13'	160	30	191	57	56	223	129	168	256	46	84	30	99	35	56	130	73	84	173	28
W14'	160	38	162	285	26	143	65	60	82	109	104	38	81	192	19	121	110	30	67	93
W15'	156	78	26	55	93	110	195	182	270	203	121	78	13	40	93	96	37	93	178	122
W16'	56	26	150	95	69	113	65	42	115	196	42	26	82	66	69	63	103	21	79	120
W17'	154	14	162	204	133	257	176	86	130	82	117	14	81	147	107	158	112	43	90	41
W18'	261	98	6	148	26	168	187	14	234	262	170	98	3	79	26	97	123	11	143	169
W19'	85	105	64	196	92	75	210	128	161	168	70	69	32	105	92	47	116	64	92	104
W20'	236	64	6	188	30	242	178	72	241	265	142	55	31	13	30	157	122	36	150	170

Table 7.4
Hard Knapsack Polynomials

$$79 + 66x + 32x^2 + 100x^3 + 82x^4 +$$
$$x^5 + 54x^6 + 11x^7 + 28x^8 + 90x^9 +$$
$$16x^{10} + 0x^{11} + 43x^{12} + 43x^{13} + 37x^{14} +$$
$$69x^{15} + 48x^{16} + 3x^{17} + 68x^{18} + 73x^{19}.$$

Now we examine only the "key" columns, namely the coefficients of x^2, x^7, x^{11}, and x^{14}, and solve the resulting easy knapsack problems:

COEFFICIENT OF X^2: 32 $\Rightarrow$ knapsack solution is $27 + 1 + 4$
$\Rightarrow$ rows with 1-bits are 4, 5, and 8;

COEFFICIENT OF X^7: 11 $\Rightarrow$ knapsack solution is $2 + 1 + 8$
$\Rightarrow$ rows with 1-bits are 7, 11, and 18;

COEFFICIENT OF X^{11}: 0 $\Rightarrow$ knapsack solution is 0
$\Rightarrow$ no additional rows with 1-bits;

COEFFICIENT OF X^{14}: 37 $\Rightarrow$ knapsack solution is $1 + 3 + 7 + 26$
$\Rightarrow$ rows with 1-bits are 1, 13, 14, and 17;

thus, in all, the rows with one-bits are 1, 4, 5, 7, 8, 11, 13, 14, 17, 18; in other words, the decrypted message is 10010 01100 10110 01100.

EXERCISE 7.6: Modify your program written to implement the Merkle-Hellman PKC to incorporate the Cooper-Patterson method.

The Chor-Rivest Knapsack-Type PKC

As we have seen, the methods of Brickell and Lagarias and Odlyzko have been successful in demonstrating the vulnerability of low-density subset-sum or knapsack-type PKCs.

However, one other knapsack PKC has been proposed that, to date, remains as a secure approach. Further, it is known that the cryptanalytic methods as described in the preceding chapter will not be successful in attacking this new method.

This subset-sum PKC was developed by Chor and Rivest [CHOR 85]. Alone among all subset-sum approaches, the Chor-Rivest PKC starts with a *general* knapsack set and not a super-increasing set.

Also, rather than using integer arithmetic as in the Merkle-Hellman knapsack PKC, we will use Galois field arithmetic as in the previous Cooper-Patterson approach.

Of course, the advantage of a superincreasing knapsack set is that such a set results in unique subset sums. This condition will not occur with general knapsack sets, but, instead, we will use a theorem by Bose and Chowla [BOSE 62] which will play a similar rôle.

THEOREM (BOSE-CHOWLA): Let p be any prime number, $n \geq 2$ an integer. There exists a sequence $A = \{ a_i \mid 0 \leq i \leq p-1, a_i \in \mathbb{Z} \}$.э.

1. $1 \leq a_i \leq p^n - 1$ $i = 0, 1, ..., p-1$

2. If $(x_0, x_1, ..., x_{p-1})$ and $(y_0, y_1, ..., y_{p-1})$ are two distinct vectors, with non-negative integral coordinates, and

$$\sum_i x_i , \sum_i y_i \leq n,$$

then:

$$\sum_i x_i a_i \neq \sum_i y_i a_i .$$

PROOF: Construct first the Galois fields $GF(p) = \mathbb{Z}_p$ and $GF(p,n)$.

Recall that $GF(p,n)$ is constructed by first considering the ring of all polynomials over $\mathbb{Z}_p$, $\mathbb{Z}_p[x]$, and then taking remainders modulo some n^{th} degree irreducible polynomial.

First we need an element $t \in GF(p,n)$ such that the minimal polynomial in $\mathbb{Z}_p[x]$ having t as its root is of degree n.

Furthermore, since the multiplicative group of any Galois field is cyclic, find a generator $g \in \, < GF(p,n)^*, \cdot >$.

Now generate the set

$$t + \mathbb{Z}_p = \{ t + i \in GF(p,n) \mid i = 0, 1, ..., p-1 \} \subseteq GF(p,n).$$

Compute the discrete logarithms for the elements of the set $t + \mathbb{Z}_p$, i.e. $\{ a_i \}$.э.

$$a_i = \log_g (t+i) \qquad i = 0, 1, ..., p-1.$$

The $\{ a_i \}$ is the sequence we seek. First of all, the a_i are all in the interval $[1, p^n - 1]$, since the powers of g generate the entire multiplicative group, and there are $p^n - 1$ distinct powers of g.

Furthermore, suppose we have two p-vectors with non-negative integral coefficients, $\xi = (x_0, x_1, ..., x_{p-1})$ and $\Psi = (y_0, y_1, ..., y_{p-1})$, with:

(1) $\xi \neq \Psi$
(2) $\sum x_i , \sum y_i \leq n$, and
(3) $\sum x_i a_i = \sum y_i a_i .$

Then, g can be raised to the power corresponding to each side of (3):

$$g^{\Sigma x_i a_i} = g^{\Sigma y_i a_i}$$

$$\Rightarrow \qquad \prod (g^{a_i})^{x_i} = \prod (g^{a_i})^{y_i}$$

But $g^{a_i} = t + i$, thus:

$$\prod (t+i)^{x_i} = \prod (t+i)^{y_i}$$

Or,

$$\begin{aligned} p_i(t) &= (t+i_1)(t+i_2) \ldots (t+i_r) \\ &= (t+j_1)(t+j_2) \ldots (t+j_s) = p_j(t), \end{aligned}$$

where $\{ i_1, ..., i_r \}$ and $\{ j_1, ..., j_s \}$ are two different non-empty sets of elements from $\{ 0, ..., p-1 \}$, with at most n elements each.

Thus the polynomial $p_i(t) - p_j(t)$ is a non-zero polynomial (since $\xi \neq \Psi$), of degree $\leq n-1$ (since the t^n terms cancel each other), with t as a root.

However, this contradicts the assumption that the minimal polynomial having t as its root is of degree n.

Q.E.D.

Defining the Cryptosystem

The first, and most critical task in constructing the PKC is to choose p and n such that the Galois field GF(p,n) is amenable to discrete logarithm computations.

Unfortunately, in general, the computation of discrete logarithms in a Galois field is another intractable problem.

(Perhaps a small example will demonstrate the difficulty. Consider $Z_5[x]$, and the irreducible polynomial $x^3 + x^2 + 2 \in Z_5[x]$.

EXERCISE 7.7: Verify that the polynomial is irreducible.

Then generate GF(5,3). Since, in this choice for GF(5,3), multiplications are modulo $x^3 + x^2 + 2$,

$$\Rightarrow \quad x^3 = 4x^2 + 3.$$

(Thus we have computed the discrete log for $4x^2 + 3$, namely 3.)

Furthermore, x is a generator of the multiplicative group, of order $p^n - 1 = 5^3 - 1 = 124$. Thus $x^{124} = 1$, but $x^{62} \neq 1$.

So how would we solve $\log_x (3x^2 + 3x + 1)$? That is, to find a .ə. $x^a = 3x^2 + 3x + 1$?

The brute force method consists of simply computing all of the powers of x. However, p and n do not need to be very large before this approach becomes unreasonable. For example, if $p = 101$, and $n = 50$, then p^n-1 has more than 100 digits. At one exponential calculation per microsecond, the brute force approach would, on average, require $\approx 10^{93}$ seconds, or 10^{84} centuries to enumerate.

(To complete the example, $\log_x (3x^2 + 3x + 1) = 83$.)

Indeed, it is known that, in general, the computation of discrete logarithms is as difficult as factoring.

We will later return to the discussion of discrete log computations.

System Generation

1. Again, recapitulating, we first make a judicious choice of p and n so that it will be feasible to compute discrete logs in GF(p,n).

2. Next, construct GF(p,n) by finding an irreducible polynomial of degree n over Z_p. (That is, find f(t) an irreducible monic polynomial of degree n in GF(p)[t] and represent GF(p,n) as GF(p)[t]/(f(t)).)

3. At random, find $t \in$ GF(p,n) such that the minimal polynomial in $Z_p[x]$ having t as its root is of degree n.

4. At random, choose g in GF(p,n), a generator of the multiplicative group $< GF(p,n)^*, \cdot >$.

5. Compute the $a_i = \log_g (t+i)$ for $i = 0, 1, 2, \ldots , p-1$.

6. Scramble the a_i's by a randomly chosen permutation of p elements, π:

$$\pi: \quad a_i \rightarrow b_i = a_{\pi(i)}.$$

7. Add noise: Choose $0 \leq d \leq p^n -2$ at random; and set $c_i = b_i + d$, for $i = 0, 1, \ldots, p-1$.

8. Now publish the keys: $c_0, c_1, \ldots , c_{p-1}$; p, n.

9. Retain as the private keys: t, g, π, d.

Encryption

The Chor-Rivest algorithm can only be used to transform p-bit strings with weight *exactly* n. Consequently, in order for the system to be useful, first a transformation must be made from all bit strings representing integers in the range $[0, C(p,n)]$ to blocks of length p and weight exactly n.

This, however, is a standard transformation and will be presented below.

To encrypt a bit string μ with weight n, add the $c_{i1}, c_{i2}, ..., c_{in}$ whose corresponding bit is 1. Send

$$E(\mu) = c_{i1} + c_{i2} + ... + c_{in} \quad (\text{mod } p^n - 1).$$

Decryption

1. Let $r(t) \equiv t^n$ (mod $I(t)$) in $Z_p[x]$, for $I(t)$ the irreducible polynomial used in defining GF(p,n).

2. Compute $s' = E(\mu) - nd$ (mod $p^n - 1$) in $Z_{p^n - 1}$.

3. Compute $p(t) = g^{s'}$ (mod $I(t)$) in GF(p,n). $p(t)$ will be a polynomial of degree n-1 in t.

4. Add $t^n - r(t)$ to $p(t)$ to get $k(t) = t^n + p(t) - r(t)$, a polynomial of degree n in $Z_p[t]$.

5. The polynomial $k(t)$ factors into linear terms over Z_p, $k(t) = (t + i_1)(t + i_2) ... (t + i_n)$. This is so because:

$$g^{E(\mu) - nd} = g^{E(\mu)} \cdot g^{-nd} \quad = g^{ci_1} g^{ci_2} ... g^{ci_n} \ g^{-nd}$$
$$= g^{(ci_1 - d)} g^{(ci_2 - d)} ... g^{(ci_n - d)}$$
$$= g^{bi_1} g^{bi_2} ... g^{bi_n}$$

and since each of the b_{ij} are discrete logarithms of some element of the set $(t + Z_p)$, we can consider that $k(t)$ is such a product of linear factors.

6. Now by trial substitution of each of the elements of Z_p, 0, 1, ..., p–1, in the expression $k(t)$, we can determine which n of them represent the roots.

7. Finally we need to apply π^{-1} to recover the positions of the 1-bits in the original message μ.

The Transformation from Integers to p-bit Strings with Weight n

First of all, we need to determine *how many* p-bit strings with weight n there are. That number is simply the combination of p things taken n at a time without replacement:

$$C(p,n) \;=\; p! \,/\, (n! \,(p\text{-}n)!\,) \quad=\quad [\,p(p\text{-}1)...(p\text{-}n\text{+}1)]\,/\,n!$$

Consequently, there is a 1-1 correspondence between all integers in the interval $[0,C(p,n)\text{-}1]$ and p-bit strings of weight n.

If we wish to be able to encrypt all bit strings, we need to choose a block length such that all integers represented by the block fall in the range $[0,C(p,n)\text{-}1]$. This means that the block length should be

$$[\,\log_2 C(p,n)\,]$$

(where the notation [x] means the greatest integer less than or equal to x).

The mapping in question is given by the following algorithm, which can be found written in Pascal code in appendix VI.

In order to draw the correspondence between p-bit strings of weight n, and integers in the interval $[1,C(p,n)]$, consider the Pascal triangle, as presented in Figure 7.2. Since the recursion formula for $C(p,n)$ relates the two proximate entries in the Pascal triangle, any positive integer up to $C(p,n)$ determines one of the two nodes in the Pascal triangle graph immediately above $C(p,n)$. If the integer k is $\leq C(p\text{-}1,n\text{-}1)$, then the node chosen is $C(p\text{-}1,n\text{-}1)$, and the path in the "northwesterly" direction is made to correspond to a 1-bit in the string to be built. If the integer is $> C(p\text{-}1,n\text{-}1)$, then the node $C(p\text{-}1,n)$ to the northeast is chosen, and a 0-bit appended. Further, k is replaced by $k - C(p\text{-}1,n\text{-}1)$, and the process is repeated.

When we eventually reach $C(0,0)$, we will have travelled "northwesterly" exactly n times, and thus there will be exactly n 1s in the bit string. Furthermore, the bit-string will be p bits long, since the distance from the node $C(p,n)$ to the node $C(0,0)$ will be exactly p.

It should be noted that messages of length $[\log_2 C(p,n)]$ will be embedded in p-bit strings, and then transformed to integers in the range $[0, p^n\text{-}1]$, in other words of length

$$[[\,\log_2 (p^n\text{-}1)\,]]$$

(where [[x]] is the least integer greater than or equal to x).

Consequently, data that is represented in $[\,\log_2 C(p,n)\,]$ bits is transmitted in $[[\,\log_2 (p^n\text{-}1)\,]]$ bits. The corresponding data expansion factor is approximately

$$(\log_2 p^n)\,/\,(\log_2 C(p,n)) \;\approx\; (n \log_2 p)/\,[\, p \cdot (p\text{-}1) \cdot ... \cdot (p\text{-}n\text{+}1)\,/\,n!\,]$$
$$\approx\; (n \log_2 p)/\,[\,\log_2 n!\ -\log_2 p!\ -\log_2 (n\text{-}p)!\,]$$

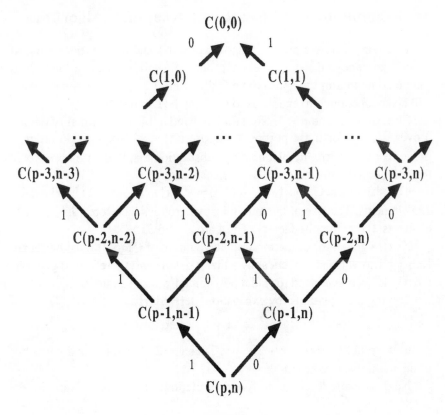

Figure 7.2
Paths Through the Pascal Triangle

and simplifying, using Stirling's formula[1]:

$$\approx (n \log_2 p)/ [\log_2 (\sqrt{(2\pi p)}) - \log_2 (\sqrt{(2\pi n)})$$
$$- \log_2 (\sqrt{(2\pi(p-n))}) + p \log_2 p - n \log_2 n$$
$$+ (p-n) \log_2 (p-n).$$

Examples of data expansion factors will be given later.

---

[1] As described in Chapter 1, $m! = \sqrt{(2\pi m)} (m/e)^m [1 + O(1/m)]$

An Example of the Chor-Rivest Knapsack Algorithm

To begin, choose a prime and prime power p and n. (It is necessary, in general, to choose these numbers appropriately so that discrete logarithms can be computed in the appropriate Galois field.) In our case, the numbers will be small enough to enable us to perform the computations.

Choose $p = 5$ and $n = 3$. Next find an irreducible polynomial of degree 3 over $\mathbb{Z}_5$ --- for these purposes, choose $t(x) = x^3 + x + 1$. (In order to prove that $t(x)$ is irreducible, note by substitution that there are no *roots* of the polynomial, thus there can be no linear factors.)

The size of the Galois field $GF(5,3) = \mathbb{Z}_5[x] / (x^3 + x + 1)$ is $p^n = 5^3 = 125$ elements. The size of the multiplicative group is therefore $125 - 1 = 124$ elements. (Note that the factors of 124 are 2^2 and 31.)

Next, a generator of the multiplicative group of $GF(5,3)$ must be found. Raising x to various powers shows that $x^{62} = 1$, and therefore to generate the whole group we need to find a polynomial whose square is x.

Solving the equations (by exhaustion) derived from:

$$(ax^2 + bx + c)^2 \equiv x \qquad (\mathrm{mod}\ x^3 + x + 1)$$

gives, eventually, $(2x^2 + x + 2)^2 = x$. Thus $g = 2x^2 + x + 2$ is a generator of the multiplicative group.

Next we have to compute five discrete logarithms for g. Namely, the solutions to:

$$
\begin{aligned}
g^{a0} &\equiv x && (\mathrm{mod}\ x^3 + x + 1)\\
g^{a1} &\equiv x + 1 && (\mathrm{mod}\ x^3 + x + 1)\\
g^{a2} &\equiv x + 2 && (\mathrm{mod}\ x^3 + x + 1)\\
g^{a3} &\equiv x + 3 && (\mathrm{mod}\ x^3 + x + 1)\\
g^{a4} &\equiv x + 4 && (\mathrm{mod}\ x^3 + x + 1).
\end{aligned}
$$

By an analysis of the powers of g, we eventually obtain:

$$
\begin{aligned}
a_0 &= 2\\
a_1 &= 68\\
a_2 &= 98\\
a_3 &= 86\\
a_4 &= 109.
\end{aligned}
$$

Now the a_i's are transformed to b_i's by a random permutation, which we choose to be $\pi : (0\ 1\ 2\ 3\ 4) \rightarrow (2\ 3\ 0\ 4\ 1)$. Then the b_i's are transformed to c_i's by adding a constant random "noise" term d, which we choose to be d = 75.

a_i :	2	68	98	86	109
b_i :	98	109	2	68	86
c_i :	173	184	77	143	161

Then the c_i, as well as the prime p=5 and the power n=3, are published.

To encrypt, one begins with a message string of length 5 with weight 3 --- suppose it is 10101. Then the zeroth, second, and fourth c_i's are added together and their sum is transmitted mod p^n -1 = mod 124. Thus, 173 + 77 + 161 = 411 ≡ 39 (mod 124).

In order to decrypt, one first computes s' = s - nd (mod p^n -1), giving s' = 39 - 3·75 ≡ 62 (mod 124).

Now, we compute the polynomial x^3 + p(x) - r(x), where p(x) = g^{62}, and r(x) = the remainder of x^3 in the Galois field.

$$g^{62} = -1 \text{ (recall that } g^{124} = 1\text{), and}$$
$$d(x) = x^3 + p(x) - r(x) = x^3 + (2x^2 + x + 2)^{62} + x + 1.$$

Now d(x) splits into linear factors (by the Bose-Chowla Theorem), and thus the roots can be computed by substituting in turn values x = 0, 1, 2, 3, 4 in d(x).

Simplifying, d(x) = x^3 + x, and 0, 2, and 3 are roots.

Thus, the final stage in decryption is the inverse of the permutation π which map 0, 2, and 3 back to 0, 2 and 4, giving the message 10101.

EXERCISE 7.8: Construct an example of the Chor-Rivest PKC using GF(11,2).

PKC Performance

In order to encrypt, n integer additions must be performed, each integer representing a bit-string of length [$\log_2 (p^n-1)$].

The decryption involves exponentiation in GF(p,n). g must be raised to a power in the range [1, p^n-1]. By the Fast Exponentiation Algorithm in Chapter 5, this represents at most 2n log p modular multiplications.

Furthermore, each GF(p,n) multiplication will require $2n^2$ $\mathbb{Z}_p$ – operations. Consequently, for a modular exponentiation, we require $4n^3$ log p operations.

In addition, there are p evaluations of a polynomial expression of degree (n-1), but this can be done using pn multiplications and pn additions, which will usually be less than $4n^3 \log p$.

Both of these computation estimates compare favorably with the complexity of encryption and decryption for the RSA and the Merkle-Hellman knapsack algorithms.

System generation is another matter. As we said above, for most choices of p and n, the computation of discrete logs is infeasible.

There are, however, some special cases. Coppersmith [COPP 84] has given an algorithm for discrete log computations for small primes. For p=2, the run-time is $e^{O(\,(3\sqrt{n})\,\log 2\,(n)\,)}$. This computation is feasible (a few hours of mainframe time) if $n \leq 200$.

There is also an algorithm by Pohlig and Hellman [POHL 78] which will be useful providing that p^n-1 has only small prime factors.

Examples of Prime Power Pairs Where p^n-1 Has Only Small Prime Factors

The table 7.5 gives a number of examples of large numbers with only small prime factors.

EXERCISE 7.9: Determine the factors of $197^{24} - 1$.

There is another consideration in the use of the Chor-Rivest cryptosystem. There is an inherent data expansion factor which is due to the necessity of only using p-bit strings with weight n. The data expansion factor was given earlier by the formula:

$$(\log_2 p^n) / (\log_2 C(p,n)) \approx (n \log_2 p)/ [\log_2 (\sqrt{(2\pi p)}) - \log_2 (\sqrt{(2\pi n)})$$
$$- \log_2 (\sqrt{(2\pi(p-n))}) + p \log_2 p - n \log_2 n$$
$$+ (p-n) \log_2 (p-n).$$

Thus, with the current examples, we have the results of table 7.6.

p	n	Largest prime factor of p^n-1
197	24	10, 316, 017
211	24	216, 330, 241
$256 = 2^8$	25	3, 173, 389, 601
$243 = 3^5$	=24	47, 763, 361

Table 7.5
Galois Fields in Which Discrete Logarithms Can Be Computed

p	n	Data Expansion Factor
197	24	1.79713
211	24	1.77646
$256 = 2^8$	25	1.74557
$243 = 3^5$	24	1.73744

Table 7.6
Data Expansion Factors for Chor-Rivest in Selected Fields

Possible Cryptographic Attacks

If we assume that parts of the secret key (t, g, π, d) become known to the attack, it is possible to reconstruct the entire secret key:

1. g AND d KNOWN:

Let $t' = g^{c0} \Rightarrow t - t' \in \mathbb{Z}_p$, and the sets $t + \mathbb{Z}_p$ and $t' + \mathbb{Z}_p$ are identical. Thus, the cryptanalyst can determine π and therefore t.

2. t AND d KNOWN:

Choose an arbitrary generator $g' \in < GF(p,n), \cdot >$. Compute the

$$a_i' = \log_{g'} (t+i).$$

Then, $\{ a_0, ..., a_{p-1} \} = L \{ a'_0, ..., a'_{p-1} \}$ where $g = g'^L$. Then L can be recovered and therefore g.

3. π AND d KNOWN:

Since the knapsack is dense, there are small coefficients .ɜ.

p	n	Density ($n/\log_2 p^n$)
197	24	1.0769191482
211	24	1.1386548038
$256 = 2^8$	25	1.28
$243 = 3^5$	24	1.2776327314

Table 7.7

Densities for Knapsacks in Selected Galois Fields

$$\Sigma \, x_i \, a_i = 0.$$

Furthermore, L^3 can find the x_i's. Thus,

$$g^{\Sigma \, xi \, ai} = 1.$$
$$\Rightarrow \quad \Pi \, (\, t + i \,)^{xi} = 1.$$

This leads to a polynomial equation of degree m-1 in t, where m = max(| Σ positive x_i's |, | Σ negative x_i's |).

All the roots of the polynomial can be found, and since t is necessarily one of the roots, the previous attack can be used.

4. USING THE LAGARIAS-ODLYZKO ATTACK:

The Lagarias-Odlyzko attack will, in general, not succeed in breaking the Chor-Rivest PKC.

This attack takes the public knapsack numbers { c_i } and a sum instance (the ciphered message) S, and constructs a (p+1)-dimensional lattice.

The cryptanalyst attempts to find a certain vector in the lattice (the one corresponding to the sum $\Sigma \, x_i c_i = S$), and if the density of the knapsack system is lower than 0.645, the aforementioned vector is the *shortest* one in the lattice.

However, the density of the Chor-Rivest knapsacks is generally much higher than 0.645.

The density for a knapsack set W = { w_1, w_2, ..., w_n } is calculated as d(W) = $n/\log_2$ max { w_i }. For a lower bound, using the four examples cited previously in Table 7.1, we can replace $\log_2$ max { w_i } by its maximum possible value, namely $\log_2 p^n$.

Variations on the RSA Algorithm

Several PKCs have been proposed based on the difficulty of factoring and the choice of public key which is a product of two secret primes.

First of all, Rabin proposed a method [RABI 79] which he did not advocate as a public-key cryptosystem, that used the difficulty of finding square roots in a modular arithmetic system as a basis for the encryption.

First, a few recollections about modular arithmetic and quadratic residues. Suppose that

$$x^2 \equiv a \qquad (\text{mod } N)$$

and suppose that N is the product of two secret primes, $N = p \cdot q$. Then, by the Chinese Remainder Theorem, we can conclude:

$$x^2 \equiv a \qquad (\text{mod } p)$$
$$x^2 \equiv a \qquad (\text{mod } q)$$

Furthermore, if the primes p and q are congruent to 3 mod 4, then the square roots of the preceding two expressions can be computed easily.

For example, if $p \equiv 3 \pmod 4$, then $(p+1) = 4k$, and $(p+1)/4$ is an integer. Since $a \in QR(p)$, we know that

$$a^{\emptyset(p)/2} \equiv 1 \qquad (\text{mod } p)$$
$$\Rightarrow \qquad a^{(p-1)/2} \equiv 1 \qquad (\text{mod } p)$$

But

$$[\, a^{(p+1)/4}\,]^2 \equiv a^{(p+1)/2} \equiv a^{(p-1)/2} \cdot a \equiv a \qquad (\text{mod } p)$$

thus x can be either

$$a^{(p+1)/4} \qquad \text{or} \qquad p - a^{(p+1)/4} \qquad (\text{mod } p).$$

Similarly, using the mod q congruence, we can conclude that x may also be either

$$a^{(q+1)/4} \qquad \text{or} \qquad q - a^{(q+1)/4} \qquad (\text{mod } q).$$

Since N has only these two prime factors, these are the only possibilities for roots.

Rabin's proposal was the following:

Choose p and q as secret primes, both congruent to 3 mod 4. Publish their product, $N = p \cdot q$. To encrypt a message μ (considered as an integer in the range [0,N-1]), square μ and reduce it mod N; send this result, $E(\mu) \equiv \mu^2 \pmod{N}$.

To decrypt the message, compute $[E(\mu)]^{(p+1)/4}$, $p - [E(\mu)]^{(p+1)/4}$, $[E(\mu)]^{(q+1)/4}$, and $q - [E(\mu)]^{(p+1)/4}$. One can determine four numbers modulo N which correspond to each of the four choices of pairs of these roots. For example, if

$$x \equiv [E(\mu)]^{(p+1)/4} \qquad \pmod{p}$$
$$\text{and} \qquad x \equiv q - [E(\mu)]^{(p+1)/4} \qquad \pmod{q}$$

one can determine a value for x mod N. Thus there will be four candidates for the decryption.

If the message to be deciphered consists of English text, the decryption can proceed. If, however, the message has no redundancy (for example, if this method is being used for key distribution), the message cannot be further deciphered. For this reason, Rabin did not propose this method as a PKC. We will, however, see an application for Rabin's method in the next Chapter.

El Gamal [ELGA 85] has used a similar idea in proposing a PKC. Suppose that parties A and B wish to exchange a secret, K_{AB}. A public large prime, p, is chosen, as well as an α, $0 < \alpha < (p-1)$.

Each of A and B choose a secret integer, x_A and x_B, respectively. A computes

$$y_A \equiv \alpha^{x_A} \qquad \pmod{p}$$

as B computes

$$y_B \equiv \alpha^{x_B} \qquad \pmod{p}.$$

Then the shared secret is computed to be

$$K_{AB} \equiv \alpha^{x_A \cdot x_B} \qquad \pmod{p}.$$

If A wishes to send a message μ to B, consider that μ is the interval [0,p-1]. Then A chooses k randomly in the interval [0,p-1], and computes $K \equiv y_B{}^k \pmod{p}$.

The encrypted message will be (c_1, c_2), where:

$$c_1 \equiv \alpha^k \qquad \pmod{p}$$

and

$$c_2 \equiv K\mu \qquad \pmod{p}.$$

To decrypt the message, first B must compute K:

$$K \equiv (\alpha^k)^{x_B} \equiv c_1^{x_B} \quad (\text{mod } p).$$

And then μ, by dividing c_2 by K.

Another method, expanding on Rabin's, is due to Williams [WILL 85]. Rather than squaring the message μ, one cubes it in the encryption.

In order to calculate the possible cube roots, it is necessary to begin with large primes p and q that are congruent to 1 mod 3, and also satisfying the condition

$$(p-1)(q-1) \equiv -9 \quad (\text{mod } 27).$$

Under these circumstances, it will be possible to publish $N = p \cdot q$, and encrypt by computing $E(\mu) \equiv \mu^3$ (mod N). the decryption will be unique, unlike in the Rabin case.

Comments on the RSA Variations

None of the above methods *per se* stand as substantial improvements the RSA algorithm. The Rabin method results in fewer computations both to encrypt and to decrypt; but as we saw, it will not give a deterministic decryption. Neither the El Gamal method nor the Williams method seems to reduce substantially the encryption/decryption.

Nevertheless, both lead to possible further strengthening of the factoring approach to public-key encryption.

Wagner's Word Problem PKC Proposal

In this survey of recent PKC proposals, the purpose has been to give the reader some sense of the type of mathematical model that can be used for the development of a PKC.

In concluding this section, we present an idea due to Wagner [WAGN 85], which uses a mathematical problem of a significantly different type than others which we have used to date.

Much of our focus to date has been on the category of **NP-complete** problems (See Appendix IV), the set of problems which probably do not have a polynomial-time algorithm for their solution. These are the problems we consdier extremely "hard" to solve.

However, in the category of all problems, there is another class, to which we can easily award the distinction of being the "hardest". The category U of **undecidable** problems consist of those problems, for which *it can be proven that there exists no algorithm that can solve them.*

In general, it is a difficult task to prove that a problem belongs to this category U. Indeed, there are only a few known examples:

- the **Turing Halting Problem**: given an arbitrary computer program, and an arbitrary input to that program, is there an algorithm which will decide whether or not the program will eventually halt when applied to that input?
- **Hilbert's Tenth Problem**: given an arbitrary polynomial equation $P(x_1, x_2, ..., x_n) = 0$, with integral coefficients, to determine whether or not it has an integral solution;
- given a context-free grammar G, is there a positive integer k such that G is an LR(k) grammar?
- a **tile** is a unit square colored on each of its four sides. A **tiling** is an arrangement of tiles so that any two common sides have the same color. Is there an algorithm which will decide, for any set of colors, C, and any collection of tiles T contained in C^4, whether or not the plane can be tiled with this collection?
- the **word problem for finitely presented groups**.

Wagner's approach relies on the last of these undecidable problems, so we will discuss it further.

Finitely Presented Groups

A **group**, as defined in Appendix II, can be described in terms of **generators** and **relations**.

To say that a group G is **generated** by elements $g_1, ..., g_n$ implies that every element of G can be written (not necessarily uniquely) as:

$$g_{i_1}^{p_{i1}} \, g_{i_2}^{p_{i2}} \cdots g_{i_n}^{p_{in}}$$

where each g_{ij} is one of the generators, and p_{ij} is an integer representing a power of g_{ij}. This string is referred to in group-theoretic terms as a **word**.

A **relation** r in G is an equation relating a word in G to the identity, e:

$$r: \qquad g_{j_1}^{p_{j1}} \, g_{j_2}^{p_{j2}} \cdots g_{j_n}^{p_{jn}} = e.$$

Sometimes an abuse of language will occur, and the expression on the left-hand side will also be referred to as the relation.

To say that a group is **finitely presented** means that it is completely described by a finite number of generators and relations.

EXAMPLE 1:

$$G = \{ \text{ generator } g \; ; \quad \text{relation } r : \; g^5 = e \}.$$

It is not difficult to see that the elements of G are $\{ e, g, g^2, g^3, g^4 \}$ and that it is in fact isomorphic to $< \mathbb{Z}_5, + >$.

EXAMPLE 2:

$$G = \{ \text{ generators } g_1, g_2 \; ; \quad \text{no relations } \}.$$

This group is an infinite group known as the **free group on two generators**. Some of the elements are: $e, g_1, g_2, g_1g_2, g_1g_2g_1, g_1g_2g_1g_2, g_1^2g_2, \ldots$

EXAMPLE 3:

$$G = \{ \text{ generators } g_1, g_2 \; ;$$
$$\text{relations } r_1 : g_1^2 = e; r_2 : g_2^3 = e; r_3 : g_1g_2g_1g_2^{-2} = e \}.$$

This group consists of six elements and is isomorphic to S_3, the symmetric group on three elements. The proof is left as an exercise.

Two words v, w in G are said to be **equivalent** if v can be transformed to w by a finite sequence of replacements (known as **Tietze transformations**). These are:

1. Replacing $x_j x_j^{-1}$ or $x_j^{-1} x_j$ by e, the identity.
2. Introducing $x_j x_j^{-1}$ or $x_j^{-1} x_j$ at any point in the word.
3. Changing relations r_j or r_j^{-1} to e for any relation r_j.
4. Introducing r_j or r_j^{-1} at any point.

The **word problem** for a group G is the problem that asks, for each word w in G, if that word is equivalent to the identity.

It is one of the most remarkable results of modern mathematics, due to Boone [BOON 59] and Novikov [NOVI 55] that there exist specific groups in which the word problem is undecidable:

THEOREM (BOONE-NOVIKOV): There does not exist an algorithm which can solve, for all finitely presented groups, G, the word problem for G, that is whether or not each word $w_1w_2\ldots w_n$ in G is equivalent to the identity element.

Furthermore, the Boone-Novikov theory constructs such groups for which the word problem is undecidable.

Proposal for a Word Problem PKC

PROPOSED CRYPTOSYSTEM:

SYSTEM GENERATION:

Find G, a finitely presented group, generators x_i, relators r_j, for which the word problem is undecidable.

Find as well, w_1, w_2, two inequivalent words in G.

Find a secret homomorphism H: $G \rightarrow G'$ such that H and G' will remain secret, and G' has an efficiently computable word problem.

The public key consists of G, w_1, and w_2. The secret key is H and G'.

ENCRYPTION:

To encrypt a bit, use the bit to choose one of w_1, w_2 and randomly apply a sequence of Tietze transformations. Obtain v, equivalent to either w_1 or w_2. Transmit v.

DECRYPTION:

Solve the word problem for H(v) in G' to decide whether it is equivalent to $H(w_1)$ or $H(w_2)$. Consequently, determine the value of the bit that was encrypted.

The weakness that prevents this cryptosystem from being practical is the following. To determine a "random sequence of Tietze transformations", we must be prepared to accept that the transformed word may grow to an arbitrarily large length. This, of course, renders the cryptosystem less than practical, but any limitation of the space from which the Tietze transformations may be chosen would in fact violate the conditions of the Boone-Novikov theory, and the resulting sub-problem would not be undecidable.

Nevertheless, although this method is not useful, it does indicate a new direction for further PKC research.

Constructing a Finitely Presented Group in Which No Solution to the Word Problem Exists

First consider subsets, S, of the integer lattice $\mathbb{Z}^n$:
S is **Diophantine** if there exists a polynomial $P(X_1, X_2, \ldots, X_n; Y_1, Y_2, \ldots, Y_m)$ such that

$(s_1, \ldots, s_n)$ is in S $\Leftrightarrow$ $P(s_1, s_2, \ldots, s_n; Y_1, Y_2, \ldots, Y_m)$ has an integer root.

Say that P **enumerates** S.

CONSTRUCTION: Assign positive integers to polynomials.
Let $\Omega : \mathbb{Z} \to \mathbb{N}$ be

$$\Omega(z) = \begin{array}{ll} 2|z| + 1 & \text{if } z \leq 0 \\ 2|z| & \text{if } z > 0 \end{array}$$

Let $X_0, X_1, \ldots, X_n, \ldots$ be a list of variables. Assign to each monomial term

$$T = cx_{i_1}{}^{e_1} \ldots x_{i_n}{}^{e_n} \quad (c \neq 0 \text{ in } Z, \text{ each } e_i \geq 1, \text{ and the } i_j\text{'s an increasing seq.})$$

The number

$$\text{ß}(T) = 2^{\Omega(c)} p_{(i_1 + 2)}{}^{e_1} \ldots p_{(i_n + 2)}{}^{e_n}$$

where p_j is the jth prime.
e.g.:

$$\text{ß}(5x_0{}^3 x_4{}^2) = 2^{10} 3^3 13^2.$$

If $P = T_1 + \ldots + T_k$, then define the Gœdel numbers:

$$\partial(P) = 2^{\text{ß}(T_1)} \ldots p_k{}^{\text{ß}(T_k)}$$

and

$$S = \{ \partial(P(X_{i_1}, \ldots, X_{i_n})) \mid P(e, X_{i_2}, \ldots, X_{i_n}) \text{ has a root when } e = \partial(P) \}$$

Then

$$G = \{ a, b, c, d \mid a^{-i} b a^i = c^{-i} d a^i, \text{ for all } i \text{ in } S \}$$

is a group which has no solution to the word problem.

NOTE: G is not finitely presented; however, using the Higman Embedding Theorem, it can be embedded in, i.e., is a subgroup of, a finitely presented group, and therefore that group is a finitely presented group for which no solution to the word problem can be found.)

Conclusions

This chapter has examined some of the major proposals for public-key cryptosystems that have been developed in addition to the Merkle-Hellman and Graham-Shamir knapsacks, and the Rivest-Shamir-Adelman PKCs.

These "experimental PKCs" have used algebraic coding theory, Galois field theory, and the word problem for finitely presented groups.

Unfortunately, only the Chor-Rivest knapsack-type algorithm seems at this point to be both secure and practical (although less practical than the RSA).

It is hoped that further research will spring from these ideas and present numerous methods by which secure PKCs can be constructed and used.

— 8 —
Other Security Problems

In addition to the classic problem of cryptography, as represented throughout the monograph by the cryptosystem χ = « K, M, C, T », there are some closely related problems which lend themselves to similar analyses.

The Authentication Problem

In an earlier chapter, the authentication problem was mentioned briefly. It differs from the encryption problem in that the message, or at least part of it, must be transformed in a way that only the sender can authenticate.

As we saw in the earlier chapter, no secret-key cryptosystem can provide authentication --- since the secret key is always shared between the authentic sender and at least one other person, that other person could always "forge" the message.

Of the public-key encryption systems described, only the RSA cryptosystem can be adapted for authentication as well as for secrecy (not at the same time, however).

Consider using the RSA algorithm for authentication alone. As with the use of the RSA for secrecy, each user, i, generates a secret key p_i, q_i of 100-digit primes, and d_i; and publishes $n_i = p_i q_i$ and $e_i = d_i^{-1}$ (mod $\phi(n_i)$).

Recall that the enciphering transformation is $E_i(m) = m^{e_i}$ (mod n_i), and the (secret) deciphering transformation is $D_i(m) = m^{d_i}$ (mod n_i).

In order to provide a message that can be authenticated, user i applies the transformation $D_i(m)$ and sends this message. The receiver of the message, in order to authenticate that the message came from i, consults the public directory and applies the transformation E_i. Consequently, the receiver obtains

$$E_i(D_i(m)) \quad = \quad m^{d_i} \ (\text{mod } n_i)$$

$$= m^{d_i \cdot e_i} \pmod{n_i}$$
$$= m.$$

Furthermore, only i could have generated the message, since only i knows the transformation D_i. There is, however, no secrecy involved, since any user of the network can attempt the decryption by trying the public key E_i.

However, RSA can simultaneously provide secrecy *and* authentication by using a double transformation. Namely, when user i wants to send a message to user j, and to authenticate it (this is often called *signing* the message), user i uses the decryption transformation D_i, and then uses user j's public key to encrypt the message for secrecy. Consequently the transformation is:

$$E_j (D_i (m)).$$

When the message is received by j, j applies his/her decryption transformation, which only j knows, followed by i's public encryption transformation for authentication. Thus:

$$E_j (D_i (m)) \quad \rightarrow \quad E_i (D_j (E_j (D_i (m))))$$
$$= E_i (D_i (m)) = m.$$

The Merkle-Hellman and Graham-Shamir knapsacks cannot be used for authentication, since the enciphering transformation maps the message space not onto itself but rather to the integers; consequently, it cannot be inverted.

However, there is a Shamir "signature-only" knapsack algorithm. It is based on the knapsack-like problem:

Given n, S $\in$ $\mathbb{Z}$, and W = (w_1, w_2, ...w_{2k}), find C = (c_1, c_2, ... c_{2k}) *such that*

$$S = CW = \Sigma c_i w_i \quad (mod \ n)$$

where each c_i $\in$ [0, log n].

n is chosen to be a (say, 100-bit) random prime number, and the pair (W,n) is the public key.

μ is a message of [log n] bits so that in binary form, it represents an integer in the range [0, n-1].

The sender constructs a k $\times$ 2k binary matrix H at random. A set of knapsack numbers are chosen to satisfy:

$$\begin{bmatrix} h_{1,1} & \cdots & h_{1,2k} \\ & \cdots & \\ h_{k,1} & \cdots & h_{k,2k} \end{bmatrix} \begin{bmatrix} w_1 \\ \cdots \\ w_{2k} \end{bmatrix} = \begin{bmatrix} 2^0 \\ \cdots \\ 2^{n-1} \end{bmatrix} \quad (\text{mod } n)$$

This system can be solved by choosing k values at random and determining the other k from the preceding equation.

For the message μ, let μ' be the message obtained by interchanging low- and high-order bits. (I.e. 111000001 becomes 100000111, etc.)

The *signature*, C, is obtained by computing

$$C = \mu' \cdot H.$$

that is, $c_j = \sum \mu'_i h_{ij}$.

The signature can be validated using the public keys since:

$$
\begin{aligned}
CW &\equiv \sum c_j w_j & (\text{mod } n) \\
&\equiv \sum (\sum \mu'_i h_{ij}) w_j & (\text{mod } n) \\
&\equiv \sum \mu'_i (\sum h_{ij} w_j) & (\text{mod } n) \\
&\equiv \sum \mu'_i 2^{i-1} & (\text{mod } n) \\
&\equiv M.
\end{aligned}
$$

As an example, choose k=3, n=7, and M to be a message in the interval [0,6].

Then generate H randomly to be:

$$\begin{bmatrix} 1 & 0 & 1 & 0 & 0 & 1 \\ 0 & 1 & 1 & 1 & 0 & 1 \\ 1 & 0 & 1 & 1 & 1 & 0 \end{bmatrix}$$

and $w_1 = 1$, $w_2 = 2$, $w_3 = 3$.

$$\begin{bmatrix} 1 & 0 & 1 & 0 & 0 & 1 \\ 0 & 1 & 1 & 1 & 0 & 1 \\ 1 & 0 & 1 & 1 & 1 & 0 \end{bmatrix} \begin{bmatrix} 1 \\ 2 \\ 3 \\ w_4 \\ w_5 \\ w_6 \end{bmatrix} = \begin{bmatrix} 1 \\ 2 \\ 4 \end{bmatrix}$$

$$
\begin{aligned}
\Rightarrow \quad & 4 + w_6 \equiv 1 & (\text{mod } 7) \\
& 5 + w_4 + w_6 \equiv 2 & (\text{mod } 7) \\
& 4 + w_4 + w_5 \equiv 4 & (\text{mod } 7) \\
\Rightarrow \quad & w_6 = 4, \quad w_4 = 0, \quad w_5 = 0. \\
\Rightarrow \quad & W = (1, 2, 3, 0, 0, 4).
\end{aligned}
$$

Let $\mu = 3$. Then $\mu = 011$ and $\mu' = 110$.

$$C = \mu' \cdot H = [1\ 1\ 0] \cdot \begin{bmatrix} 1 & 0 & 1 & 0 & 0 & 1 \\ 0 & 1 & 1 & 1 & 0 & 1 \\ 1 & 0 & 1 & 1 & 1 & 0 \end{bmatrix} = [1\ 1\ 2\ 1\ 0\ 2]$$

For the authentication, one multiplies C by W, giving

$$\begin{aligned} C\,W &= [1\ 1\ 2\ 1\ 0\ 2]\,[1\ 2\ 3\ 0\ 0\ 4] \\ &= 1 + 2 + 6 + 8 \equiv 17 \equiv 3 \qquad (\text{mod } 7). \end{aligned}$$

The system as it stands is not secure, since an attacker might be able to determine the matrix H after examining enough messages.

However, if messages are randomized before being signed, this can be avoided.

Generate a random binary vector $R = (r_1, r_2, ..., r_{2k})$. Then, transform μ to μ^*:

$$\mu \;\longmapsto\; \mu^* = (\mu - RW) \quad (\text{mod } n).$$

μ^* is signed as before, giving C'. Then the signature of μ is computed from C' by adding R, giving C = C' + R.

$$\begin{aligned} C\,W &\equiv & (C' + R)\,W \\ &\equiv & (C'W + RW) \\ &\equiv & (\mu^* + RW) \equiv \mu \qquad (\text{mod } n) \end{aligned}$$

EXERCISE 8.1: Construct a 4 × 8 Shamir signature-only knapsack example.

The Ong-Schnorr-Shamir Schemes

A class of signature schemes using polynomials modulo n has been described by Ong, Schnorr, and Shamir [ONG 84], [ONG 85].

The original form of this scheme involved the quadratic equation modulo n:

$$s_1^2 + k \cdot s_2^2 \equiv \mu \qquad (\text{mod } n)$$

where μ is the message to be authenticated, in the interval [0,n-1], n (as usual) is the product of two large secret primes p and q, and k forms the public key. The signature is the pair $S = (s_1, s_2)$.

In other words, in the protocol, each user A, B, ... would have a secret key, yet to be described. When A wishes to send a message, A computes its signature for the message in some fashion, and sends (μ, s_1, s_2).

It is possible to operate this system more efficiently choosing one large modulus n for all users in the system, with only the system manager knowing how to construct n. Indeed, we will see that knowledge of the factors of n does not play a rôle in the use of the system.

What is important is that each user be able to generate a secret key and a public key, and that anyone be able to verify a user's signature using the public key, and in addition no one save the person with the secret key is able to produce the signature for a given message.

The secret key for each user, in this version, will be an invertible transformation of coordinates from the pair (s_1, s_2) to a pair (x_1, x_2) given by:

$$\begin{bmatrix} x_1 \\ x_2 \end{bmatrix} = \begin{bmatrix} 1 & u^{-1} \\ 1 & -u^{-1} \end{bmatrix} \begin{bmatrix} s_1 \\ s_2 \end{bmatrix}$$

In effect, u can be any invertible element modulo, so such a u can be easily found. The public key for this user will be $k \equiv -u^{-2} \pmod{n}$, easily computable from the known u^{-1}. Computing the inverse of this transformation gives:

$$\begin{bmatrix} s_1 \\ s_2 \end{bmatrix} = \begin{bmatrix} 2^{-1} & 2^{-1} \\ 2^{-1}u & -2^{-1}u \end{bmatrix} \begin{bmatrix} x_1 \\ x_2 \end{bmatrix}$$

The transformation above, when applied to the equation

$$s_1^2 + k \cdot s_2^2 \equiv \mu \pmod{n}$$

produces the simpler equation:

$$(2^{-1}x_1 + 2^{-1}x_2)^2 + k \cdot (2^{-1}ux_1 - 2^{-1}ux_2)^2 \equiv \mu \pmod{n}$$

or

$$x_1 \cdot x_2 \equiv \mu \pmod{n}.$$

Now the user can choose x_2 at random from the invertible elements of $\mathbb{Z}_n$, compute $x_1 \equiv \mu \cdot x_2^{-1} \pmod{n}$, perform the transformation above to the coordinates (s_1, s_2), and then send the triple (μ, s_1, s_2).

To authenticate the message, any one who receives the message merely verifies that

$$s_1^2 + k \cdot s_2^2 \equiv \mu \pmod{n}$$

since k is the public key for the user.

However, for anyone else to forge the message, they would have to be able to determine u, which is as difficult as determining $\sqrt{-k}$, which seems as difficult as factoring n.

Unfortunately, although it was felt initially that determining $\sqrt{-k}$ was difficult, Pollard [POLL 84] showed that the above quadratic equation could be solved in reasonable time, yielding k.

Consequently, in the second paper by Ong, Schnorr, and Shamir, whose results are still valid, the problem has been cast in a more general setting. Now to produce such a signature scheme, one begins with a polynomial equation:

$$P(s_1, s_2, ..., s_d) \equiv m \pmod{n}$$

and seeks a linear transformation (i.e. a d × d invertible matrix) to a set of coordinates $(x_1, x_2, ..., x_d)$, yielding a transfomation of the polynomial P to:

$$x_1 \cdot P'(x_2, x_3, ..., x_d) \equiv P(s_1, s_2, ..., s_d) \equiv m \pmod{n}.$$

Then the signature is the n-tuple $(s_1, s_2, ..., s_d)$. The authentication takes place by evaluating $P(s_1, s_2, ..., s_d)$. Forging is not possible because the transformation A, and therefore the x_i's, remain secret.

Pollard's attack based on the ability to solve the original quadratic equation does not seem to extend to higher degree polynomial equations.

The Oblivious Transfer

There are situations when a probabilistic encryption is sufficient, that is, one party encrypts, and another party decrypts the cipher with a probability p that the procedure results in the recovery of the message.

This is called the **oblivious transfer** because the sender is oblivious as to whether or not the message has been received. Under certain objectives for the transfer of information, this model might be entirely sufficient.

The Rabin protocol described in the previous chapter can be used for an oblivious transfer with probability $1/2$: That is, A will send a message to B, and B will decrypt this message with a probability $1/2$ of recovering the message.

Also, B will know whether or not the message has been received; A will be oblivious of this result.

The method is the following:

1. A chooses large primes p and q and computes $N = p \cdot q$. p and q are the secrets to be transmitted to B.

2. B chooses a number x randomly in the interval [1,N-1] .ə. gcd(x,N) = 1, and B sends the square of x mod N, x^2 (mod N), to A.

3. A can compute the four roots of x^2 (mod N), say x, N-x, y, and N-y. A chooses one of the four at random and sends it to B. (There must *be* four roots of x^2, since the original x^2, reduced mod p and reduced mod q, generates elements of QR(p) and QR(q), thus two roots each.)

4. If B receives y or N-y, B can compute p and q since the gcd(x+y,N) = p or q. If B receives x or N-x, B learns nothing.

WHY IS gcd(x+y,N) = p OR q?

First of all, since both x and y are square roots of the same number mod N,

$$\Rightarrow \qquad (x^2 - y^2) \equiv 0 \qquad \qquad (\text{mod } N)$$
$$\Rightarrow \qquad (x^2 - y^2) = k \cdot N \qquad \qquad (\text{for some } k)$$
$$\Rightarrow \qquad (x + y) \cdot (x - y) = k \cdot p \cdot q \qquad (p, q \text{ primes})$$

There are several possible implications of the preceding equation. First of all, $N = p \cdot q$ might divide $(x + y)$. This would imply that $x \equiv N-y$ (mod N). But this is not possible since the four roots (x, N-x, y, N-y) must be distinct. Another possibility is that N divides (x - y). This must also be ruled out since it would imply that $x \equiv y$ (mod N), again a contradiction.

Thus, since N does not divide either factor on the left hand side, it must be the case that p divides one of the factors, and q divides the other. Thus, either p or q must divide $(x + y)$, and thus gcd(x + y, N) = p or q. (The gcd cannot be N since *only one* of the two factors can divide (x + y).)

So, B, after receiving y or (N - y), can compute (x + y), and therefore the gcd, and one of the two primes p or q.

EXERCISE 8.2: Find four distinct values of x such that:

$$x^2 \equiv 737 \quad (\text{mod } 1763).$$

Oblivious Transfer for Coin Flipping by Telephone

One (possibly) practical application of the oblivious transfer protocol is to enable two parties to perform a coin toss by telephone (or by mail). If either one of the two parties is not honest, it is not possible to perform a fair coin toss by telephone.

DISHONEST COIN FLIP BY TELEPHONE - VERSION 1: A tosses a coin; B chooses heads. B announces the choice to A, who then says, "no, the results was tails".

DISHONEST COIN FLIP BY TELEPHONE - VERSION 2: A tosses a coin, and tells B, "the result is heads". B replies, "oh, that's exactly what I chose".

However, the coin toss (or its probabilistic equivalent) can be performed in this way:

1. A chooses large primes p and q, and forms their product, $p \cdot q = N$. A sends N to B.

2. B checks to see if: (a) N is prime, using a primality test; (b) N is a prime power, by extracting roots, and, if N is a power (say $N = x^a$), by testing primality of x; or (c) N is even. Under any of these circumstances, A is deemed to have cheated and therefore loses.

Otherwise, B chooses x at random in the interval $[1, N-1]$ and sends x^2 (mod N) to A.

3. A computes the four roots of x^2 (mod N), picks one at random, and sends it to B.

4. B wins if B can factor N. (From the previous discussion, B has two chances out of four of winning.)

Mental Poker

Another example of a problem involving the necessity of verifying information that could be falsified in a normal prototcol is the game of **mental poker**.

In other words, imagine that N players wish to play poker, but all are connected via telephone lines. As with the coin flipping example above, a way must be found to deal the cards, and to announce hands, without cheating.

One usually makes several assumptions about the game of mental poker. First of all, the deals are fair: each player knows his or her own cards, and no one else's; all of the hands are disjoint (that is, no two players will have the same card); and all possible hands are equally likely to occur. (One might point out that these conditions do not *always* occur in the game of "physical poker".)

Suppose that the N players are A_1, A_2, A_3, ..., A_N. Of course, N cannot be very large, if we are playing with only one "mental deck" of cards. Indeed, to simplify the example, let us suppose that N = 2.

Each player creates in some fashion a **public encrypting function**, E_{A1} and E_{A2}, perhaps constructed by the RSA algorithm using the product of two secret primes. In addition, each player maintains a **secret decrypting function** D_{A1} and D_{A2}.

The same algorithm must be used for the encrypting and decrypting functions, and further it must ensure that these functions are commutative —— that is, that for any message μ,

$$E_{A1} (E_{A2} (\mu)) = E_{A2} (E_{A1} (\mu)).$$

There will be 52 messages that we will enumerate in some fashion, for example,

$$\mu_1 \leftrightarrow \text{"TWO OF CLUBS"} \quad \leftrightarrow 2 \; \clubsuit$$
$$...$$
$$\mu_{52} \leftrightarrow \text{"ACE OF HEARTS"} \quad \leftrightarrow A \; \heartsuit.$$

Suppose that A_1 is chosen as the "dealer".

Then A_1 computes $E_{A1} (\mu_i)$, $\forall i = 1, ..., 52$, and sends all 52 of these messages, in some random order, to A_2. Then A_2 selects at random 5 of these messages (a poker hand has 5 cards), and returns them to A_1. Suppose these messages are $E_{A1} (7 \; \clubsuit)$, $E_{A1} (3 \; \heartsuit)$, $E_{A1} (K \; \diamondsuit)$, $E_{A1} (J \; \spadesuit)$, and $E_{A1} (7 \; \heartsuit)$. (This will be A_1's hand.) A_1 is able to determine the hand using the decryption function D_{A1}, yielding $D_{A1}(E_{A1} (7 \; \clubsuit)) = (7 \; \clubsuit)$, and so on.

A_2 then selects five more messages at random, say $C_1 = E_{A1}(8 \; \spadesuit)$, ..., $C_5 = E_{A1}(10 \; \diamondsuit)$, and computes C'_1, ..., C'_5 as:

$$C'_j = E_{A2} (C_j) \qquad j = 1, 2, ..., 5.$$

(This will represent A_2's hand.) These C'_j are sent to A_1.

Now consider the situation. What do A_1 and A_2 know and what can they pretend? A_1 now sends the C'_j back to A_2 after applying the deciphering function:

$$D_{A1}(C'_j) \quad = \quad D_{A1}(E_{A2}(C_j))$$
$$= \quad D_{A1}(E_{A2}(E_{A1}(\mu_i)))$$
$$= \quad D_{A1}(E_{A1}(E_{A2}(\mu_i)))$$
$$= \quad E_{A2}(\mu_i).$$

A_2 deciphers using D_{A2} to discover his or her hand. A_2 can ensure that A_1 has not cheated in returning the original hand by comparing against the original C_j, that A_2 selected.

Consequently, each player can announce his or her own hand, and the other player has a way of verifying that the hand being announced is true.

Unfortunately, this simple protocol has not proved satisfactory for even a two-player poker game. A method has been determined, by Lipton [LIPT 81], to determine one bit of the cards (messages). This could be used to determine, for example, the colors of the cards that have been dealt. Fortune and Merritt [FORT 85], in a clever article describing the history of this problem, have referred to this as a "marked deck".

Lipton's observation was that exponentiation modulo n preserves quadratic residues. Thus, the dealer, knowing which cards represent quadratic residues (in all probability about half of them, since approximately half the cards will be quadratic residues), and comparing these with the cards returned by the other player, will be able to determine one bit worth of information from the opponent's hand.

The preceding protocol apparently cannot be improved to eliminate this problem. Goldwasser and Micali [GOLD 82] later demonstrated what is to date a secure protocol for two-player mental poker; no protocol has yet been demonstrated for secure, n-player mental poker.

One-Way Encryption Functions

A one-way cipher is an *irreversible function* f: M → C. In other words, there is no way of decrypting a cipher text $f(\mu)$. Again, in some cases, this may be perfectly adequate.

The principal class of examples again arise from situations where the ciphertext need not be examined, but that it need be compared with the encryption of a given message text. For example, encrypted passwords are used in many operating systems for the verification of proper user identification.

Encrypted passwords may be stored, and when a login attempt is made, with an attempted password μ for user A, $f(M)$ may be compared with the encryption of the password for A to determine whether or not login is valid.

It is clear that one requirement for a one-way cipher, is that it be a *monomorphism* to the cipherspace. However, unlike a normal cryptographic protocol, there is no requirement that the function be invertible, i.e. an *isomorphism*.

Purdy [PURD 74] has suggested a method using the difficulty of finding roots of polynomials mod p as a one-way encryption function.

Choose a large prime, p, and a sparse polynomial function f on all messages in the range [0,p-1]:

$$f(\mu) \equiv \mu^n + a_{n-1}\mu^{n-1} + ... + a_1\mu + a_0 \qquad (\text{mod } p)$$

Use this function f as the one-way function. To compute μ knowing the value $f(\mu)$ requires $O(n^2 (\log p)^2)$ operations, which, if n is large, will not be feasible.

Threshold Schemes

A **threshold scheme** is an approach to key management that may find application with groups of users in large networks.

Motivation for the concept of a threshold scheme may come from the public-key model of cryptography --- where the complete key is broken into two pieces, one piece being made public, and the other left secret.

Another model to consider is the bank safety deposit key. Two keys are created; one is in the possession of the depositor, the other in the possession of the bank. The safety deposit box cannot be opened by one key; both keys must simultaneously be applied for the lock to open.

Suppose a key K can be divided into n pieces $K = (k_1, k_2, ..., k_n)$. Each piece will be called a **shadow**.

If the key K has the property that :
1. Any m of the shadows $k_{i1}, ..., k_{im}$ are sufficient to reconstruct K;
2. No set of (m-1) of the shadows are sufficient to reconstruct K;
then the scheme is called an (m,n) threshold scheme.

The utility of such a concept is that if one or a few persons in the system lose their part of the key, the total key K can still be reconstructed; in addition, the system will have the security of having at least m members of the group participate before the key can be used.

An example of an (m, n) threshold scheme was given by Shamir using the Lagrangian interpolation polynomial, a method for reconstructing an mth-degree polynomial curve given n points.

The key to be generated comes from an arbitrary $(m-1)^{st}$ degree polynomial

$$h(x) = a_{m-1}x^{m-1} + \dots + a_1x + a_0 \quad (\text{mod } p).$$

p is chosen to be a prime larger than all of the coefficients. The complete key K is the constant term a_0.

The shadows are obtained by evaluating the polynomial at m points,

$$k_i = h(x_i) \quad\quad i = 1, 2, \dots, m-1$$

Given m shadows, m points uniquely determine a polynomial of degree m-1, and therefore $K = a_0$ can be reconstructed using the Lagrangian interpolation polynomial:

$$h(x) = \sum_{s=1}^{m} k_{is} \left(\prod_{\substack{j=1 \\ j \neq s}}^{m} (x - x_{ij})/(x_{is} - x_{ij}) \right) \quad (\text{mod } p)$$

Consider an example, with m = 3, n = 5, p = 17, and K = 13. Choose

$$h(x) = 2x^2 + 10x + 13 \quad (\text{mod } 17)$$

Then five shadows $k_1, \dots k_5$ are:

$$k_1 = h(1) = (2 + 10 + 13) \equiv 8 \quad (\text{mod } 17)$$
$$k_2 = h(2) = (8 + 20 + 13) \equiv 7 \quad (\text{mod } 17)$$
$$k_3 = h(3) = (18 + 30 + 13) \equiv 10 \quad (\text{mod } 17)$$
$$k_4 = h(4) = (32 + 40 + 13) \equiv 0 \quad (\text{mod } 17)$$
$$k_5 = h(5) = (50 + 50 + 13) \equiv 11 \quad (\text{mod } 17).$$

In order to reconstruct K from three shadows, say k_1, k_3, and k_5, compute the Lagrangian:

$$h(x) = \sum_{s=1}^{m} k_{is} \left(\prod_{\substack{j=1 \\ j \neq s}}^{m} (x - x_{ij})/(x_{is} - x_{ij}) \right) \quad (\text{mod } p)$$

$$= \quad 8\,(x\text{-}3)\,(x\text{-}5)/((1\text{-}3)(1\text{-}5)) + $$
$$10\,(x\text{-}1)\,(x\text{-}5)/((3\text{-}1)(3\text{-}5)) + $$
$$11\,(x\text{-}1)\,(x\text{-}3)/((5\text{-}1)(5\text{-}3))$$
$$= 8 \cdot 8^{-1}\,(x\text{-}3)(x\text{-}5) + 10\cdot(\text{-}4)^{-1}\,(x\text{-}1)(x\text{-}5) + 11 \cdot 8^{-1}\,(x\text{-}1)(x\text{-}3)$$

$$= 19x^2 - 92x + 81 \equiv 2x^2 + 10x + 13 \quad (\text{mod } 17).$$

Thus K is recovered.

The Asmuth-Bloom Threshold Scheme

Another approach to the threshold problem has been presented by Asmuth and Bloom [ASMU 83].

The (m, n) version of the Asmuth-Bloom scheme, to keep as a secret any number up to K, is constructed by choosing a large prime, p, and n numbers modulo p: { $d_1, d_2, ..., d_n$ }, subject to the following conditions:

1. $p > K$;
2. The d_i's are in increasing order: $d_1 < d_2 < ... < d_n$;
3. Each d_i is relatively prime to p: $\gcd(p, d_i) = 1, \forall\, i = 1, .., n$;
4. The d_i's are pairwise relatively prime: $\gcd(d_i, d_j) = 1, \forall\, i, j = 1, ..., n, i \neq j$;
5. $d_1 \cdot d_2 \cdot ... \cdot d_m > p \cdot d_{n-m+2} \cdot d_{n-m+3} \cdot ... \cdot d_n$.

The last condition implies that n/p is greater than any (m-1) of the d_i's.

To distribute the shadows, choose at random $r \in [0, (n/p) -1]$. Then compute $K' = K + rp$. The n shadows will be

$$K_i \equiv K' \quad (\text{mod } d_i) \quad\quad i = 1, 2, ..., n.$$

How Can m Users Recover the Secret K?

Suppose the m users have shadows $K_{i1}, K_{i2}, ..., K_{im}$. Then, by the Chinese Remainder Theorem, K' is known modulo $n' \equiv d_{i1} \cdot d_{i2} \cdot ... \cdot d_{im}$. Since $n' \geq n \Rightarrow K'$ is known.

How Is It That (m-1) Users Cannot Recover the Secret?

(m-1) users can only recover K' modulo $n_2 = d_{i1} \cdot d_{i2} \cdot ... \cdot d_{im-1}$, but $n/n_2 > p$, and the $\gcd(n_2, p) = 1 \Rightarrow K'$ cannot be computed.

EXERCISE 8.3: Construct a (9,3) Asmuth-Bloom threshold scheme.

Blakley's Threshold Scheme

Blakley [BLAK 79] described a simple (m, n) - threshold scheme involving the analytic geometry of an m-dimensional real vector space, $\mathbb{R}^m$.

The key or secret is embedded in the coordinates of a point $(x_1, x_2, ..., x_m)$ in the vector space.

The n shadows are the equations of n (m-1)-dimensional hyperplanes, the intersection of any two of which results in an (m-2)-dimensional hyperplane (just as the intersection of any two non-parallel, non-coincident two-dimensional planes in three-dimensional space results in a one-dimensional line).

The equation of an (m-1) dimensional hyperplane is given by a linear equation of the form:

$$a_1 \cdot x_1 + a_2 \cdot x_2 + \ldots + a_m \cdot x_m \quad = \quad b.$$

We must also ensure that the point hiding the secret is coincident with every one of the n shadows or hyperplanes.

Then, since the intersection of any m such hyperplanes, in m-space, yields a point, any m shadows together will reveal the secret. However, less than m hyperplanes (shadows) taken together will in the intersection being at least a line, and not a point, and therefore the coordinates of the hidden point will remain hidden.

EXERCISE 8.4: Give a geometric interpretation of a (3,3) Blakley threshold scheme.

The Karnin-Greene-Hellman Threshold Scheme

Karnin, Greene, and Hellman [KARN 83] have devised another scheme using matrix multiplication.

(n+1) vectors of m dimensions are chosen, say V_0, V_1, ..., V_n, such that any possible m × m − matrix formed using these vectors as column vectors will have rank m. Then U is a row vector of dimension m+1.

The secret will be the matrix product $U \cdot V_0$. The n shadows will be $U \cdot V_i$, for i = 1, 2, ..., n.

Any m of the shadows being known permits the solution of an m × m system of linear equations with the unknowns being the components of U. Knowing U, $U \cdot V_0$ can be computed, revealing the secret. Knowing less than m shadows yields an underdetermined system, and the coefficients of U cannot be found.

A Generalization

Kothari [KOTH 85] has shown that all four of the above schemes can actually be described as particular cases of a general linear threshold scheme which he defines using the geometry of linear varieties.

Ramp Schemes

An elaboration of the concept of a threshold scheme has been presented Blakley and Meadows in an idea known as a **ramp scheme** [BLAK 85].

A ramp scheme, or more particularly, a **(d,m,n) ramp scheme**, is a protocol designed to allow d inputs, and m − d other, predetermined types of inputs, to be combined to produce n outputs, in such a fashion that the d inputs can be reconstructed from any m outputs.

An (m,n) threshold scheme is, in fact, a (1, m, n) ramp scheme. That is, there are n outputs (the shadows); and any m of these outputs or shadows can be used to reconstruct the 1 input, namely the secret. Furthermore, the probability of determining the output is 1 if m shadows are used; whereas the probability is 0 if less than m outputs are used.

In a (d,m,n) ramp scheme, it is assumed that partial information will be obtained (part of the secret) if at least d, but less than m, shadows are known. However, we will assume that the utility or convenience of returning partial information is worth the effort of the construction.

EXAMPLE:

Consider some large finite field, GF(p,r). Consider also a t-dimensional vector space over this field, to be denoted $V = GF(p,r)^t$, and an s-dimensional vector space $W = GF(p,r)^s$, with s < m < t, where m is taken from the fact that this will be a (d, m, n) ramp scheme.

One could begin to construct an (m, n) threshold scheme using such a vector space, and n hyperplanes, each having an equation of the form:

$$a_1 \cdot x_1 + a_2 \cdot x_2 + \ldots + a_m \cdot x_m = b,$$

where this equation is taken in the field GF(p,r).

Just as with ordinary Euclidean geometry, the intersection of any m hyperplanes will completely determine the coordinates of the point, revealing the secret. However, if (m-1) hyperplanes intersect, they will intersect in a line. Since there are only a finite number of points on a line in a vector space over a finite field, we will have compromised the perfect security of the threshold scheme.

So, in our case, we will map V onto W, via a vector space surjection π:

$$\pi: \quad V \rightarrow W.$$

Choose a point $w \in W$, and a point $v \in \pi^{-1}(w) \subseteq V$. To the point $v \in V$ so chosen, associate n shadows/hyperplanes, with the following properties:

1. The intersection of any m shadows is $\{v\}$.

2. For $l = m - s$,

a) the restriction of π to the intersection of any l shadows is surjective;

b) knowledge about $w = \pi(v)$ increases in a regular way with knowledge of each shadow after l shadows (for example, the image of any $l+1$ shadows could be a subspace of W of dimension s-1; the image of any $l+2$ shadows could be a subspace of W of dimension s-2; and so on.

Now, using the result of combining any number of shadows $\leq d$ is to gain no information at all. Since we are trying to locate w, all we know is that $w \in W$.

Applying between d and m shadows, we continually gain knowledge about the location of w, namely that it is in a certain subspace of W. Finally, knowing m shadows gives us the coordinates of w.

Encryption in Data Bases

At present, most database management systems are unable to maintain data in an encrypted form.

Especially in a relational model of data management, the amount of data to be processed in order to retrieve the answers to arbitrary queries is usually so great that standard encryption methods are precluded at this time.

However, through the control mechanism of the database management system which provides access to the data, it is possible to achieve a certain degree of security, by defining password encryption schemes based on varying levels of authorization to various fields in the database.

In particular, the method of Cooper, Hyslop, and Patterson [COOP 84b] uses irreducible polynomials and the Chinese Remainder Theorem in Galois fields to enable each user, with any combination of authorized fields, to have his (her) separate password.

An Application of the Chinese Remainder Theorem to Multiple-key Encryption in Data Base Systems

In a data base environment, data must be shared among many users subject to constraints. In particular, these constraints include minimizing data redundancy, ensuring integrity, validity, and security and maintaining independence of the data from application programs [DATE 82].

Since each user is given access to a subset of the entire data base, it is necessary for each user to possess a password that will unlock the encrypted data he or she is permitted to see. Because some fields of information are mutually available, and others are not, this means that users must have different passwords for data access. With most encryption algorithms, each user must have a separately encrypted portion of the data base, and a price must be paid for the double encryption of those fields mutually available; or, alternatively, each subfield of a record is individually encrypted and each user given a data path to the passwords that encrypt his particular set of fields [HSIA 79].

Cooper, Hyslop, and Patterson have presented an encryption algorithm that provides a single encryption of each record in the data base which, upon decryption, will present to the user only those fields he or she is entitled to see.

Consider that the data base in question consists of fixed-length character strings made up of substrings, subsets of which are available to the various users of the data base. These character strings are to be encrypted in such a way that all or any part of them of interest can be decrypted given an appropriate password. This decryption algorithm will be the same for all users.

The algorithm to be employed is the following: Let $S = s_1 s_2 ... s_n$ be a representative character string consisting of the concatenation of the substrings $\{s_i, i=1,...n\}$. We assume that all the records to be encrypted are of this form. Each user is entitled to access a character string S_j consisting of a subset of the substrings which make up S, perhaps permuted in order.

The Encryption Process

The algorithm for encryption proceeds as follows:

1. Choose a prime p greater than or equal to the number of characters in the plaintext alphabet. The plaintext alphabet can be increased, if its size is not already prime, by the duplication of frequently-occurring letters. Create a bijection from the plaintext alphabet to the integers modulo p ($\mathbb{Z}_p$). Therefore each user's representative substring can be viewed as a sequence of the integers from 0 to p-1.

2. Use each sequence of integers to form a polynomial in the indeterminate x of degree one less than the length of the representative sequence. Thus, for example, the sequence {1,2,3,4} becomes the polynomial $x^3 + 2x^2 + 3x + 4$. We shall represent the polynomial for the representative sequence S_k as $S_k(x)$.

3. For each polynomial $S_k(x)$ formed above, find a finite field that contains the polynomial as a field element. This finite or Galois field will be one of the choices for GF(p,k), dependent on the choice of irreducible polynomial.

4. In each finite field GF(p,k) invented in step 3, choose a secret polynomial $R_k(x)$. Multiply the polynomial $S_k(x)$ by $R_k(x)$ within the field GF(p,k) to produce a new polynomial $T_k(x)$. We denote this operation as:

$$S_k(x) \cdot R_k(x) \quad \equiv \quad T_k(x) \qquad \text{mod } (p, I_k(x))$$

where $I_k(x)$ is the irreducible polynomial that was selected to generate the field GF(p,k).

5. Use the Chinese Remainder Theorem (as in Appendix III) to find a polynomial A(x) which is the solution to the set of linear congruences:

$$A(x) \quad \equiv \quad T_k(x) \qquad \text{mod } (p, I_k(x))$$

for each k. This A(x) is the required encryption for the representative record S. Since all other records in the data base have the same record format, the polynomials $I_k(x)$ and $R_k(x)$ are sufficient to encrypt the entire data base.

The Decryption Process

Suppose we wish to decrypt A(x) to return the sequence S_k for user k.
1. Divide A(x) by $I_k(x)$. The remainder is $T_k(x)$.
2. Multiply $T_k(x)$ by $[R_k(x)]^{-1}$ to obtain $S_k(x)$.

3. Replace the coefficients in $S_k(x)$ by the plaintext characters according to the inverse of the original bijection.

Remarks

The cost of the algorithm consists of the overhead required to generate the irreducible polynomials for the finite fields involved, and in the selection of the secret polynomial passwords and the generation of their inverses, which need only be done once as part of the data base definition. Multiplying and dividing polynomials, which is basically all that is required for the encryption and decryption, is relatively fast. The implemented package requires as input the column definitions of the concatenated fields to be used as subsets to be retrieved by each individual user under the control of a database administrator, who assigns to the users the passwords they require for access.

For those interested in actually implementing the algorithm, it is recommended that section 4.6 of Knuth's Seminumerical Algorithms [KNUT 69] be read. An extremely good general work on finite fields is the book by Lidl and Niederreiter [LIDL 83].

Some of the algorithms needed for implementation are also discussed in [COOP 80] and [COOP 84a].

— 9 —

Standardization of Public-Key Encryption

This monograph has examined many of the research questions that have arisen in the field of cryptology over the last ten years. We have seen an extraordinary effort in the attempts by many investigators to explore the seemingly fertile ground of public-key cryptography, and we have seen in the last chapter how many of the ideas arising from public-key cryptosystems have found applications in related types of security problems.

This chapter will discuss the question of standardization of public-key cryptosystems and report on recent progress in this regard.

In 1984, the International Standards Organization established a Working Group in one of the organization's technical committees for the purpose of attempting to devise a standard for public-key encryption.

Known officially as the ISO/TC 97/SC 20/WG2 working group on "Public Key Cryptosystems and Applications", the group prepared its first annual report in December 1984 [ISO 85].

Why Standardize?

There is an interesting dynamic in the world of computer science concerning research and standardization. In some sense, the two represent divergent objectives. The researcher always looks at the *status quo*, and attempts to modify it by changing assumptions, accepted methodology, or varying the hypothesis.

In the computer industry, constantly changing techniques, although they may result in improved equipment, software, or practice, also result in a loss of productivity because of the costs involved in "retrofitting" ---

bringing equipment, software, or personnel practice up to a current level of sophistication.

There are several classic examples of this struggle in the discipline of computer science. Perhaps one of the most interesting centers around the programming language Pascal (used in all the coding examples in this monograph).

Pascal, developed in the early 1970s by Niklaus Wirth, is a programming language that incorporated many of the evolving concepts of structured programming of the era. As a consequence, Pascal became extremely popular in universities, and most computer science students in North America today learn Pascal as a first language.

However, Pascal as a language, although at the time of its inception representing the state-of-the-art in block-structured programming languages, nevertheless had no strong momentum in terms of industry-wide standardization bodies. Consequently, it was many years before standards were developed for Pascal. (Indeed, most references today to a Pascal standard are to the book published by Jensen and Wirth defining the language [JENS 74], which of course was not the product of national or international standards bodies.)

As a result, even though Pascal is still extremely popular in universities, it has made almost no penetration into industry --- Horowitz [HORO 83] reported on a survey taken of business computing environments, finding that Pascal was used by only 1.2% of the respondents. COBOL, FORTRAN, and PL/I, however, being languages supported, and to a large degree developed, by various sectors of the computing industry (especially IBM), moved much more quickly to being established as national and international standards, consequently permitting these languages to have a greater acceptance by industry.

A second class of example involves the operating system UNIX,[1] developed by the Bell Laboratories, again in the early 1970s. Although standards bodies do not concern themselves with the standardization of operating systems, since operating system design is usually targeted for a specific computer, by a specific vendor, UNIX stands out as an exception.

Since UNIX makes a reasonable claim as a truly **portable** operating system, i.e., one that can be relatively easily implemented on many different computers, UNIX users have recently begun to call for standard versions of

---

[1]UNIX is a trademark of the American Telephone and Telegraph Company.

UNIX to be adopted by the designers of customized UNIX and UNIX-like operating systems.

UNIX is also a product of several fertile research environments, particularly at the Bell Laboratories and at the University of California at Berkeley. As new concepts for operating system design were incorporated into UNIX, it too evolved over the years.

Finally, another example of standardization comes from the work in data encryption in the early 1970s. We saw in Chapter 2 how LUCIFER, developed at IBM, eventually evolved into the Data Encryption Standard as adopted by the National Bureau of Standards in 1977.

It is not an exaggeration to say that the adoption and promotion of the DES as a standard for secret-key cryptography has, by and large, stifled further research in the area. For better or for worse, secret-key cryptography has all its eggs in one basket. That is why the following chapter, in discussing recent attempts to cryptanalyze the DES, is important to consider.

Many people now feel that the time is ripe to provide a similar floor for public-key cryptography via the standardization process.

Who Standardizes?

Standardization bodies are generally supported either by national governments, industry associations, individual industries, international governmental organizations, or any combination of the above.

The best known of the standardization bodies are probably **ANSI (The American National Standards Institute), ISO (International Standards Organization), and NBS (The National Bureau of Standards)**.

ANSI is an industry-supported instiute in the United States. It has been heavily involved in the standardization of programming languages, for example FORTRAN, COBOL, and Ada.[2]

ISO is an international body, whose secretariat is in France. ISO has developed standards for Pascal.

---

[2] Ada is a trademark of the United States Department of Defense, Ada Joint Programming Office.

The NBS, of course, adopted the standard for secret-key encryption, the DES.

In all of these cases, the standards bodies operate in much broader fields than just the computing industry.

Other standards bodies are the CCITT (Comité Consultatif International de Téléphone et Télégraphe), the United States Department of Defense, and the Canadian Standards Association.

Who's Working on Standardizing Public-Key Encryption?

The ISO began a project to develop a standard for public-key cryptosystems and their mode of use in 1984. The task was assigned to the prosaically-named ISO/TC97/SC20/WG2. This can be decrypted to mean "International Standards Organization, Technical Committee 97, Subcommittee 20, Working Group 2".

This group produced its first annual report in December of 1984, essentially outlining its view of the state of knowledge about publiic-key encryption to that date. The target for the Working Group to produce a draft standard is two years (although it is not stated whether the two year-period dates from the 1984 Annual Report or the formation of the Working Group).

The balance of this chapter will discuss the contents of the first Annual Report, and will quote heavily from [ISO 85]. The quotes will be offset and in a different (Helvetica) typeface.

Scope of the Working Group

The task given to the Public-Key Cryptosystem Working Group is the following:

> ISO/TC97/SC20/WG2 "Public key cryptosystems and applications" has been given three specific tasks:
> 1. Specification of public-key cryptosystems, including algorithms, key generation and auxiliary functions;
> 2. Study the requirements for authentication and data integrity using public-key cryptosystems;
> 3. Study the requirements for digital signatures using public-key cryptosystems.

Classification

As a preliminary to the discussion of PKCs, the Working Group has presented an interesting classification of various cryptosystems. It is perhaps interesting to give this classification as presented by the Working Group:

Cryptosystems can be characterized by functional properties. We shall assume that one is given a set of functions:

$$y = f(x,k)$$

parametrized by the key k. Observe that we use here a general function f, which shall become P or S when it possesses the appropriate properties.

The various relevant properties are gathered in the following table [represented here as Figure 9.1]. That table examines various properties of functions useful for cryptographic purposes; the first important property is the existence of a left inverse function g such that:

$$x = g(f(x,k), k),$$

and the relative ease with which it is possible to compute one of the parameters x, y, or k from the two others. Furthermore, a function f(x,k) with a left inverse g(y,k) is said to be invertible if it satisfies:

$$y = f(g(y,k), k).$$

Using the symbol ∘ to denote function composition and the symbol I to denote the identity mapping, we can express the invertibility by:

$$f \circ g = g \circ f = I.$$

If that property is satisfied, we write f^{-1} instead of g.

In general, function composition is not a commutative operation, and we say that two functions f_1 and f_2 commute if:

$$f_1 \circ f_2 = f_2 \circ f_1.$$

The table leads to the definition of various types of functions characterized by subsets of the complete set of properties. These particular classes have been selected for two reasons: on the one hand, their cryptographic significance is well known, *[sic]* on the other hand, we know at least a representative of each

Quality of scheme \ Class of scheme	Symmetric Crypto systems	One-way functions	Commutative pairs of functions	PKC s
$y = f(x,k)$ easy to compute	⊗	⊗	⊗	⊗
given (x,y), k difficult to compute	⊗	⊗		⊗
given (y,k), x difficult to compute		⊗		
$f(x,k)$ has a left inverse $g(y,k)$	⊗	--		⊗
easy to derive g from f	⊗			
trapdoor information allows the derivation of g from f				⊗
commutativity			⊗	

Figure 9.1
Classifications of Cryptographic Schemes

class (see below). In the table, we assumed that f(x,k) can always be computed efficiently; we used furthermore the shortened phrase "g can be derived from f" to mean that it was possible to derive an efficient algorithm for g from f. In [Figure 9.1] the symbol '⊗' means that the class of functions associated with its column possesses the property associated with its row. The dash '—' indicates an optional property.

Symmetric [private-key or secret-key] cryptosystems are characterized by the fact that there exist efficient algorithms both for f and g and that these algorithms are easily deduced from each other. We included the difficulty of retrieving the key from a matching cleartext-ciphertext pair to cover the known text attack...

Besides symmetric systems, [Figure 9.1] shows that it is possible to define a number of function classes:

• **one way functions**: such as the exponential in some finite field:

$$y = a^x \text{ in } GF(q),$$

or the power function in the ring of integers modulo a composite number n, the factorization of which is kept secret:

$$y = x^a \text{ mod } n.$$

The corresponding inverse functions are the discrete logarithm and the root extraction. A typical use of one way functions is the one sided identification.

• **commutative pairs of functions**: as an example the exponential forms a commutative pair with itself; the remarkable fact is that it can be used for key distribution and identification by using only the properties of the commutative pairs and without resorting to the other properties of the exponential. Commutative pairs of functions can be used for key distribution, one and two sided identification.

• **public key privacy schemes**: the secret function is the left inverse of the public function. In these schemes the public function is used to encipher and the secret one to decipher. Anyone can send a confidential message to an identified receiver. Various implementations have been proposed using the ring of integers modulo a composite number n, the factorization of which is kept secret (the RSA scheme), using the knapsack problem (MERKLE-HELLMAN) or even using GOPPA codes (McELIECE).

• **public key signature schemes**: the public function is the left inverse of the secret function. In this scheme the secret function is used to sign while the public one is used to check the signed message. Anyone can verify the integrity of the message and the identity of the sender. Various implementations have been proposed using also the ring of integers modulo a composite number the factorization of which is kept secret (RSA, Rabin scheme, OSS scheme), or using the knapsack problem (Shamir).

REMARK: The RSA scheme is involved in both the public key schemes; this property is due to the invertibility of the basic functions.

Requirements for Applications

Of the various applications to which PKCs may be placed, there are different technical requirements for privacy, for integrity, and for digital signatures. The Working Group has summarized these as follows:

2.2 Requirements for Privacy

The purpose of privacy is to protect against passive attacks. It is necessary to keep secret the information interchanged in a communication network or stored in memory. Data encipherment provides privacy.

It seems that the running time of public key encipherment prevents its use in some applications. However, a hybrid scheme can be defined in which the text encipherment is provided by a symmetric system, keys for the latter being exchanged under the protection of a public key system.

2.3 Requirements for Integrity

In some applications (banking, electronic mail, etc.) it is necessary that the entity which receives a message can be sure of the data having arrived unaltered and of the sender's identity. These two requirements are combined in our use of the term integrity.

Public key cryptosystems lend themselves conveniently to assuring the integrity of messages.

2.4 Requirements for Digital Signatures

The digital signature is a way to achieve person and message integrity so that it is possible to convince of the authenticity a third party having no prior knowledge of the security system. A signature must be the basis of a proof that the receiver can show to a judge.

A digital signature must have a number of features that provide it with legal significance.

It must:

- be permanent,
- be inviolable,
- identify the signatory,
- be negotiable between signer and receiver,
- be significant (and alert the signer to its significance),
- evoke immediate trust (eg as the basis for an act of business).

The following implementable technical qualities of digital signatures should be discerned:

A - A third party must not be able to change the text so that its receiver or its sender cannot detect the change.

B - Neither the sender nor the receiver of a signed text must be able to manipulate it and thus deceive the partner.

C - The signature must be authenticable to a trusted third party.

D - The documentation must be negotiable without reliance on a witnessing third party (a secret must not be detectable, not even to the trusted third party).

E - A signed document must not be copiable.

F - The signing and authenticating method must be sufficiently robust.

Smart Cards

One of the important applications being developed in financial transaction networks is the so-called "smart card". A **smart card** is a computer, on a plastic card, like a credit card or automatic teller machine (ATM) card, with an implanted microprocessor, and a series of electrical contacts for an I/O interface.

Such cards exist today; they are being produced, for example, by the CCETT for Cie. Schlumberger of France. Indeed, the International Association for Cryptologic Research, the society of researchers in cryptology, uses a smart card as a membership card (although the card itself is not usable as a "smart" card at present).

In the future, machines like automatic teller machines will in fact serve as I/O devices for the tiny computers or smart cards which will be inserted into the familiar slots.

Naturally, since the loss or the theft of a smart card will be quite feasible, a security and authentication system must be devised so that someone who comes into the possession of a smart card will not have access to the financial information nor the financial authority that comes with the card.

Public key authentication may be used in smart cards. For example:

> In a negotiation with a [smart] card, the local (point-of-sale terminal) or distant (service provider) device must decide the authenticity of the card: the card must contain a parameter generated by the issuing authority.
>
> In a negotiation involving a transmission network and a central controller, a random value chosen by the controller is submitted to the card for a cryptographic computation. The right result convinces the remote controller. Such a procedure cannot be used in POS terminals; a large dissemination of secrets must be avoided.
>
> In the specified solution for local payments, the issuer computes an identity certificate and writes it in the card. Let I be a 160-bit parameter related to the card, and J a 320-bit parameter formed by the repetition of I. The identity certificate is the cubic root of J modulo a composite number N, the factorization of which is only known to the issuer.
>
> Each card tester knows the number N, and can thus test the genuineness of an identity certificate delivered by a card by raising it to the cube modulo N. Nobody can forge dummy certificates without knowing the factors of N. Additional tests are made by the card tester to verify the genuineness of the card itself.

Examples

Another set of examples is available for the description of potential uses of public-key cryptosystems. These examples include caller identification in a public data network, OSIS (Open Shops for Information Services), and key management for symmetric (secret-key) ciphers.

Caller Identification in a Public Data Network:

The telephone network does not provide the called party with the identification of the calling line; so in order to generalize some facilities now restricted to on-line users, the public data network must identify the caller through the switched telephone network.

On TRANSPAC, at the opening of the TELETEX service, a first-level protocol will be available by the beginning of 1985. An identity certificate, issued by the network authority, is transmitted by the TELETEX terminal to the network in an XID frame at call establishment. This first-level protocol does not protect against an active attack by repetition of a recorded identity certificate.

So a second-level protocol will be introduced as an optional additional step; the controller chooses a random parameter and requires the caller to perform a cryptographic computation on this parameter. This cryptographic computation is made by a security device, such as a smart card, connected to the terminal....

In the actual smart cards, a secret key algorithm is implemented; by checking the identity certificate the controller obtains a card serial number from which he reconstructs the subscriber secret key. But this second-level protocol is fully compatible with the substitution of the secret key algorithm by a public key algorithm. The user composite number is then obtained by checking the identity certificate. Future smart cards will implement the secret function of public key cryptosystems.

OSIS:

OSIS (Open Shops for Information Services) is a ... (international) project conducted by tele-information services, banks, and telecommunications research institutions. It consists of the following consecutive sub-projects:

• OSISinf - telecommunication system with an immediate on-line payment-for-service option,

• OSISpay - generalized payment system,

• OSIScon - generalized telecommunication system for contract exchange.

Payments are effected by signing payment messages (e.g. electronic cheques). The signature is digital and meets the requirements specified above... Such payment transactions need not be limited to telecommunication systems, but can also be used in any payment system (OSISpay), as e.g. point-of-sale terminals. The use of signatures need not be limited to payment messages, but can be an option (OSIScon) of open communications systems, as e.g. Teletex.

Signatures are effected by the OSIS token, a credit card sized device issued by a bank, similar to a chipcard, but in addition providing a foil key input and display. The token is carried by its owner. He keys in the payment message and his PIN (Personal Identification Number). The token authenticates him by his PIN. A positive authentication result activates the token to sign the (payment) message. After signing the message the token is deactivated.

The signature is effected in the token by an asymmetric encipherment algorithm and the token's secret key, the (condensed) payment message being the cleartext input and the signature the ciphertext output. The token concatenates the message, the signature, and its own identifier, consisting of a token's public key, PKtoken, the latter's signature by the issuing bank's secret key, the bank's public key PKbank, and the latter's signature by the OSIS central bank's secret key. For authentication purposes every token stores the bank's public key PKbank, which in turn authenticates the signing token's public key, PKtoken, which in turn authenticates the signature. For the encipherment algorithm the RSA scheme is being used at present.

The token must be tamper-resistant and prevent exhaustive PIN search. It must give warning of attempts at intrusion. After three wrong PIN inputs, it must destroy its secret information.

Key Management for Symmetric Ciphers:

Whatever the sophistication of a key management system for data encipherment using a symmetric cipher, the fundamental problem is usually one of establishing master keys at the communications parties to allow for the secure exchange of session keys. The general solution to this problem involves a physical action to install the master keys; a secure key transport module may be used or the keys can be transported in printed form. In large networks the setting up of master keys operating between many pairs of communicating parties can be a very onerous task. In all cases, the master key must be kept secret.

If a public key cryptosystem is also available to the system designer, the key management task can be transformed. What is then needed is a reliable source of public keys for each participating user. Given such a reliable source, it is possible to encipher master keys for symmetric ciphers using public keys.

This enables a hybrid cipher system to be operated - using public keys for master key protection (with the simplified key management thereby available) and a symmetric cipher for the exchange of session keys and for data encipherment (with the higher operating efficiency of the symmetric cipher). The vital issue in such a system is the need for absolute integrity of the source of public keys.

Technical Properties

Technical properties of public-key cryptosystems that may, in the future, match legal requirements are:

Permanance: The limiting factor is the perpetuation of magnetically recorded information. The problem has been solved for data processing in general.

Immutability: Quality A is sufficient for immutability of the text signed. Immutability of the document signed requires also quality E.

Identification: The signing key must not be determinable by public information; its owner must keep it secret and must not make it available to anyone else. Quality C (including qualities A-B) is sufficient for identification.

Negotiability: This property is provided by quality C. Partners must not conspire. Quality F provides for the negotiability (against conspiring partners) of a signature witnessed by a notary.

Significance: A signature must be significant enough to change a legal situation; it must promote a warning to the signer that he is about to commit something important. Effecting an electronic signature requires attention, e.g. it may only be achieved if one activates one's signing device (by putting in a PIN) and presses a key to sign and another key to transmit the message.

Immediate trust: The receiver must be able to trust the signature *prima facie*. The digital signature not only can be *prima facie* authenticated with the attached public key; full authentication with a trusted third party's authentic public key need not take much longer; for this purpose the attached public key can be authenticated by the trusted third party.

Quality D cannot be provided by a handwritten signature, and therefore, neither may be required for its substitute. Quality F is used for any of the above legal requirements.

Comparing handwritten signatures and those effected on data by cryptographic techniques shows that the latter can be superior to the former.

Further Information on the Security of Available Public-Key Algorithms

The Factorization Problem:

Factorization of the modulus breaks the RSA algorithm; more generally factorization breaks all schemes based on rings of integers modulo a large composite number.

The following table gives a rough idea of progress in factorization; each entry indicates the maximum size of factorizable numbers. The times of factorization are not explicit stated, but a solution within hours is implied.

YEAR	NO. OF DIGITS FACTORIZED	NO. OF BITS FACTORIZED
1970	43	142
1980	50	166
1982	55	182
1983	62	206
1984	72	239

A projection of the number to be factorized in 1985 is 85 digits or 282 bits... Progress in factorization must be carefully monitored in order to determine the safe lower limit on modulus size.

In addition to the size constraint on the modulus, conditions on every prime component of the modulus have been proposed; let x be a prime factor of the modulus, then additional conditions can be summarized as follows:

      x - 1 shall have a large prime factor y,
      y-1 shall have a large prime factor,
      x+1 shall have a large prime factor.

The working group will study the value of such constraints.

The Discrete Logarithm Problem:

The security of cryptosystems using exponential function is strongly dependent upon the difficulty of computing discrete logarithms.

The field $GF(2^n)$ and particularly the Mitre system based on $GF(2^{127})$ should be rejected: operands of 660 digits (2,200 bits) are required to obtain a security comparable with the RSA scheme with a modulus of 200 digits (665 bits). At this size the execution effort is too much.

The field $GF(p)$ (p prime and p-1 with a large prime factor) is more interesting: a modulus length of 135 bits or 450 bits provides a security equivalent to RSA at 200 digits. Odlyzko gives another practical comparison: in about one day on a computer Cray IMP, one can factor integers about 2^{250} and compute discrete logarithm in fields $GF(p)$, with p about 2^{130}.

Hardware and Software Implementation

The importance of the RSA system, already used in various applications as mentioned in section 2, makes it a likely candidate for implementation and for standardization. It is possible that the ElGamal system, recently invented, may also be a candidate. The Diffie-Hellman key distribution system must not be forgotten, because it provides a convenient way to exchange secret keys.

A number of RSA implementations are at present under development, both in hardware (custom design chips) and in software...

The most we can say at present is that apart from microprocessor-based implementations and custom-designed chips, a number of software implementations are available on mainframe computers. Their portability is poor as they generally require machine code routines. These implementations are relatively slow.

We observe two tendencies at present. Where speed is essential large machines or custom built devices are used. Where security is essential attempts are being made to use hardware such as a mono-chip, for instance in a smart card, it should allow portability and low power-consumption.

Conclusions

The Working Group has reached the following conclusions to date:

[The Working Group is] unanimously convinced that:
- public key cryptosystem standardisation is strongly needed,
- public key cryptosystem standardisation is a realistic goal.

In the opinion of the working group the RSA public key cryptosystem is the most likely candidate for standardisation, though very little has yet happened towards this end. This algorithm has survived public scrutiny and debate better than any other candidate and it is particularly appropriate for signature generation. However, we expect that other public key algorithms will eventually emerge, together with specialised algorithms, such as those used only to generate signatures.

To reach the goal of standardisation and to clarify the situation during the standardisation process, contributions (from members of the working group and other qualified persons) are warmly invited on the following subjects:
- random numbers: generation, implementation, evaluation,
- prime numbers: methods of production (including constraints), performance of generators,
- composite numbers: methods of production, size and classes, number of factors, implementation, performances,
- public exponent: 3, $2^{32} + 1$, other; discrimination between signature exponent and privacy exponent,
- modes of operations,
- hash functions: for signature,
- methods of factorisation, influence of *a priori* knowledge of generation methods,
- other methods for signature and key distribution,
- implementation and protection of secret functions, software and hardware.

WG2 will endeavor to clarify the problems of patents and licences in this field.

A two-year period is needed to produce a first working draft and to submit it to SC20 for ballot as a Draft Proposal.

Finally, W.L. Price, the Standards Editor for the Working Group [PRIC 86], has requested "short contributions ... from those active in the field of data security standards." Persons interested in contacting the working group may communicate with Mr. Price at the National Physical Laboratory, Teddington, Middlesex, TW11 0LW, United Kingdom; or the Working Group secretariat, at the Association française de normalisation, Cedex 7, 92080 Paris La Défense, France.

— 10 —
Attempting to
Cryptanalyze the DES

Unquestionably, the Data Encryption Standard (henceforth called DES) has had the greatest impact of any encryption method upon information security since its adoption almost ten years ago. However, in addition to the success in its use, the DES has drawn more than its share of critics. Indeed, it now appears, in mid-1986, that DES devices will no longer be certified by the National Security Agency after 1987, and the National Security Agency has developed a new and controversial program for the certification of cryptographic devices to be used for government security (the CCEP or Commercial COMSEC Endorsement Program). Consequently, the future of the DES, even now that it is just beginning to be used in a widespread fashion, is in doubt.

The DES has only very recently come into widespread commercial use. (It has never, coincidentally or not, achieved successful adoption by the U.S. military establishment.)

For example, HBO (Home Box Office) is now encrypting cable television signals for the first time in that industry, using an encryption device based on DES.

The CIRRUS international banking network [GIFF 85] uses a Racal-Vadic encryption device for electronic funds transfer which is based on the DES.

The DES was adopted as a standard for inter-agency electronic funds transfer by the United States Government in 1984.

An issue that has continued to be of interest to scholars in this area is whether or not the DES can be cryptanalyzed in a time shorter than, or at a cost less than, the Hellman attack as described in Chapter 2.

In 1985, two significant efforts were undertaken towards the cryptanalysis of the DES. At MIT, a group led by Kaliski, Rivest, and Sherman [KALI 85a], [KALI 85b] devised a number of "cycling experiments" intended to confirm or reject certain group-theoretic assumptions about the DES.

A little bit later, Adi Shamir, at the Weitzmann Institute in Israel, began an analysis into certain symmetries he discovered in the functions that make up the DES.

The purpose of this chapter is to describe these new attempts at the cryptanalysis of the DES.

Description of the DES in Group-Theoretic Terms

Earlier in the monograph, we gave a functional description of the Data Encryption Standard. For the purposes of the current approach to the attempts at cryptanalysis, it will be useful to look at the DES from a group-theoretic perspective.

For a given key k, the transformation t_k defines an invertible transformation on M_{64}, the set of all 64-bit messages; consequently, an element of the (symmetric) group of all permutations on M_{64}, $S(M_{64})$. Recall that this group has cardinality

$$(2^{64})\,!$$

The key space, K_{56} ($= K$), of cardinality 2^{56}, therefore generates a subset Ω_{DES} of $S(M_{64})$, since every key generates a permutation of M_{64}.

Can we say any more about the structure of this set Ω_{DES} ? For example, is it a subgroup? Does it contain the identity element? Does it contain inverses? Is it closed under composition?

In general, the answer to all of these questions is, "we don't know". In fact, we know very little about the structure of this set Ω_{DES}.

Here is a summary of existing knowledge:

1. Let G_{DES} be the group generated by Ω_{DES}. $G_{DES} \subseteq A(M_{64})$, the alternating subgroup of $S(M_{64})$.

2. THE COMPLEMENTATION PROPERTY. Let x^c represent the logical NOT of a boolean string (i.e. element of M_n). Then, for every key k and every message μ in DES:

$$t_{DES}\,(\mu^c,k^c) \;=\; (t_{DES}(\mu,k))^c.$$

In order to demonstrate the above, recall the functional definition of the DES transformation:

$$t_{DES}(\mu,k) = IP^{-1} \circ T_{16} \circ T_{15} \circ ... \circ T_2 \circ T_1 \circ IP\ (\mu,k)$$

First, it is a trivial remark that permutation commutes with complementation. Consequently, IP, IP^{-1}, PC-1, PC-2, P, and LS_i all commute with complements.

Next, we establish the following identities related to the exclusive-or operation:

$$\text{(a)}\quad A \oplus B^c = (A \oplus B)^c$$
$$\text{(b)}\quad A \oplus B = (A^c) \oplus (B^c)$$

by computing the appropriate Boolean expressions:

A	B	$A \oplus B$	A^c	B^c	$A \oplus B^c$	$(A \oplus B)^c$	$(A^c) \oplus (B^c)$
0	0	0	1	1	1	1	0
0	1	1	1	0	0	0	1
1	0	1	0	1	0	0	1
1	1	0	0	0	1	1	0

Since IP and IP^{-1} commute with complements, it will suffice to show that

$$(T_j(k,\mu))^c = T_j(k^c,\mu^c) \qquad j = 1, 2, ..., 16.$$

Recall that T_j can be described as a function on the left- and right-halves of the input message, $\mu_{i-1} = (L_{i-1}, R_{i-1})$:

$$T_j(k,\mu) = (R_{j-1}, P(\ S(\ E(R_{j-1}) \oplus k_j\ )\ )\ ) \oplus L_{j-1}\ ).$$

a. $(k_j)^c = (k^c)_j$: The functions that generate k_j are a sequence of permutations (PC-1, LS_j, PC-2), consequently they commute with complements.

b. $(R_{j-1}{}^c) = (R^c)_{j-1}$ and $(L_{j-1}{}^c) = (L^c)_{j-1}$.

c. Assume that $(\mu_{j-1}{}^c) = (\mu^c)_{j-1}$. Then

$$
\begin{aligned}
(\ T_j\ (\ \mu_{j-1}, k_j\ )\ )^c &= (\ R_{j-1}, P(\ S(\ E(R_{j-1}) \oplus k_j\ )\ )\ ) \oplus L_{j-1}\ )\ )^c \\
&= (\ (R_{j-1})^c,\ (P(\ S(\ E(R_{j-1}) \oplus k_j\ )\ )\ ) \oplus L_{j-1})^c\ ) \\
&= (\ (R^c)_{j-1},\ P(\ S(\ E(R_{j-1}) \oplus k_j\ )\ )\ ) \oplus (L^c)_{j-1}\ ) \\
T_j\ ((\mu^c)_{j-1}, (k^c)_j\ )) &= (\ (R^c)_{j-1}, P(\ S(\ E((R^c)_{j-1}) \oplus (k^c)_j\ ))\ ) \oplus (L^c)_{j-1}\ )
\end{aligned}
$$

Thus the result will be demonstrated if we can show that

$$P(\ S(\ E(R_{j-1}) \oplus k_j\ ) = P(\ S(\ E((R^c)_{j-1}) \oplus (k^c)_j\ )\ )\ )$$

or

$$S(E(R_{j-1}) \oplus k_j \; = \; S(E((R^c)_{j-1}) \oplus (k^c)_j)$$

E also commutes with complementation, since E injects 32 bits into a 48-bit string by repeating some of the bits. Thus we will show

$$
\begin{aligned}
E(R_{j-1}) \; \oplus \; k_j \;\; &= \;\; (E(R_{j-1}))^c \oplus \; (k_j \;)^c \\
&= \;\; E(\; (R_{j-1})^c \;) \; \oplus \; (k^c)_j \\
&= \;\; E((R^c)_{j-1} \;) \; \oplus \; (k^c)_j
\end{aligned}
$$

which was the result required. The reader might also note that this is also the solution to exercise 2.4.

3. EXISTENCE OF WEAK KEYS. There exist at least four distinct keys k [MEYE 82] such that

$$t_k^2 \; = \; Id.$$

These are (written in hex with parity bits):

01	01	01	01	01	01	01	01
1F	1F	1F	1F	1F	1F	1F	1F
E0	E0	E0	E0	E0	E0	E0	E0
FE	FE	FE	FE	FE	FE	FE	FE

4. EXISTENCE OF SEMI-WEAK KEYS. There exist at least six distinct pairs keys $k_1 \neq k_2$ [MEYE 82] such that

$$t_{k1} \, t_{k2} \; = \; Id.$$

These are (written in hex with parity bits):

E0	FE	E0	FE	F1	FE	F1	FE
FE	E0	FE	E0	FE	F1	FE	F1
1F	FE	1F	FE	0E	FE	0E	FE
01	FE	01	FE	01	FE	01	FE
1F	E0	1F	E0	0E	F1	0E	F1
01	E0	01	E0	01	F1	01	F1

FE	1F	FE	1F	FE	0E	FE	0E
E0	1F	E0	1F	F1	0E	F1	0E
FE	01	FE	01	FE	01	FE	01
E0	01	E0	01	F1	01	F1	01
01	1F	01	1F	01	0E	01	0E
1F	01	1F	01	0E	01	0E	01

Some Further Group-Theoretic Terminology

There are a number of natural group-theoretic concepts which can be extended to statements about cryptosystems.

For example, a cryptosystem is **faithful** $\Leftrightarrow$ every key represents a distinct transformation. In other words, the mapping from the key space to the group of all permutations in the message space is an *injection*.

A cryptosystem χ is **closed** $\Leftrightarrow$ the subset t_χ is closed under composition.

A cryptosystem χ is **pure** $\Leftrightarrow$ for every T_0 in t_χ, the set $T_0^{-1}t_\chi$ is closed. (Closed implies pure but pure does not imply closed.)

For any $\tau \subseteq S_M$, for any $m \in M$, the τ-**orbit of m** is the set:
$$B_m = \{ T_k(m) \mid T_k \in \tau \}.$$
The τ-**stabilizer** of m is the set
$$H_m = \{ T_k \in \tau \mid T_k(m) = m \}.$$
τ **acts transitively** on M $\Leftrightarrow$ for every pair of messages m, n $\in$ M, $\exists$ a transformation $T_k \in \tau$.$\ni$. $T_k(m) = n$.

It is unknown whether or not DES is faithful, closed, or pure.

Attacks on the DES

As was earlier discussed in chapter 2, Diffie and Hellman [DIFF 77] proposed an attack on the DES using exhaustive key search. Their cost analysis of DES encryption showed that a special-purpose "DES-breaking" machine could be built for $20,000,000.

Because of this potential weakness of the DES, we also saw suggestions concerning the enlargement of the key size to 112 bits. Principal among these are the suggestions of Tuchman [TUCH 78] and sequential multiple encryption. However, no extension to 112-bit keys has been adopted as part of the standard.

Group Properties of the DES

One of the more interesting questions about the DES is, what are the characteristics of the subgroup of $S(M_{64})$ generated by the set of DES transformations?

A related question is, is the set of all DES transformations, Ω_{DES}, a group in and of itself? If the answer were to be yes, then the composition of two DES transformations would also be a DES transformation; thus both the sequential multiple transformation and the Tuchman extension would reduce to single 56-bit encryption; and the Hellman and Diffie attack could defeat either.

Furthermore, if the DES is a group, Kaliski, Rivest and Sherman demonstrate an algorithm (the "meet in the middle" algorithm) [KALI 85a] to cryptanalyze the DES in $2^{28} \approx 250,000,000$ steps.

The Birthday Paradox

Now we will turn to a discussion of the cycling experiments at MIT [KALI 85a],[KALI 85b], perhaps the first large-scale attempt to gain useful experimental information on the possible cryptanalysis of the DES.

One of the strongest tools used in the cycling experiments at MIT derives from the well-known "Birthday Paradox". The Birthday Paradox is usually stated in this way:

If r people are selected at random, what is the chance that no two of them will have the same birthdate (not the same year)? For example, in a class of 30 students, what is the chance that no two students will have the same birthdate? Intuition, for most of us, would say that since $30/365 \approx 8\%$, the chances are about 8%.

To calculate the true probability of no two persons having the same birthdate, think of a method whereby one student after another announces their birthdate, and we consider each such event as an independent event, with the assumption that birthdays are uniformly distributed over the 365 days of the year (a good enough assumption, as well as the assumption about ignoring leap years).

Then, the probability that the first event is *successful* (i.e. where success is defined as the result of no same birthdays being announced), is 1. The probability that the second event is successful is 364/365, since only the first student's birthday being called would result in failure. Similarly,

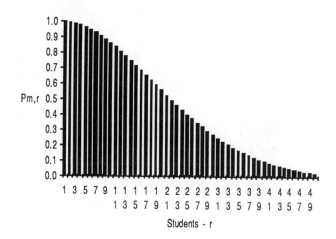

Figure 10.1
A Graph of Birthday Paradox Probabilities as a Function of r (≤50)

with the 3rd student, the probability of success would be 363/365 (since, in order to reach the third student, the first two would have to have distinct birthdays). One continues in this way, so on down to 336/365 for the 30th student.

The probability that no two students will have the same birthday is the probability of the occurrence of all of the afore-mentioned events, namely:

$$p = \frac{365 \cdot 364 \cdot 363 \cdot \ldots \cdot 336}{365 \cdot 365 \cdot 365 \cdot \ldots \cdot 365} = \frac{365!}{335! \cdot (365)^{30}}$$

or, in general,

$$P_{m,r} = \frac{m!}{(m - r)! \cdot m^r}.$$

We would like to examine the behavior of this probability $p_{m,r}$ (and therefore also the probability of at least two people having same birthdays,

$q_{m,r} = 1 - p_{m,r}$, particularly when r is expressed as a function of m, $r = f(m)$ $= m^c$. This is shown in Figure 10.1.

In other words, the point at which the probability is $1/2$ that there will be two simultaneous birthdays occurs in a class with ≈ 23 students.

Now let us attempt to compute the comparable function $p_{m,r}$ for general values of m and r.

By Stirling's formula, one can replace:

$$m! = (2\pi)^{1/2} \, m^{1/2} \, (m/e)^m \, [\, 1 + O(1/m) \,]$$

$$\Rightarrow \quad \log p_{m,r} = \log (m!) - \log ((m-r)!) - \log (m^r)$$
$$= \log ((2\pi m)^{1/2} \cdot (m/e)^m) -$$
$$\log ((2\pi(m-r))^{1/2} \cdot ((m-r)/e)^{(m-r)}) - r \log m$$
$$= (1/2) \log (2\pi m) + m \log (m/e) - (1/2) \log (2\pi(m-r))$$
$$+ (m-r) \log ((m-r)/e) - r \log m$$
$$= ((1/2) + m - r) \cdot \log m \quad - m \, -$$
$$((1/2) + m - r) \cdot \log (m-r) + m - r$$
$$= ((1/2) + m - r) \cdot (\log (m/(m-r))) - r$$

for all r sufficiently small.

If we wish to analyze the behavior of the function $p_{m,r}$, then it is instructive to transform the variable r by replacing it by $r = f(m) = m^c$, where c will lie in the range $0 \le c \le 1$.

The table 10.1 gives the results of these calculations, indicating that a probability of 1/2 for success in the birthday problem comes approximately where the value of $c \approx 0.5$. In other words, the "breakeven point" for the birthday problem comes approximately where $r = \sqrt{m}$. This analysis will prove to be useful in the next, and related probability problem we will consider.

Table of values of $p_{m,r}$ for various values of c and m

m \ c:	0.06	0.12	0.18	0.24	0.30	0.36	0.42	0.48	0.54	0.60	0.66	0.72
100	0.9979	0.9936	0.9853	0.9697	0.9418	0.8929	0.8112	0.6830	0.5018	0.2889	0.1069	0.0176
120	0.9982	0.9943	0.9865	0.9719	0.9449	0.8967	0.8144	0.6829	0.4949	0.2747	0.0932	0.0126
140	0.9983	0.9948	0.9876	0.9736	0.9474	0.8999	0.8172	0.6829	0.4892	0.2630	0.0825	0.0093
160	0.9985	0.9952	0.9884	0.9750	0.9496	0.9026	0.8196	0.6831	0.4843	0.2531	0.0739	0.0071
180	0.9986	0.9955	0.9891	0.9762	0.9514	0.9049	0.8218	0.6833	0.4801	0.2445	0.0669	0.0054
200	0.9987	0.9958	0.9897	0.9773	0.9530	0.9070	0.8238	0.6835	0.4764	0.2369	0.0609	0.0043
220	0.9988	0.9961	0.9902	0.9782	0.9544	0.9089	0.8255	0.6838	0.4731	0.2301	0.0559	0.0034
240	0.9989	0.9963	0.9906	0.9790	0.9557	0.9106	0.8272	0.6840	0.4701	0.2240	0.0515	0.0027
260	0.9989	0.9964	0.9910	0.9797	0.9568	0.9121	0.8287	0.6843	0.4673	0.2185	0.0477	0.0022
280	0.9990	0.9966	0.9914	0.9803	0.9579	0.9136	0.8301	0.6846	0.4648	0.2134	0.0444	0.0018
300	0.9990	0.9968	0.9917	0.9809	0.9588	0.9149	0.8314	0.6848	0.4624	0.2087	0.0414	0.0015
320	0.9991	0.9969	0.9920	0.9814	0.9597	0.9161	0.8327	0.6851	0.4602	0.2044	0.0387	0.0013
340	0.9991	0.9970	0.9922	0.9819	0.9605	0.9172	0.8338	0.6854	0.4582	0.2003	0.0364	0.0010
360	0.9992	0.9971	0.9925	0.9824	0.9612	0.9183	0.8349	0.6856	0.4563	0.1966	0.0342	0.0009
380	0.9992	0.9972	0.9927	0.9828	0.9619	0.9193	0.8360	0.6859	0.4545	0.1930	0.0323	0.0007
400	0.9992	0.9973	0.9929	0.9832	0.9626	0.9202	0.8369	0.6861	0.4528	0.1897	0.0305	0.0006

Table 10.1

Calculations for $p_{m,r}$ in the Birthday Paradox

Meet-in-the-Middle Methods

The "meet-in-the-middle" problem is related to the birthday problem. Stated simply, the "meet-in-the-middle" problem is this:

Given a universe of m elements. Two samples, X and Y, of size r, are to be drawn at random, and without replacement, from this universe. What is the probability that the two sets, X and Y, so chosen, will be disjoint?

The analysis proceeds much as before. Also as before, call the probability that the two sets will be disjoint $p_{m,r}$. When the first sample for X is drawn from the universe, the probability is m/m of success in ensuring that the sets are disjoint. When the first sample for Y is drawn, the probability is (m-1)/m of success, since there are m choices for Y, and only one will result in failure.

When the second sample is drawn from X, the probability of success is (m-2)/(m-1); since there are now (m-1) choices for X; and (m-2) of these choices will result in success --- all but Y's first choice. When the second sample is drawn for Y, the probability is (m-3)/(m-1) ... there are still (m-1) choices for Y, but only (m-3) will result in success, the two already chosen from X not leading to success.

Continuing this argument, the resulting probability for $p_{m,r}$ becomes:

$$p_{m,r} = \frac{m(m-1) \ldots (m-2r)}{(\, m(m-1)\ldots(m-r) \,)^2}$$

$$= \frac{m! \cdot (\, (m-r)! \,)^2}{(m-2r)! \cdot (\, m! \,)^2} = \frac{(\, (m-r)! \,)^2}{(m-2r)! \cdot m!}$$

Again relying on the Stirling formula for approximating n!, we can compute log $p_{m,r}$ as:

$$\log p_{m,r} = (1 + 2m - 2r) \, \log (m-r) - (1/2 + m - 2r) \log (m-2r)$$
$$- (1 + m) \log m \qquad - r$$

which becomes, to a first term approximation (for r $\ll$ m), $-2r^2/m$.

The substitution r = f(m) = m^c will be made once again, to find an approximate value of c which will lead to the probabillity of success in the "meet-in-the-middle" problem to be 1/2.

Again, as in the previous example, a value of c approximating 1/2 will give a probability of $e^{-2m^0} = e^{-2} \approx 14\%$ of finding a match. In other words, a value of m^c nearing the square root of m will lead to reasonable expectations for matches in the sample.

The MIT Experiments

Consider devising an experiment to enable us to decide whether or not the DES cryptosystem χ_{DES} is *closed*. Recall that a cryptosystem is closed if the set of encryption transformations is closed under functional composition.

If χ_{DES} is closed, then it is reasonable to expect that for any key $k \in K$, that we can find two other keys a, b $\in$ K such that $T_k = T_a \circ T_b$. Indeed, if two sets of keys $a_1, ..., a_r$ and $b_1, ..., b_r$ are selected at random, then we look for a pair a_i, b_j such that $T_k = T_{ai} \circ T_{bj}$. To try to find this match, we can precompute $c = T_k^{-1}(\mu)$, for some message μ, and then compute $x_i = T_{ai}(\mu)$ for all $i \leq r$, and $y_j = T_{bj}^{-1}(\mu)$ for $j \leq r$. Then, we look for matches $x_i = y_j$.

PROPOSITION 10.1: If χ_{DES} is closed, then there are exactly m pairs of keys i and j such that $T_i \circ T_j = T_k$, where m is the order of the cryptosystem. If the χ_{DES} consists of random permutations in S(M), then the expected number of pairs i and j such that $T_i \circ T_j = T_k$ is $m^2/(|M|)!$

PROOF: If χ_{DES} is closed, then composition by T_i permutes the operators T_k, thus for each T_i, we can find one T_j such that $T_i \circ T_j = T_k$. Thus there are always m pairs giving the required result. In particular, if the cryptosystem is *faithful*, then the value m will be the cardinality of the key space, |K|. In any case, m ≤ |K|.

If χ_{DES} is random, then there are m^2 possible pairs of the form $T_i \circ T_j$, and |M|! permutations of M altogether. Thus the probability of a transformation being represented by a $T_i \circ T_j$ pair is $m^2/(|M|)!$

Q.E.D.

It is possible that a match $x_i = y_j$ will not result in the equality $T_k = T_{ai} \circ T_{bj}$, but this can be tested easily by using a few other test messages $\mu_1, \mu_2, \mu_3, ...$

If χ_{DES} is closed, the procedure will find a match with probability $q_{m,r} \geq 1 - e^{-3r^2/m}$, since this is the probability, computed above, for a match when two samples of size r are drawn from a universe of m elements producing disjoint samples. In this case, the value of m is the size of the key space, 2^{56}. Consequently, we would have a 0.5 expectation of finding a match if

$$0.5 \;=\; 1 - e^{-2r^2/(2^{56})}$$

or, solving for r,

$$r \;\approx\; 0.59 \cdot 2^{28}.$$

In other words, the probability becomes 0.5 of finding a match approximately when the size of the sample is the square root of the size of the key space.

On the other hand, if χ_{DES} is not closed, then the probability that K would contain a pair a, b $\in$ K such that $T_k = T_a \circ T_b$ would be $|K|^2 / (|M|!)$, which is very small.

Thus, if we conduct this test, and do not find a match after samples of size r $\approx 2^{28}$, we have evidence to confirm the likelihood that χ_{DES} is not closed.

This test is one that is within theoretical computational bounds, since $2^{28} = 268, 435, 456$. The computational complexity of this test will involve the sorting and storing of two lists of length r $= 2^{28}$. Of course, using quicksort, the sorting can be done in r log r time. The actual test conducted at MIT is somewhat more compact, but along the same lines.

The Cycling Closure Test

A more compact test for the closure of DES consists of trying to determine cycle lengths in the group generated by the DES, G_{DES}, which is a subgroup of A(M) $\leq$ S(M).

Let m $= |\, G_{DES}\,|$. We will compute a pseudo-random walk in G_{DES}. In other words, we will find a pseudo-random function ρ which will determine a sequence of keys. Then the walk in G_{DES} will consist of beginning with a certain group element, multiplying by another group element as determined by the pseudo-random function, and so on until we find a cycle in the group.

In particular, let the first group element be $\gamma_0 = e$. Then $\gamma_i = (T_{k_i}) \circ \gamma_{i-1}$, where each key k_i is chosen by applying ρ to the previous key: $k_i = \rho(k_{i-1})$.

If the DES is closed, then the order of $G_{DES} \leq 2^{56}$, the size of the key space. Consequently, trying to find a cycle, being analogous to trying to find matching birthdays in the birthday paradox, would be expected to produce a result in $\sqrt{|G_{DES}|} = \sqrt{2^{56}} = 2^{28}$ steps.

On the other hand, if the DES is random, then in all probability $|G_{DES}| \approx A(M) = (2^{64})! / 2$.

Rather than computing this pseudo-random walk in G_{DES}, we will take the walk in the message space, M by computing $\mu_1, \mu_2, \mu_3, \ldots$ where

$$\mu_i = \gamma_i (\mu),$$

where μ is some initial message chosen at random.

In this case, since the size of the message space is 2^{64}, we would expect to find a cycle in approximately $\sqrt{(2^{64})} = 2^{32}$ steps.

This is in fact the experiment conducted at MIT. Using a variation of the Floyd Two-Finger algorithm (discussed below) to determine cycles, many tests have been done. All preliminary results seem to support the hypothesis that indeed, the DES constitutes a random set of permutations in A(M).

To carry out the experiments, the MIT group modified an IBM Personal Computer, and attached a DES encryption device. The details of this design are also described later.

The Floyd Two-Finger Algorithm

The Floyd "two-finger" algorithm is not only used extensively in the MIT cycling experiments, but is also integral to the Pollard ρ-algorithm, one of the key steps in recent advances in the factoring of large integers.

The Two-Finger Algorithm makes its appearance in the literature as problem 21, on page 7, of the second volume of Knuth (where else!) [KNUT 69]. There it is introduced through the following question:

PROPOSITION: Given a sequence of non-negative integers $X_0, X_1, X_2, \ldots$ with the property that $X_n \leq m$, $\forall$ n. Suppose there exists a function f on the interval [0,m] with the property that it maps each element of the sequence to its successor, $f(X_n) = X_{n+1}$, $\forall$ n $\geq$ 0. Then $\exists$ λ, m .϶.

$$X_0, X_1, \ldots, X_{m-\lambda-1} \text{ are distinct}$$

and
$$X_{n+\lambda} = X_n.$$

PROOF: Since the values $X_0, X_1, X_2, \ldots$ take their values in a bounded interval, at most the first m of these will have distinct values. Let the index

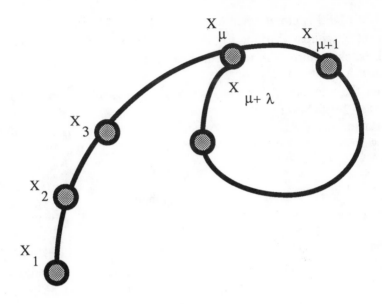

Figure 10.2
Why It Is Called the Pollard Rho-Algorithm

of the first occurrence of the first value to be repeated be n-λ; let the second occurrence of the value $X_{n-\lambda}$ be X_n. Then we will further have:

$$X_{n+1} = f(X_n) \quad = \quad f(X_{n-\lambda}) \quad = \quad X_{n-\lambda+1},$$

and, in general,

$$X_{n+j} \quad = \quad X_{n-\lambda+j}, \quad \forall j \geq 1,$$

thus

$$X_{n+\lambda} \quad = \quad X_{n-\lambda+\lambda} \quad = \quad X_n.$$

Q.E.D.

With the above proposition demonstrated, prove the following:

$\exists \, n > 0 \,$.э. $\, X_n = X_{2n}$, and the smallest such number lies in the range $\mu \leq n \leq \mu + \lambda$.

Finally, given the above two results, the two-finger algorithm *finds* such a value of n in $O(\mu+\lambda)$ steps, using a bounded number of memory locations.

(For those curious as to the nomenclature, one imagines using two fingers, one to point to each of X_n and X_{2n} as the algorithm is traced. Eventually the two "fingers" will collide.)

The algorithm is simply a loop (say, indexed by i) going from 1 to n, and at each step comparing X_i to X_{2i}. At each step, the function f is applied to the previous value X_i, and the function $g = f \circ f$ is applied to X_{2i} The previous proposition guarantees that the algorithm will terminate after at most $\mu + \lambda$ loops.

Thus this algorithm is linear in the cycle length, and consequently, as applied to the previous cycling test, should determine a cycle in either approximately 2^{28} steps (DES closed hypothesis) or 2^{32} steps (DES random hypothesis). As opposed to the previous "meet-in-the-middle" test, however, the Floyd algorithm eliminates the need for large storage requirements.

Custom Hardware for the MIT Cycling Experiments

Rivest and the group at MIT have carried out many of the computations described above. They have modified an IBM PC by adding a wire-wrap board. This board contains a micro-programmable finite-state controller, that operates a byte-oriented Advanced Micro Device AmZ8068 DES chip. A 512-byte PROM is used to generate the pseudo-random next-key function.

It has previously been estimated that the best known results for DES encryption in software, using an IBM PC, are about 200-300 encryptions per second.

On a VAX 11/780 (in software), this can be improved to about 2500 encryptions per second.

However, the modified IBM PC, as described above, can perform 41,000 encryptions per second, or about 2.5 million per minute, or about 3.6 billion encryptions per day. Since 3.6 billion is between 2^{31} and 2^{32}, and since we will often expect cycle length to be in the vicinity of 2^{32}, this device can be reasonably expected to accomplish our task.

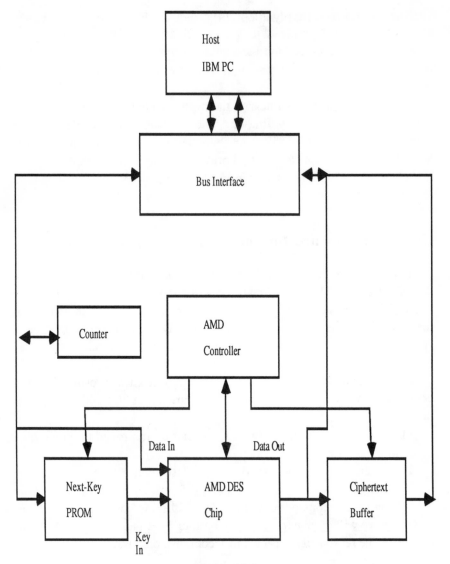

Figure 10.3
Hardware for MIT Cycling Experiments

Shamir's Remarkable Symmetries

We conclude this chapter by presenting some ideas as described by Adi Shamir at the Crypto '85 Conference in Santa Barbara, in August 1985 [SHAM 85].

Some recent research has demonstrated remarkable symmetries in certain aspects of the DES which seem to pose many questions.

First of all, to discuss the DES, we will review some of the (already published) observations about the DES:

1. One of the features of the algorithm is the short size of the key. It is known (Hellman and Diffie) that a $20,000,000 investment could produce a machine to break DES in half a day. Various estimates on machine cost, and algorithm analysis have raised or lowered these estimates slightly. Furthermore, because of the short key, even shaving few bits off the key (say, from 56 bits to 50 bits), then the cost might be lowered from $20 M to $16,000.

2. Other attacks have shown that there is trade-off between time and memory that can be achieved.

3. DES is closed under complementation. (That is, $(T_j(k,\mu))^c = T_j(k^c,\mu^c)$.)

4. The permutations in DES are highly structured. (Davies gave a description of PC-2 as three Hamiltonian graphs. [MEYE 82]) This is not necessarily a negative feature of DES as the rôle of the permutation is not to provide security but rather to distribute bits.

5. The crucial step in encryption is in the S-boxes. Furthermore, Desmedt has shown that S_4 is 75% redundant [DESM 84]. However, this fact by itself does not give a handle on cryptanalysis, since even assuming that S_4 were the identity transformation would not give substantial information since the combination of all the S-boxes is what's important.

6. A few instances of weak keys have been found.

As is well known, the design criteria for the S-boxes (indeed, the entire algorithm) have never been declassified. Nevertheless, again referring to published literature and known results, one can make a number of statements about known design criteria for the S-boxes:

1. Each S-box contains four permutations of the integers in the range [0,15]. (This is a trivial remark from observation of the S-boxes.)

2. The S-box transformations, as mappings from Z_6 to Z_4, are non-linear and non-affine.

3. One change in input always causes at least two changes in output.

4. (According to Meyer and Matyas) The S-boxes demonstrate higher than usual boolean complexity.

5. There is a balanced distribution of 0 and 1.

In order to try to discover some symmetry in the S-boxes, one could, for example, examine the distribution of the least significant bit in the output of the S-boxes; or similarly, the distribution of the most significant bit. However, neither of these approaches demonstrates anything other than a seemingly random distribution of these elements.

However, if the set {0, ..., 15} partitioned into those elements with even and odd weights (when thought of as 4-bit strings) something remarkable happens.

The integers in the set {0, ..., 15} with even weight are 0 (weight 0), 3, 5, 6, 9, 10, 12 (all with weight 2), and 15 (weight 4).

When the output of the S-boxes S_1, S_2, S_5, S_7, and S_8 is examined with respect to this partition of the integers, and the S-boxes themselves bisected along a vertical axis, the distribution of the S-box outputs is as follows (See Figures 10.4 and 10.5):

S-BOX	LEFT HALF	RIGHT HALF
S_1	7	25
S_2	10	22
S_5	6	26
S_7	9	23
S_8	8	24

The probability that this might occur at random is approximately 2^{-35}.

Suppose that the circled and uncircled spots in the S-boxes are considered as boolean values, and suppose that the six bit positions of input to the S-boxes are labelled ABCDEF, most significant to least significant.

Then constructing Karnaugh maps for each of the S-boxes will give the following polynomials:

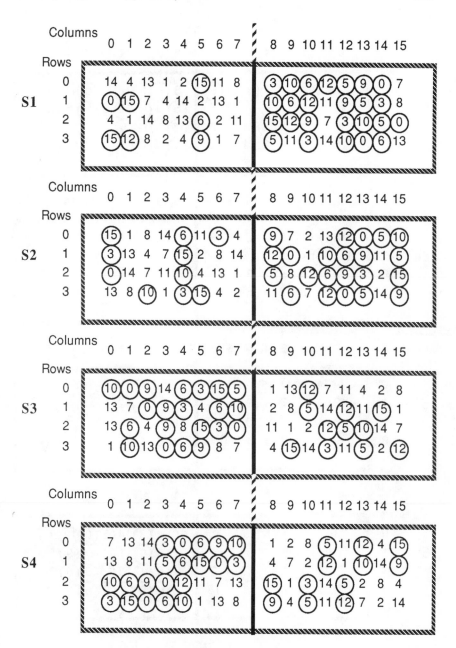

Figure 10.4
Shamir Symmetries in S-Boxes S_1 to S_4

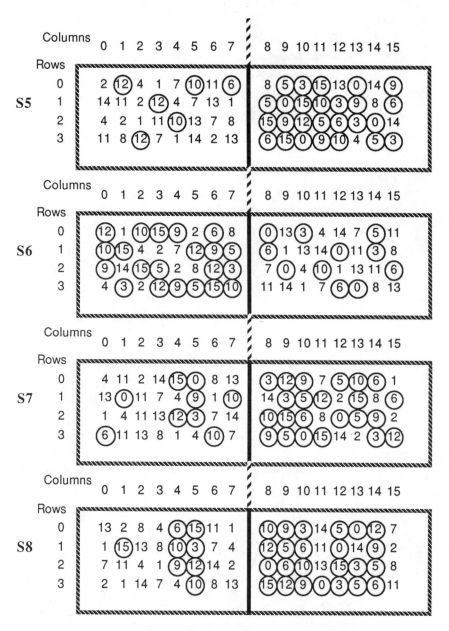

Figure 10.5
Shamir Symmetries in S-Boxes S₅ to S₈

S-box	Karnaugh polynomial	No. of errors
S_1	$B^c \oplus BDE \oplus B^cD^cE$	8 errors out of 64
S_2	$B^c \oplus BDE^c \oplus B^cD^cE^c$	10 errors out of 64
S_5	B^c	12 errors out of 64
S_7	$B^c \oplus BDEF^c \oplus B^cC^cD^cF^c$	10 errors out of 64
S_8	$B^c \oplus BDE \oplus B^cCD^c$	4 errors out of 64

We can compute some probabilities of these functions occurring at random.

The number of boolean functions with 6 variables is: 2^{64}.

The number of boolean functions with one linear and two 3rd degree terms is: $\approx 2^{17}$.

The number of functions described by a single polynomial with $\le k$ errors is:

$$\approx \quad C(64,k).$$

$\Rightarrow$ the probability that a random function is described by such a polynomial is:

$$\approx \quad C(64,k) \times 2^{17} / 2^{64}.$$

Thus, in the five cases above, we can compute:

$$
\begin{aligned}
S_1: &\qquad 2^{-15}\\
S_2: &\qquad 2^{-10}\\
S_5: &\qquad 2^{-20}\\
S_7: &\qquad 2^{-8}\\
S_8: &\qquad 2^{-28}
\end{aligned}
$$

And the probability that *all* of these functions could be random is the product, which is $2^{-(15+10+20+8+28)} = 2^{-81}$.

As yet, it does not seem to be possible to draw any conclusions about these remarkable observations. However, the observation of this degree of symmetry may be a very large clue to the eventual cryptanalysis of the DES.

— Appendix I —
Modular Arithmetic

In general, for any set S, a subset R of S × S is called a **relation** on S. A relation is an **equivalence relation** if the following three proprties are satisfied:

(1) REFLEXIVITY: $(s,s) \in R, \forall s \in S$.

(2) SYMMETRY: $(s,t) \in R \Rightarrow (t,s) \in R$.

(3) TRANSITIVITY: $(s,t) \in R, (t,u) \in R \Rightarrow (s,u) \in R$.

Often, an equivalence relation R will use the notation $s \sim t$ rather than $(s,t) \in R$.

Suppose that $\mathbb{Z}$ represents the set of integers. For any natural number $n > 0$, we can define a relation on $\mathbb{Z}$ in the following way:

$$a \sim b \iff (a - b) \text{ is divisible by } n$$
$$\iff (a - b) \text{ has remainder } 0 \text{ when divided by } n.$$

It can be easily checked that "~" is an equivalence relation, and the corresponding quotient set, called $\mathbb{Z}_n$, consists of the n equivalence classes corresponding to the n possible remainders r, $0 \le r < n$. Normally we will simply denote the elements of $\mathbb{Z}_n$ as 0, 1, 2, ..., n-1.

The operations of addition and multiplication on $\mathbb{Z}$ respect equivalence classes. In other words, if $a \sim b$, and $c \sim d$, then $(a+c) \sim (b+d)$; and similarly for multiplication. Consequently, the operations on $\mathbb{Z}$ induce operations, which we will also call additon and multiplication, and for which we will use the common notation "+" and "·".

The set $\mathbb{Z}_n$, together with the two binary operations + and ·, defines the system of **modular arithmetic** or **arithmetic modulo n**. To avoid confusion, equality in this system is called **congruence**, and is usually written in this fashion:

$$(x + y) \equiv z \pmod{n}$$

There is one important distinction in the types of algebraic systems defined by arithmetic modulo n depending on the value of n:

EXERCISE I.1: Prove the following statement. In arithmetic modulo n (Z_n)*, every non-zero element has a multiplicative inverse if and only if n is a prime number.*

(x has a multiplicative inverse means that there exists a y $\in$ Z_n such that x · y $\equiv$ 1 (mod n).)

EXERCISE I.2: Find the invertible elements of Z_{15}*.*

— Appendix II —
Groups

A mathematical object that we will want to use frequently is the **group**.

A *group* is an ordered pair $<G, \cdot >$, where G is a set, and $\cdot$ is a **binary operation** on G, that is a mapping $\cdot : G \times G \to G$. In addition, the mapping, which may also be written $\cdot(g,h)$ and $g \cdot h$, must have the properties:

1. (ASSOCIATIVITY) For all g,h, k in G,

$$(g \cdot h) \cdot k \ = \ g \cdot (h \cdot k)$$

2. (IDENTITY) There exists a special element i in G, such that, for all g in G,

$$i \cdot g \ = \ g \cdot i \ = \ g$$

3. (INVERSE) For each g in G, there exists a special element g^{-1} such that:

$$g \cdot g^{-1} \ = \ g^{-1} \cdot g \ = \ i.$$

There are many examples of groups:

(a) Additive group of the integers, $< \mathbb{Z}, + >$. The identity element is 0; the inverse of any element n in $\mathbb{Z}$ is -n. $(n+(-n) = (-n)+n = 0.)$

(Note: *Multiplication* on the integers does *not* form a group.)

EXERCISE II.1: Prove that $< \mathbb{Z}, \cdot >$ is not a group.

(b) The additive group of the integers modulo n, $< \mathbb{Z}_n, + >$. The identity element is 0; the additive inverse of a is that (unique) b such that $a + b \equiv 0 \pmod{n}$.

(c) For n = p any prime number, the multiplicative group of the integers modulo p, excluding the 0 element, $< \mathbb{Z}_p - \{0\}, \cdot >$. The identity element is 1; any non-zero element a is relatively prime to p; that is, GCD(a,p) = 1. By the Euclidean algorithm, there exist integers x and y such that $a \cdot x + p \cdot y = 1$. Thus $a \cdot x \equiv 1 \pmod p$, and x is the inverse of a in this group.

(If the modulo is not prime, there exist elements in $< \mathbb{Z}_p\text{-}\{0\}, \cdot >$ which do not have inverses. For example, let 6 be the modulo. Since $2 \cdot 3 = 6$, 2 and 3 cannot have inverses modulo 6. Suppose there were an element 2^{-1}. Then $2^{-1} \cdot 2 \equiv 1 \pmod 6$; therefore:

$$(2^{-1} \cdot 2) \cdot 3 = 1 \cdot 3 \equiv 3 \pmod 6.$$

On the other hand,

$$2^{-1} \cdot (2 \cdot 3) = 2^{-1} \cdot 0 \equiv 0 \pmod 6,$$

which is a contradiction.) See also exercise I.1.

4. Let S_X (sometimes written $S(X)$) be the set of all permutations of a set X. The composition of two permutations is a permutation; and $< S_X, \circ >$ forms a group. The identity element of the group is the identity mapping. The inverse of any permutation is simply that permutation which returns the set to its original order. This group is also called the **symmetric group**. It depends only on the cardinality of the underlying set X. Indeed, the symmetric group on a set of n elements is usually written S_n.

In fact, the set of all permutations of a set is a generic object in group theory, since every group can be shown to be contained in one of these permutation groups.

EXERCISE II.2: Suppose α represents the permutation $(a\ b\ c) \longmapsto (c\ a\ b)$, and β represents the permutation $(a\ b\ c) \longmapsto (b\ a\ c)$. Show that any permutation of the three objects a, b, and c can be represented as a composition of α's and β's.

Consequently construct a "multiplication table" for S_3.

Subgroups and Homomorphisms

Suppose H is a subset of the underlying set, G, of a group $< G, \cdot >$. Then the binary operation is defined on H as well. If:

(1) H is closed under the operation (in other words $h_1 \cdot h_2$ is always in H as well as being in G); and if

(2) $< H, \cdot >$ is a group;

then $< H, \cdot >$ is said to be a **subgroup** of $< G, \cdot >$. We sometimes write $< H, \cdot > \leq < G, \cdot >$, or, when the operation is understood, $H \leq G$.

A mapping between groups $< G, \cdot >$ and $< H, * >$ is said to be a **homomorphism** if it is *operation-preserving*; that is, if $\emptyset(g \cdot g') = \emptyset(g) * \emptyset(g')$ for all g, g' in G.

EXERCISE II.3: Prove that a homomorphism always maps the identity element of the domain group to the identity element of the image group.

If a homomorphism is *1-1*, it is said to be a **monomorphism**; if a homomorphism is *onto*, it is said to be an **epimorphism**. A homomorphism which is both a monomorphism and an epimorphism is said to be an **isomorphism**.

THEOREM II.1. Every group G can be imbedded in a permutation group S_X.

PROOF: Let $X=G$. Then there exists a monomorphism $\emptyset : G \to S_G$ given by $\emptyset(g) = f_g$, where f_g is the permutation of G given by left multiplying every element of G by g: $f_g(h) = g \cdot h$.

It must be demonstrated that (1) $\emptyset$ is a homomorphism, i.e. that $\emptyset(g_1 \cdot g_2) = \emptyset(g_1) \circ \emptyset(g_2)$; (2) that $\emptyset$ is 1-1; i.e. that $\emptyset(g) = $ Id implies that $g = i$. These proofs are left to the reader.

Q.E.D.

For a finite group (i.e., a group whose underlying set is finite), the cardinality of the underlying set is said to be the **order** of the group. The order of the group G is written $|G|$.

THEOREM II.2. For a finite set X, the order of S_X is $(|X|)!$

PROOF: Left to the reader.   Q.E.D.

A property found in certain groups is the property of **commutativity**. If, for all g, $h \in G$, $g \cdot h = h \cdot g$, then the group G is said to be **commutative** or **abelian**. Examples (a) - (c) are examples of abelian groups.

For any group that is written with a "multiplication-like" notation, repeated operations with the same element are written in a "power" notation. In other words, $a \cdot a \cdot a \cdot a = a^4$. It should be noted that the previous expression is written without parentheses; the associativity of the operation "$\cdot$" guarantees that the expression $a \cdot a \cdot \ldots \cdot a$ is unambiguous.

Cyclic Groups

If a group G has the property that, for all $g \in$ G, there exists some h for which $g = h^n$ for some $n \in \mathbb{Z}$, then the group is said to be **cyclic**, and h is said to be a **generator** of G. G may also be written as « h ».

Exercise II.4: Prove that $< \mathbb{Z}, + >$ and $< \mathbb{Z}_n, + >$ are cyclic groups with generator 1.

For any element g of any group G, the set $\{..., g^{-2}, g^{-1}, g^0 = i, g, g^2, ...\}$ forms a subgroup of G. If this subgroup « g » is finite, then the order of « g » is said to be the **order of the element g in the group G**.

THEOREM II.3. If H is a subgroup of G, then the relation R_H on G defined by: $(a,b) \in R_H \Leftrightarrow a = b \cdot h$ for some $h \in$ H; is an equivalence relation.

PROOF: it is necessary to show that R_H is *reflexive, symmetric,* and *transitive.*

REFLEXIVE: $i \in$ H; since $a = a \cdot i \Rightarrow (a,a) \in R_H$.

SYMMETRIC: If $(a,b) \in R_H$, then $a = b \cdot h$ for some $h \in$ H;
$$\Rightarrow a \cdot h^{-1} = b \cdot h \cdot h^{-1} = b$$
$$\Rightarrow b = a \cdot h^{-1} \Rightarrow (b,a) \in R_H.$$

TRANSITIVE: If $(a,b), (b,c) \in R_H$, then $a = b \cdot h$, $b = c \cdot h'$, for some $h, h' \in$ H;
$$\Rightarrow a = c \cdot h \cdot h' \Rightarrow (a,c) \in R_H.$$

∴ R_H is an equivalence relation.

Q.E.D.

Cosets and the Index of a Subgroup

The equivalence classes under the relation R_H are called the **left cosets of H (in G)**. One may similarly define (by the relation $(a,b) \Leftrightarrow a = hb$) the **right cosets of H**.

THEOREM II.4: If H is a finite subgroup of G, then every (left or right) coset of G modulo H has the same number of elements as H.

PROOF: Let $aH = \{ ah \mid h \in$ H $\}$, and $bH = \{ bh \mid h \in$ H $\}$ be two (left) cosets of G.

The group element $x = b \cdot a^{-1}$ defines a mapping, through left multiplication, from $aH \rightarrow bH$. Prove that this mapping is 1-1 and onto.

Q.E.D.

Two other theorems merit mention at this time:

If a subgroup H of a group G divides G into only finitely many left (or right) cosets, then the number of cosets is called the **index of H in G**. It is written index(G:H).

THEOREM II.5: The order of a finite group G is equal to the product of the order of any subgroup H and the index of H in G. Thus the order of H divides the order of G; and the order of any element a $\in$ G divides the order of G.

PROOF. Since |G| is finite, the number of cosets, being bounded by |G|, is finite. The elements of the left coset iH are exactly the elements of H; thus |aH| = |H|.

Since Theorem 4 showed that all cosets have the same number of elements; and since R_H, being an equivalence relation, partitions all of G into cosets, then the number of elements in all the cosets must be |G|; in addition, it also must be (number of cosets) · (number of elements in one coset) = index (G:H) · |H|.

Thus, |H| | |G|; further, since the order of the element a is the order of the cyclic subgroup «a», this also must divide |G|.

Q.E.D.

THEOREM II.6: (a) Every subgroup of a cyclic group is cyclic.

(b) In a finite cyclic group «a» of order n, the element a^i generates a subgroup of order n/GCD(i,n). (GCD = greatest common divisor)

(c) If d is a positive divisor of the order n of a finite cyclic group «a», then «a» contains one and only one subgroup of index d; and «a» contains one and only one subgroup of order d. Finally, «a» contains $\emptyset$(d) elements of order d. The function $\emptyset$ is the **Euler $\emptyset$-function**, or **totient**, defined as the number of integers c, with GCD(c,d)=1 and $1 \le c \le d$.

(d) A finite cyclic group «a» of order n has $\emptyset$(n) generators, that is elements a^r such that «a^r» = «a». These elements are the elements a^r such that GCD(r,n) = 1.

PROOF: (a) Suppose that the group in question is «a», and the subgroup H.

Let m be the smallest positive power of a .∋. $a^m \in$ H. Then, H = «a^m».

Certainly, all a^m, a^{2m}, a^{3m}, .. will be in H. Suppose there is some *other* element $a^k \in$ H, where k is not a multiple of m.

If m = 1, then H = «a», and the result is proved.

If m > 1 and m ∤ k, then ∃ r, 0 < r < m, .∋. k = bm + r.

$\Rightarrow$ $a^r = a^k \cdot ((a^m)^b)^{-1} \in$ H, which is a contradiction since r < m.

$\therefore$ every element of H is of the form a^{km}, $k \neq 0$;

$\Rightarrow$ H is cyclic.

(b) Let r be the smallest power of a which can be expressed as a power of a^i. Then $a^{p \cdot i} = a^r$, or $a^{p \cdot i} = a^{q \cdot n + r}$, thus $p \cdot i = q \cdot n + r$, $\Rightarrow$ GCD(i,n)=r.

$\therefore$ «a^i» = «a^r» $\Rightarrow$ index «a^i» = index «a^r» = GCD(i,n)

$\Rightarrow$ order «a^i» = n/GCD(i,n).

(c) If d | n, then $k \cdot d = n$. Then «a^d» is a subgroup of index d (and order k); and «a^k» is a subgroup of order d (and index k).

These subgroups must be unique. If not, let H be a subgroup of «a» of index d, and let a^j be the element of smallest positive power in H.

Then the subgroup must be a^j, a^{2j}, a^{3j}, ..., $a^{kj} = 1 \Rightarrow j = d$.

Divide n by d, suppose that n/d = k. Consider «a^k».

In «a^k», $a^{j \cdot k}$ is a generator if GCD$(j,d) = 1$

$\Rightarrow$ j is counted in $\phi(d)$.

$\therefore$ the number of generators of «a^k»

= number of elements of «a» of order d = $\phi(d)$.

(d) From (b), for every number k < n such that GCD$(k,n) = 1$, «a^k» = «a». Therefore, the element a^k is also a generator of «a», and there must be $\phi(n)$ of these.

Q.E.D.

EXERCISE II.5: Find all the subgroups of S_3, the symmetric group on three elements.

For readers interested in further study in the theory of groups, the references [BIRK 53] or [McCO 75] are suggested.

— Appendix III —
Elementary Number Theory

We have already seen an application of the mathematical objects known as groups to the study of cryptosystems. We will see also that the study of the properties of the integers and modular arithmetic systems will also come into play.

The study of these properties is known as elementary number theory.

Fast Exponentiation

It is often important to be able to raise an integer (or an element of $\mathbb{Z}_n$) to a power in an efficient fashion. Such an algorithm is known as **fast exponentiation**, and it is embodied in the following theorem.

THEOREM III.1: a^m (mod n) can be computed using at most $2 \cdot (\log_2 (m+1))$ multiplications.

PROOF: Write m in its binary form, $m = b_k b_{k-1} ... b_0$. Now, perform the following loop:

{ Initialize } j := k, and PRODUCT := a.

While $j \geq 0$,

    begin

        if $b_j = 0$,

        then square the product;

        else   **if** $b_j = 1$,

            then square and multiply by a.

        In either case, reduce mod n and decrement j by 1.

    end.

The while loop will be executed at most k ($= \log_2(m+1)$) times; on each pass, at most two multiplications will be performed.

Q.E.D.

A program to carry out fast exponentiation is found in Appendix VI.

Next we have a number-theoretic version of a theorem we have developed in a group-theoretic context.

THEOREM III.2: If GCD(a,n)=1, then there exists an integer b, $0<a<n$, such that $a\cdot b \equiv 1 \pmod n$.

PROOF: First of all, we will show that for GCD(a,n) = 1, $a\cdot i \equiv a\cdot j \pmod n$, $\forall\ 0 \le i < j < n$.

Assume the contrary. Then, for some pair i,j, we have

$$a\cdot i \equiv a\cdot j \qquad \pmod n$$
$$\Rightarrow \qquad a\cdot(i-j) \equiv 0 \qquad \pmod n$$
$$\Rightarrow \qquad n \mid a(i-j)$$
$$\Rightarrow \qquad n \text{ divides } i-j, \text{ since GCD(a,n)=1.}$$

But this is a contradiction, since i-j must be $< n$.

Now, because of the above, the products $a\cdot i$, i=1,2,...,n-1 take on (n–1) separate values in $\mathbb{Z}_n - \{0\}$; thus one of the products must have the value 1; hence the theorem is proven.

Q.E.D.

The Euler ø-function

The collection of all of the values $a \in \mathbb{Z}_n - \{0\}$ which are relatively prime to n is called the **reduced set of residues** modulo n. Also the **Euler ø-function**, or **totient**, is defined, for all n>1, as the set of all natural numbers between 1 and n that are relatively prime to n. Thus, for example, if p is a prime, $ø(p) = p-1$.

THEOREM III.3: If n is the product of two primes, $n = p \cdot q$, then $ø(n) = ø(p)\cdot ø(q) = (p-1)\cdot (q-1)$.

PROOF: The set of all the residues mod n is $\{0,1,2,...,pq-1\}$. The only residues which are *not* relatively prime to n are p, 2p, 3p,..., (q-1)·p; q, 2q, 3q, ..., (p-1)·q; and 0.

Adding these up gives $ø(n)$
$$= pq - (\ (p-1) + (q-1) + 1\ )$$
$$= pq - (p+q) - 1$$
$$= (p-1)\cdot (q-1)$$
$$= ø(p)\cdot ø(q).$$

Q.E.D.

Another important result is a general statement about the orders of elements in the modulo groups. This theorem is due to Fermat, who lived in the 17th century, and who produced many of the great theorems of number theory, including the famous Fermat's Last Theorem[1].

THEOREM III.4: (FERMAT) For every $a \neq 0 \in \mathbf{Z}_p^* = \, < \mathbf{Z}_p - \{0\}, \cdot >$, $a^{p-1} \equiv 1 \pmod{p}$.

Instead of proving III.4, we prove a generalization:

THEOREM III.5: (EULER) For every $a \neq 0 \in \mathbf{Z}_n^*$.э. GCD(a,n)=1, $a^{\emptyset(n)} \equiv 1 \pmod{n}$.

PROOF: Let $\{ a_1, a_2, ..., a_{\emptyset(n)} \}$ be the reduced set of residues mod n, such that $0 < a_i < n$, and i=1,...,$\emptyset(n)$.

Then the set $\{ a \cdot a_1 \bmod n, a \cdot a_2 \bmod n, ..., a \cdot a_{\emptyset(n)} \bmod n\}$ is a permutation of $\{ a_1, a_2, ..., a_{\emptyset(n)} \}$. Thus,

$$\prod_{i=1}^{\emptyset(n)} (aa_i) \equiv \prod_{i=1}^{\emptyset(n)} a_i \qquad (\bmod\ n)$$

$$\Rightarrow \quad a^{\emptyset(n)} (\prod_{i=1}^{\emptyset(n)} a_i) \equiv \prod_{i=1}^{\emptyset(n)} a_i \qquad (\bmod\ n)$$

$$\Rightarrow \quad a^{\emptyset(n)} \equiv 1 \qquad (\bmod\ n).$$

Q.E.D.

One of the first practical problems usually encountered in computing in mod systems is the difficulty of computing inverses. If we know the value of $\emptyset(n)$, then the fast exponentiation algorithm gives us a method of computing inverses. For, $a^{\emptyset(n)} = a \cdot a^{\emptyset(n)-1} \equiv 1 \pmod{p}$; thus, $a^{\emptyset(n)-1}$ is the inverse of a, and it can be computed using the fast exponentiation algorithm.

And, if the mod system is based on a prime p, we know from the above that the totient is (p-1).

---

[1] Fermat's Last Theorem: There exist no sets of integers x,y,z > 0, n>2, such that the equation $x^n + y^n = z^n$ has a solution. Fermat claimed to have found a solution in a marginal comment found in his last writing. Only in *1983* was a *partial* solution to his theorem discovered, by the German mathematician Gerhard Faltings.

The Euclidean Algorithm

Another method for computing inverses is based on the Euclidean algorithm. First, the Euclidean algorithm for computing GCDs:

EUCLIDEAN ALGORITHM FOR GCDS:

begin { Compute GCD(a,n) }

Suppose that $a \leq n$.

    { Set } $p := a$ and $q := n$.

    While $p \neq 0$,

        begin

                { set } $p' := q \bmod p$ and $q' := p$;

                { then set } $p := p'$ and $q := q'$

        end

    The GCD is q

end.

The algorithm terminates, since p is finite and non-increasing; furthermore, p decreases unless $p = q$, in which case, the algorithm will terminate in the next step.

A variation of the Euclidean algorithm can be used to compute inverses:

EUCLIDEAN ALGORITHM FOR INVERSES:

begin { To compute the inverse of a mod n: }

    { Set } $g_0 := n$; $g_1 := a$; $u_0 := 1$; $u_1 := 0$; $v_0 := 0$; $v_1 := 1$; $i := 1$.

    While $g_i \neq 0$,

        begin:

                $y := g_{i-1}$ **div** g_i;

                $g_{i+1} := g_{i-1} - y \cdot g_i$;

                $u_{i+1} := u_{i-1} - y \cdot u_i$;

                $v_{i+1} := v_{i-1} - y \cdot v_i$;

                $i := i + 1$;

        end;

    { Set } $x := v_{i-1}$.

    If $x \geq 0$

    then x is the inverse;

    else x+n is the inverse

end.

Linear Equations

The ability to compute inverses allows one to solve linear equations in mod systems. However, unlike with the arithmetic of the integers or the reals, the equation $ax \equiv b \pmod{n}$ has either no solutions or many solutions if $GCD(a,n) \neq 1$.

THEOREM III.6: Let $g = GCD(a,n)$. Then if $g \mid b$, the equation

$$ax \equiv b \pmod{n}$$

will have g solutions of the form

$$x \equiv (b/g)x_0 + t(n/g) \pmod{n}, \quad t = 0, ..., g\text{-}1$$

where x_0 is the solution of $(a/g)x \equiv 1 \pmod{n/g}$.

PROOF: 1. Each of the values $(b/g)x_0 + t(n/g)$, $t = 0, ..., g\text{-}1$ is a solution:

Since $a[\,(b/g)\,x_0 + t\,(n/g)\,] \quad = \quad b\,(a/g)\,x_0 + at\,(n/g)$

$$\equiv \quad b \qquad (\bmod\ n/g).$$

If $\qquad a[\,(b/g)\,x_0 + t\,(n/g)\,] \equiv \quad b \qquad (\bmod\ n/g)$,

then (n/g) divides $a[\,(b/g)\,x_0 + t\,(n/g)\,] - b$, which implies that n divides $a[\,(b/g)\,x_0 + t\,(n/g)\,] - b$, which implies

$$a[\,(b/g)\,x_0 + t\,(n/g)\,] \quad \equiv \quad b \qquad (\bmod\ n).$$

2. All of the values $(b/g)x_0 + t(n/g)$, $t = 0, ..., g\text{-}1$ are distinct: Suppose that

$$(b/g)x_0 + i(n/g) \quad \equiv \quad (b/g)x_0 + j(n/g) \qquad (\bmod\ n)$$

for $i \neq j$, $0 \leq i, j \leq g\text{-}1$.

$\Rightarrow \qquad i(n/g) \equiv j(n/g) \qquad\qquad (\bmod\ n)$

$\Rightarrow \qquad (i\text{-}j)(n/g)$ is divisible by n, say $(i\text{-}j)(n/g) = kn$

$\Rightarrow \qquad (i\text{-}j)/g = k \quad \Rightarrow \qquad (i\text{-}j)$ is a multiple of g.

But this is a contradiction since i,j and therefore $(i\text{-}j)$ are $< g$.

                                                                    Q.E.D.

THEOREM III.7: Let $d_1, d_2, ..., d_k$ be pairwise relatively prime, and let $n = d_1\, d_2\, ...\, d_k$. Then

$$f(x) \equiv 0 \qquad (\text{modulo } n)$$

$$\Leftrightarrow \qquad f(x) \equiv 0 \qquad (\text{modulo } d_i) \quad \forall\ i.$$

PROOF: $n \mid f(x) \Leftrightarrow n \mid d_i$, $\forall\ i$, since the d_i are pairwise relatively prime.

                                                                    Q.E.D.

THEOREM III.8: (CHINESE REMAINDER THEOREM) Let d_1, d_2, ..., d_k be pairwise relatively prime, and let $n = d_1 d_2 ... d_k$. Then the system of equations

$$x \equiv x_i \qquad (\text{modulo } d_i) \qquad i = 1, 2, ..., k$$

has a common solution x in the range [0, n-1].

PROOF: For $i = 1, 2, ..., k$, $\text{GCD}(d_i, n/d_i) = 1$.

$\therefore \exists y_i .\ni. (n/d_i)y_i \equiv 1 \pmod{d_i}$.

Also, $(n/d_i)y_i \equiv 0 \pmod{d_j}$ if $i \neq j$, since $d_j \mid (n/d_i)$.

Let

$$x \equiv \sum_{i=1}^{k} (n/d_i)y_i x_i \ (\text{modulo } n).$$

Then x is a solution of each of the k given equations, since

$$x \equiv (n/d_i)y_i x_i \equiv x_i \qquad (\text{modulo } d_i).$$

Q.E.D.

Quadratic Residues

Various computations in the text use the Chinese remainder theorem. Another set of computations we will use are from the theory of **quadratic residues**. Consider the arithmetic system $\mathbb{Z}_n{}^*$. Let a be an invertible element in $\mathbb{Z}_n{}^*$. (In other words, $\text{GCD}(a,n)=1$.) Then a is said to be a **quadratic residue modulo n** $\Leftrightarrow \exists$ x such that:

$$x^2 \equiv a \qquad (\text{modulo } n).$$

If a is not a quadratic residue modulo n, it is said to be a **quadratic nonresidue modulo n**. We will call the set of quadratic residues modulo n, QR(n), and QNR(n) the set of quadratic nonresidues.

THEOREM III.9: For p, a prime number > 2, and $0 < a < p$, the equation

$$x^2 \equiv a \qquad (\text{modulo } p).$$

has at least *two* solutions if $a \in$ QR(p) and zero otherwise.

PROOF: Obviously if $a \in$ QNR(p) there are no solutions.

Suppose x_0 is one solution if $a \in$ QR(p). Then, $p-x_0$ is also a solution:

$$\begin{aligned}
(p - x_0)^2 &\equiv p^2 - 2px_0 + x_0^2 && (\text{modulo } p) \\
&\equiv x_0^2 \equiv a && (\text{modulo } p).
\end{aligned}$$

The solutions are distinct since if $x_0 \equiv p - x_0 \pmod{p}$, we would have to have $2x_0 \equiv 0 \pmod{p}$ which is not possible since p is odd.

Q.E.D.

THEOREM III.10: For any prime $p > 2$, $|QR(p)| = |QNR(p)| = (p-1)/2$.

PROOF: The $(p-1)/2$ residues $1^2, 2^2, ..., ((p-1)/2)^2$ are quadratic residues. There can be no additional residues, since for every $a \in QR(p)$, at least one of its roots x_0 or $p-x_0$ lies in the interval $[1, (p-1)/2]$.

Q.E.D.

THEOREM III.11: For any prime $p > 2$, and $0 < a < p$:

$$a^{(p-1)/2} \equiv 1 \pmod{p} \qquad \text{if } a \in QR(p)$$
$$a^{(p-1)/2} \equiv p-1 \pmod{p} \qquad \text{if } a \in QNR(p).$$

PROOF: By Fermat's Theorem (III.4),

$$a^{(p-1)} - 1 \equiv 0 \pmod{p}.$$

Since p is odd, we can factor $a^{(p-1)} - 1$, giving

$$(a^{(p-1)/2} + 1)(a^{(p-1)/2} - 1) \equiv 0 \pmod{p}.$$

Thus either p divides $(a^{(p-1)/2} + 1)$ or $(a^{(p-1)/2} - 1)$. (It cannot divide their difference, since the difference is 2.)

Thus,

$$a^{(p-1)/2} \equiv -1 \pmod{p}.$$

If $a \in QR(p)$, then there exists an x such that $a = x^2 \pmod{p}$,

$$\Rightarrow \quad a^{(p-1)/2} \equiv (x^2)^{(p-1)/2} \equiv x^{p-1} \equiv 1 \pmod{p}.$$

So, the $(p-1)/2$ quadratic residues mod p are solutions of

$$a^{(p-1)/2} \equiv 1 \pmod{p}.$$

There cannot be other solutions since the equation, being of degree $(p-1)/2$, can have no more than $(p-1)/2$ solutions. Thus, the $(p-1)/2$ quadratic nonresidues must be solutions of

$$a^{(p-1)/2} \equiv -1 \equiv p-1 \pmod{p}.$$

Q.E.D.

EXERCISE III.1: *Write a program to compute quadratic residue sets for small numbers (say, $n < 10000$).*

EXERCISE III.2: Using the program written in the previous exercise, try to find correlations between the size of the set $QR(n)$ and the factorization of n. (For example, show that $QR(2p) = p$ where p is a prime.)

Readers interested in further reading in number theory are referred to [LEVE 56].

— Appendix IV —
Computational Complexity and
the Theory of NP-Completeness

The search for public-key cryptosystems has led to a careful study and application of mathematical problems that are, in some fashion, inherently difficult to solve. Chapters 4 and 5 have discussed two such examples, namely the knapsack problem and the problem of factoring large integers.

Before the widespread interest in *computational* mathematics brought about by the development of the computer, not a great deal of thought was given to the *degree of difficulty* of solving a given mathematical problem.

Within the past twenty years, however, computer scientists and mathematicians have begun to realize what defines a problem as easy, difficult, essentially impossible, or formally impossible.

From a computer science point of view, one may think of a problem as being essentially impossible to solve if a computer program written to solve the problem cannot complete its execution in any reasonable or acceptable amount of time.

For example, suppose that the "problem" to solve is that of printing out all of the first N natural numbers. Suppose also that N may be described mathematically in different ways: as $N = n^5$, as $N = 2^n$, and as $N = (n!)$.

Depending on the value of n, a judgement can be made as to whether or not attempting a solution is reasonable.

(Note: We may assume that the space requirements involved on a computer are not a constraint. Were we to use a linked list representation for very large integers, we could certainly handle an integer of $\log_{10} N$ digits with $2 \cdot (\log_{10} N)$ words. Furthermore, the execution of instructions other than the PRINT instruction would certainly take far less machine time than the time required for the output --- our algorithm would simply increment the last digit by 1; if the digit were 9, it would increment the next to last, and so on.)

	n^5	2^n	$n!$
$n = 10$	100 secs.	10.28 secs.	36,000 secs. $\cong$ 10 hours
$n = 100$	10^8 secs. $\cong$ 3 years	$\cong 10^{28}$ secs. $\cong 10^{20}$ years	$\cong 10^{190}$ secs. $\cong 10^{180}$ centuries
$n = 1000$	10^{13} secs. $\cong$ 300,000 years	$\cong 10^{290}$ years	$\cong 10^{2980}$ centuries

Table IV.1
Comparison of Execution Times

We will make one last assumption: that printing each natural number in the sequence requires .01 second on our fastest printer --- a reasonable assumption for a laser printer.

Then the execution times, for various values of n and N, will be as in table IV.1.

We would certainly agree that for n as small as 10, it would be feasible to run the program for each of the functions n^5, 2^n, and (n!). However, everyone would agree also that for n = 100, only the function n^5 is effectively computable; and for n = 1000, possibly none of the three are computable --- although improvements in technology might render the n^5 computation feasible.

The necessity for a consistent type of measurement and analysis of the difficulty of computing a solution to a given problem, as indicated by the above, has led to the development of a branch of mathematics known as **complexity theory**, and more specifically, to a theory known as **the theory of NP-completeness**.

A very detailed introduction to this subject is found in [GARE 76]. This Appendix will treat the subject very concisely.

How to Measure the Complexity of a Problem

The solution to a computational problem can always be described by an algorithm --- in other words, by a procedure that is guaranteed to terminate in a finite number of steps.

To study how complex an algorithm is, we need a consistent notation in order to be able to compare different algorithms which solve the same problem. Then, with this standard method of measurement, the complexity of a problem can be defined as the minimum complexity of any algorithm which solves the problem.

Of course, in addition, the solution of a *problem* implies that the algorithm is capable of solving any of the *instances* (i.e. input data sets --- possibly infinite in number) of the problem.

Therefore, first we need a method of representing these data sets. An **encoding scheme** is a mapping from the set of all input data sets of a given problem, to a finite string over some fixed alphabet.

For example, if the problem in question is the previous problem of printing out a set of natural numbers, the only input data required is the *last* number to be printed in the series. Consequently, the encoding scheme might map one data set, i.e. one integer, to the character string consisting of the digits of that integer (over the fixed alphabet $\Sigma = \{0,1,...,9\}$); or, more probably, to the bit-string representing the binary form of that integer (over the alphabet $\Sigma = \{0,1\}$).

If the problem were somewhat more complex, say the problem of finding a Hamiltonian circuit[1] in a graph, an encoding scheme would have to describe the input graph in some way. Two common ways are (1) to list the labels for vertices, and then the edges as unordered pairs of these vertices; and (2) to list the entries of a boolean square matrix, where the order of the matrix corresponds to the number of vertices; a '1' entry at the (i,j) position in the matrix corresponds to the existence of an edge between the ith and the jth vertex.

For example, given the graph shown in figure IV.1, two encoding schemes might be:

---

[1] A Hamiltonian circuit in a graph is a cycle that visits every vertex in a graph exactly once (and terminates in the vertex at which it originated).

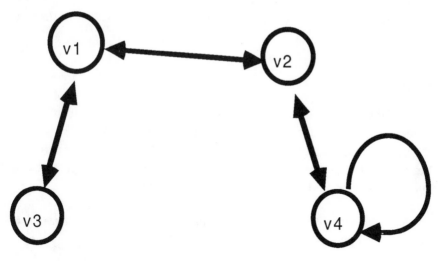

Figure IV.1
A Graph with Four Vertices

v(1)v(2)v(3)v(4)(v(1),v(2))(v(1),v(3))(v(2),v(4))(v(4),v(4))

or

0110,1001,1000,0101.

If assumptions are made about the nature of the encoding scheme, in particular that the string does not contain irrelevant or redundant information, then the function determined by the length of the encoding scheme string gives one variable in measuring the complexity of the algorithm.

The **time complexity function** of an algorithm is the amount of time that is necessary to execute the algorithm, as a function of the length of the encoding scheme string.

It is clear that there are a number of indeterminate quantities in the statement above. Since there could be many encoding schemes for an algorithm, and since the algorithm could be executed using an infinite variety of possible computer programs, on a wide variety of possible machines, there clearly cannot be a unique value of the time complexity function for a given problem instance.

However, one of the nice aspects of this theory is that under reasonable assumptions, all of the potential encoding schemes, programs, and computer configurations will give essentially equivalent values of the time complexity function.

Big-Oh

For any two functions, f, g : $\mathbb{N} \to \mathbb{R}$, f is said to be **big-oh of g(n)**, written O(g(n)), if $\exists$ a constant $c \geq 0$.э. $f(n) \leq c \mid g(n) \mid$, $\forall$ n $\in$ $\mathbb{N}$.

Usually, the complexity of an algorithm will be given by computing its big-oh function, where n represents the length of the string given by an encoding scheme, and f(n) is the time to execute the algorithm.

Exercise IV.1: Show that matrix multiplication is a problem whose complexity is $O(n^3)$.

Exercise IV.2: Show that the backtracking solution to a general maze problem is $O(n!)$.

Polynomial Time Complexity and the Category P

In general, it is considered that if an algorithm can be found that will solve a problem with a time complexity function which is big-oh of some *polynomial* function in n, then the problem is **tractable**, or it admits of a computational solution.

Exercise IV.1 above shows that matrix multiplication is essentially a tractable problem. Exercise IV.2 tells us only, however, that the backtracking algorithm *solution* to a general maze problem has complexity greater than polynomial complexity. Of course, we might be able to find some other algorithm which would solve the maze problem and yet have polynomial complexity.

Now we can make an approximate definition of the complexity of a *problem*. A problem π is said to be in the category P (a mnemonic for "problems solvable in polynomial time") if there exists an algorithm to solve π, for some encoding scheme for π, which has a polynomial time complexity function in the length of the encoding scheme[2].

---

[2] Technically speaking, the program in question and its time of execution is usually considered to be a deterministic one-tape Turing machine, and its "execution time" the number of steps before halting.

The Other Extreme: Undecidable Problems and Category U

We have embarked upon a classification scheme for the complexity of problems. After defining P, we move to the other extreme and define a category U, the category of all problems *for which it can be proven that there does not exist an algorithm giving a solution.*

It has proven to be a rather remarkable fact of twentieth-century mathematics that one can show that certain problems, in effect, do not have algorithms to solve all possible input data.

The first such result is due to Alan Turing, who proved that it is not possible to describe an algorithm which, given an arbitrary program and an arbitrary input to that program, will decide whether or not the program will halt when the program is run on that input.

About twenty years later, in the 1950's the Boone-Novikov theorem of group theory was proved, showing that it is not possible to find an algorithm which will determine whether or not a group, defined with a finite number of generators and relations[3], is actually the trivial group { i } [LYND 83].

A third in this category of undecidable problems is the so-called "Hilbert's tenth problem" on the solvability of polynomial equations over the integers.

Consequently, we will call this latter category of problems the category U (for undecidable).

Non-polynomial Problems (NON-POLY)

Since we have concluded that the category of problems that have tractable (computable) solutions is the category P, it seems reasonable to define a category NON-POLY --- for the category of all problems which cannot be solved by polynomial time algorithms.

It is a trivial remark that NON-POLY $\neq \varnothing$, the empty set, since clearly U $\subseteq$ NON-POLY. (If an algorithm can't be found, then certainly a polynomial time algorithm cannot be found.)

---

[3] A **relation**, in this context, is an equation of the form $g_i^{ai} g_j^{aj} \ldots g_k^{ak} = i$.

Consequently, NON-POLY problems are the intractable ones. However, a more precise definition was given by Stephen Cook [COOK 71].

Cook defined a category called NP, the class of problems that can be solved in **polynomial time** on a **non-deterministic computer**, or a computer that can execute a non-deterministic algorithm.

A non-deterministic algorithm divides a problem into a "solution" part and a "verification" part. For example, consider the maze problem again. A non-deterministic algorithm, in order to execute in polynomial time, requires that the **verification** procedure execute in polynomial time (think also of having all of the solution stages operating in parallel). Clearly it is possible to verify that a given path is a successful path through a maze in polynomial time. Thus maze-running falls into this NP category.

Factoring also falls into the NP category, since if someone alleges that x and y are factors of some integer n, a verification proof (i.e. multiplying x and y) can be carried out in polynomial time.

So, we now have the hierarchy of problems:

$$P \rightarrow NP \rightarrow NON\text{-}POLY \rightarrow U$$

Note that NON-POLY consists of harder problems than NP, since NP problems, as defined, *may* admit polynomial time algorithms.

The category that is truly interesting is NP - P, since problems in this category would be truly intractable. Unfortunately, it is not known even whether or not NP - P = $\varnothing$!!

NP-Completeness

Cook also defined a most interesting category of problems called NP–complete problems.

Problems are said to be **polynomially time equivalent** if there is a polynomial time complexity function which maps every instance of one problem to an instance of the other, and vice versa.

Finally, a problem π is said to be **NP-complete**, if $\pi \in$ NP, and every other problem π' to which π is polynomially time equivalent, is also in NP.

So NP-complete problems are the category on which we wish to focus, in particular for the following reasons:

1. Techniques are available to show that many problems are NP–complete.

2. If any single NP-complete problem is ever shown to have a polynomial time solution, then polynomial time solutions can be constructed for all other problems in the category!!!

The reference cited at the beginning of this Appendix [GARE 76] lists more than 300 problems which have been proven to be NP-complete. A few of the familiar problems in this category are:

1. The traveling salesman problem: Given a list of cities to visit, and distances between each, find a path visiting all the cities which minimizes the total mileage travelled.

2. The Hamiltonian circuit problem: Find a cycle in a graph that visits all of the nodes once and once only (except for the origin).

3. Integer programming: Given a function

$$f = c_1 x_1 + c_2 x_2 + \ldots + c_n x_n$$

and a set of constraints

$$a_{11} x_1 + a_{12} x_2 + \ldots + a_{1n} x_n \leq b_1$$
$$a_{21} x_1 + a_{22} x_2 + \ldots + a_{2n} x_n \leq b_2$$

$$\cdot$$
$$\cdot$$

$$a_{m1} x_1 + a_{m2} x_2 + \ldots + a_{mn} x_n \leq b_m$$

(a_{ij}'s, b_j's integers). Find *integer* values for the x_i's which satisfy the constraints and maximize the function f.

4. Knapsack problem (See Chapter 4.)

5. Quadratic Residues: Given positive integers a,b,c. Is there a positive integer $x < c$ such that $x^2 \equiv a \pmod{b}$?

NP-Complete Problems as Bases for Cryptosystems

NP-complete problems are a natural source for potential cryptosystems. First of all, they have inherently the property that a general case is unlikely to admit a general algorithmic solution.

As an example, the knapsack problem was used to define the first public-key cryptosystem.

A potentially fruitful line of research is to analyze the known NP-complete problems to see if any do admit of further PKCs.

— Appendix V —
Galois Fields

A **field** «F, +, ·» is an algebraic object of much interest in the study of cryptosystems.

In essence, a field is a set with *two* binary operations defined --- in the notation above, "+" and "·".

With the first operation, denoted by "+", $< F,+ >$ is an abelian group.

If the identity element (which we will denote by 0 since the symbol "+" is being used for the group operation) under $< F,+ >$ is removed from the set, giving F* = F - {0}, the structure $< F*,· >$ is also an abelian group.

In addition, the operations must *distribute* one over the other in the following way:

$$x · (y + z) \ \ = \ \ (x · y) + (x · z).$$

EXAMPLES OF FIELDS:

1. F = {0,1}, with binary operations:

+	0	1			0	1
0	0	1		0	0	0
1	1	0		1	0	1

2. F = $\mathbb{Q}$, the set of rational numbers, with ordinary addition and multiplication, and identities 0 and 1 respectively.

3. F = $\mathbb{R}$, the set of real numbers, with ordinary addition and multiplication, and identities 0 and 1 respectively.

4. F = $\mathbb{C}$, the set of complex numbers, defined (in one way) as an extension of the real numbers by adding a new element i, with the property that $i^2 = -1$, and a general element of $\mathbb{C}$ written as a + bi, where a,b $\in \mathbb{R}$.

5. F = $\mathbb{Z}_p$, where p is a prime number, and addition and multiplication are taken modulo p.

Why Study Fields?

Fields are of interest because the structural requirements of two operations, related by distributivity, reveal a great deal about the structure of fields. Furthermore, certain problems remain very difficult to solve inside of even small fields, leading to methods of developing functions difficult to invert, and hence leading to public key cryptosystems.

Our analysis here will actually demonstrate the key structure theorem for finite fields. In orer to arrive at that result, first we need to begin with a more general algebraic structure on a set with two operations, namely the **ring**.

Rings

DEFINITION; A **ring** « R, +, · » is a set with two binary operations .Э.

1. < R, + > is an abelian group.
2. The operation · is associative:

$$a \cdot (b \cdot c) = (a \cdot b) \cdot c \qquad \forall\ a,b,c \in R.$$

3. The operation · has the distributive property with respect to + :

$$a \cdot (b + c) = a \cdot b + a \cdot c$$
and $$(b + c) \cdot a = b \cdot a + c \cdot a \qquad \forall\ a,b,c \in R.$$

EXAMPLE 1: The ring of integers « $\mathbb{Z}$, + , · ».
EXAMPLE 2: Any field, « F, +, · », is a ring.

There is a hierarchy of algebraic structures between the ring structure and the field structure. We will have occasion to refer to these.

DEFINITION: A ring R is a **ring with identity** if there exists an element $1 \in R$.Э. $1 \cdot a = a \cdot 1 = a, \forall\ a \in R$.

DEFINITION: A ring R is a **commutative ring** if $a \cdot b = b \cdot a$, $\forall\ a, b \in$ R.

DEFINITION: A commutative ring, with identity, R is an **integral domain** if $a, b \in R$, $a \cdot b = 0 \Rightarrow$ either $a = 0$ or $b = 0$.

DEFINITION: In a ring with identity R, an element r is called a **unit** if $\exists\ r' \in R$.Э. $r \cdot r' = r' \cdot r = 1$. The set of all units in a ring form a group, called the **group of units**.

DEFINITION: A ring with identity I is a **division ring** if, $\forall\ a \neq 0 \in I$, $\exists\ b \in I$.Э.

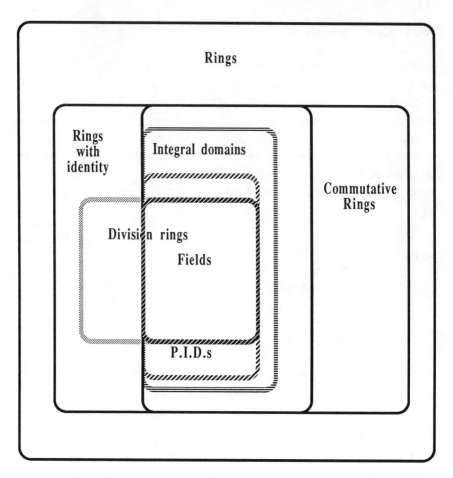

Figure V.1

Hierarchy of Algebraic Structures with Two Binary Operators

$$a \cdot b = b \cdot a = 1.$$

In other words, the group of units consists of all elements of R except 0. The set of non-zero elements of a ring R is often denoted R*.

In particular, the definition of a division ring implies that the multiplicative structure contained in the ring or integral domain structure is a group; if this group were to be an abelian group, then the structure is necessarily a field.

Consequently, the only division rings that are not fields are those wherein the multiplicative group is non-abelian.

THEOREM V.1: Every *finite* integral domain is a field.

PROOF: Let the non-zero elements of I be a_1, a_2, ..., a_n. Then consider any element $a \neq 0 \in I$, and consider the products:

$$a \cdot a_1, a \cdot a_2, ..., a \cdot a_n.$$

These n products are distinct, for, if not, there exists some a_i and a_j such that

$$a \cdot a_i = a \cdot a_j$$
$$\Rightarrow \quad a \cdot (a_i - a_j) = 0$$
$$\Rightarrow \quad \text{a has a zero divisor}$$
$$\Rightarrow \quad \text{I is not an integral domain.}$$

Thus, of the n distinct products, one of these (say $a \cdot a_k$) must be the value $1 \in I$. Thus a_k is the inverse of a. Similarly every other non-zero element of I has an inverse, and so the multiplicative operation forms a group. Since this group must be commutative, I is a field.

Q.E.D.

Subrings

A subset R' of a ring R is a **subring** if
1. $< R',+ >$ is a subgroup of $< R,+ >$;
2. «R',+,·» is a ring.

A subring $I \subseteq R$ is an **ideal** if $\forall i \in I, r \in R$, both $i \cdot r$, and $r \cdot i \in$ R. To be more precise, when both of the products are in I (for all i and r), the ideal is called a two-sided ideal; if only the first (second) product is in I, the ideal is a left (right) ideal. Since we will mostly deal with commutative rings, we will in this context ignore the distinction in ideal types.

EXAMPLES:

1. $R = \mathbb{Z}$, $I = \{ \text{ even numbers } \} = \{ 2z \mid z \in \mathbb{Z} \}$. I is an ideal because, for any $z \in \mathbb{Z}, y \in I$,

$$\Rightarrow z \cdot y = 2 \cdot z \cdot x = 2 \cdot x \cdot z = y \cdot z, \quad \text{which is even}$$
$$\Rightarrow z \cdot y = y \cdot z \in I.$$

2. $R = \mathbb{Q}$ (rational numbers). $R' = \mathbb{Z}$ is a subring but *not* an ideal, since $1/2 \in \mathbb{Q}, 3 \in \mathbb{Z}$, but $3 \cdot 1/2 = 3/2 \notin \mathbb{Z}$.

3. $R = \mathbb{Z}_{15}$. R is a ring but not an integral domain since $3 \cdot 5 = 0 \cdot I = \{0, 3, 6, 9, 12\}$ is an ideal since I consists of multiples of 3; multiplying one of these by any other $\mathbb{Z}_{15}$ element still results in a multiple of 3.

REMARK: For any ring R, $r \in R$, (r) is an ideal where:

$$(r) = \{ r' \cdot r + n \cdot r \mid r' \in R, n \in \mathbb{Z} \}.$$

(The proof is left to the reader.) Any ideal I = (r) is called a **principal ideal generated by r**. The partition of a ring R into disjoint sets by an ideal I is the division of R into **residue classes**.

PROPOSITION V.2: Let R be a ring, $I \subseteq R$ an ideal in R. Then the set of residue classes of R, denoted R/I, forms a ring with operations

$$(a + I) + (b + I) = a + b + I,$$
$$(a + I) \cdot (b + I) = a \cdot b + I.$$

PROOF: Left to the reader. Use the results of Appendix II to show that <R/I,+> is an abelian group.

THEOREM V.3:   Let p be a prime number, and $\mathbb{Z}$ be the ring of integers. Then the set of residue classes of $\mathbb{Z}$ with respect to the principal ideal (p) forms a field $\mathbb{Z}/(p)$ (to be denoted $\mathbb{Z}_p$).

PROOF: By theorem V.1 and proposition V.2, since $\mathbb{Z}/(p)$ is finite, we need only show that $\mathbb{Z}/(p)$ is an integral domain. Therefore, suppose that

$$(a + (p)) \cdot (b + (p)) = 0 + (p).$$

This means that $\exists\, k_1, k_2, k_3 \in \mathbb{Z}$.э.

$$(a + k_1 p) \cdot (b + k_2 p) = 0 + k_3 p$$
$$\Rightarrow \quad ab = (k_3 - k_1 b - k_2 a)\, p$$
$$\Rightarrow \quad \text{either a or b divides p, since p is a prime.}$$

Suppose a divides p; then $a = k_4 p$, say, and

$$\Rightarrow \quad a + (p) = 0 + (p).$$

This contradiction implies that $\mathbb{Z}/(p)$ is an integral domain.

Q.E.D.

DEFINITION: Let R be a ring, and n the smallest positive integer .э. nr = 0, $\forall\, r \in R$. Then n is called the **characteristic** of R, written char(R). If no such n exists, we say that the ring R has **characteristic zero**.

THEOREM V.4:   A non-zero ring R with identity, having positive characteristic, and no zero divisors, must have prime characteristic.

PROOF: Since R is non-zero, the characteristic of R must be at least 2. Suppose that $n = \text{char}(R)$, and that n is composite and factors into proper factors as $n = km$. Then

$$0 \ = \ n \cdot 1 \ = \ (km) \cdot 1 \ = \ (k \cdot 1) \cdot (m \cdot 1)$$
$\Rightarrow$ either $(k \cdot 1) = 0$ or $(m \cdot 1) = 0$, since there are no zero divisors;
$\Rightarrow$ either $(k \cdot 1 \cdot r) = 0, \ \forall \ r \in R$, or $(m \cdot 1 \cdot r) = 0, \ \forall \ r \in R$.

In either case, we would have a value for the characteristic strictly smaller than n, a contradiction. Thus n must be a prime number.

Q.E.D.

COROLLARY V.5: A finite field has prime characteristic.

PROOF: Let F be a finite field, with multiplicative identity 1. Then there are only finitely many distinct elements $\Rightarrow \ \exists \ k > 1 \ni k \cdot 1 = 0$. Then, for any other element $f \in F$, $k \cdot f = k \cdot 1 \cdot f = 0$. Thus the characteristic of F is positive (at most k). Thus, by theorem V.4, the characteristic must be a prime.

Q.E.D.

DEFINITION: An ideal I of a ring R is a **prime ideal** if $\forall \ a,b \in R$, $a \cdot b \in I \Rightarrow$ either $a \in I$ or $b \in I$.

An ideal I of R is a **maximal ideal** if $J \supseteq I \Rightarrow J = I$, or $J = R$.

DEFINITION: A ring R is a **principal ideal domain** (PID) if:
1. R is an integral domain; and
2. every ideal of R is a principal ideal.

THEOREM V.6: Let R be a commutative ring with identity. Then:
1. An ideal M of R is a maximal ideal $\Leftrightarrow$ R/M is a field.
2. An ideal P of R is a prime ideal $\Leftrightarrow$ R/P is an integral domain.
3. Every maximal ideal of R is a prime ideal.
4. If R is a PID, then R/(p) is a field $\Leftrightarrow$ p is a prime element of R.

PROOF: Part 1:

[$\Rightarrow$] If $a \notin M \Rightarrow I = \{ ar + m \mid r \in R, m \in M \}$ is an ideal of R, and $I \supset M \Rightarrow I = R$.

$\Rightarrow ar + m = 1$, for some $r \in R, m \in M$.

$\therefore$ if $a + m \ (\neq 0 + m) \in R/M$, then $(a + M) \cdot (r + M) \ = \ a \cdot r + M \ = \ (1 - m) + M \ = \ 1 + M.$

$\Rightarrow$ R/M is a field.

[$\Leftarrow$] Let $I \supseteq M$, $I \neq M$ be an ideal of R. Then, for $a \in I - M$, $a + M$ has an inverse since R/M is a field. Thus,

$$(a + M)(r + M) \ = \ 1 + M$$

$\Rightarrow \ ar + m \ = \ 1$ for some $m \in M$

$\Rightarrow \ 1 \in I$ $\Rightarrow \ I = R$ $\Rightarrow$ M is maximal.

PART 2:

[$\Rightarrow$]   Let p be a prime ideal.

$\Rightarrow$ R/P is a commutative ring with identity, $\quad 1 + P \neq 0 + P$. Suppose R/P is not an integral domain, and $(a+P)(b+P) = 0+P$.

Then, $ab \in P$,

$\Rightarrow$ either $a \in P$ or $b \in P$

$\Rightarrow$ R/P has no zero divisors

$\therefore$ R/P is an integral domain.

[$\Leftarrow$]   Let R/P be an integral domain. Let $a \cdot b \in P$. Then $(a+P)(b+P) = 0+P$. Since R/P is an integral domain, either $(a+P)$ or $(b+P) = 0+P$. Thus either a or $b \in P$,

$\Rightarrow$ P is a prime ideal.

PART 3: Follows from parts 1 and 2.

Q.E.D.

Polynomial Rings

One of the more interesting ring structures is that obtained by beginning with a ring R (or field F), and constructing the ring of all polynomials over R (or F). This structure is defined algebraically exactly as ordinary real polynomials in a single variable are defined: namely, to add polynomials, coefficients of like degree terms are added, and to multiply polynomials, the products of terms of degree m and n lead to terms of degree m+n. Formally,

DEFINITION: For any ring R, the **polynomial ring** «R[x],+,·» is defined as:

As a set,

$$R[x] \ = \ \{ \ a(x) = a_0 + a_1 x + a_2 x^2 + ... + a_n x^n \ | \ a_i \in R, i = 0, 1, ..., n \ \}.$$

For $a(x) = a_0 + a_1 x + a_2 x^2 + ... + a_n x^n$, $b(x) = b_0 + b_1 x + b_2 x^2 + ... + b_r x^r \in R[x]$, addition is defined as:

$$c(x) = a(x) + b(x) = \ c_0 + c_1 x + c_2 x^2 + ... + c_s x^s,$$

where $s = \max(n,r)$, $t = \min(n,r)$, $c_i = a_i + b_i$, $i = 0, 1, ..., t$; $c_j = a_j$ or b_j, for $j = t+1,...,s$, depending on whether $n > r$ or $r > n$.

To define multiplication, we will first define the operation for monomials:

$$a_j x^j \cdot b_k x^k \;=\; a_j b_k \, x^{j+k},$$

and then extend the definition by the distributive property. Thus,

$$a(x) \cdot b(x) \;=\; a_0 b_0 + (a_0 b_1 + a_1 b_0)\, x + (a_0 b_2 + a_1 b_1 + a_2 b_0)\, x^2 + \dots$$

An alternative notation sometimes used for polynomials is a coordinate form notation, for example,

$$a(x) = (a_0, a_1, a_2, \dots, a_n).$$

If the underlying ring of R[x] (also called the **ground ring**) has an identity, 1, then so does the ring R[x], namely the element $1 + 0 \cdot x + 0 \cdot x^2 + \dots$

The highest (non-zero) coefficient of a polynomial a(x), a_n, is called the **leading coefficient** of a(x). The term a_0 is referred to as the **constant term**. The value n, of the exponent of the highest non-zero term, is called the **degree** of a(x). Finally, if the leading coefficient is a unit in the ring R, then the polynomial is said to be **monic**.

THEOREM V.7: Let R be a ring. Then:

1. R[x] is commutative $\Leftrightarrow$ R is commutative;
2. R[x] is a ring with identity $\Leftrightarrow$ R is a ring with identity;
3. R[x] is an integral domain $\Leftrightarrow$ R is an integral domain.

PROOF: Left to the reader. Note that Part 2 is proved above; also that any ring R is isomorphic to a subring of its polynomial ring R[x], namely that subring consisting of all polynomials with only constant terms.

THEOREM V.8: Let F be a field, and $g(x) \neq 0 \in$ F[x]. For any $f(x) \in$ F[x], $\exists$ polynomials q(x), and $r(x) \in$ F[x] .$\ni$.

$$f = q \cdot g + r \qquad \text{where } \deg(r) < \deg(g).$$

PROOF: The ordinary long division algorithm of arithmetic can be used to demonstrate this result. For example, the first term of the quotient q(x) is found by comparing the leading terms of f(x) and g(x), say $f_n \cdot x^n$ and $g_m \cdot x^m$, then the leading term of the quotient will be $f_n \cdot g_m^{-1} \cdot x^{n-m}$. Subtracting $f_n \cdot g_m^{-1} \cdot x^{n-m} \cdot g(x)$ from f(x) will leave a remainder of degree at most n-1. Then the process is repeated, to eventually give a remainder r(x) of degree less than deg(g).

Q.E.D.

THEOREM V.9: For F a field, F[x] is a principal ideal domain. For every ideal $I \neq 0 \subset$ F[x], $\exists$ an uniquely determined monic polynomial $g \in$ F[x] .$\ni$. I = (g).

PROOF: Theorem V.7 $\Rightarrow$ F[x] is an integral domain.

Let I $\neq$ 0 be an ideal, and let h(x) be a non-zero polynomial of *least* degree in I; let h_n be the leading coefficient of h(x); and let $g(x) = h_n^{-1} \cdot h(x)$. Then g(x) $\in$ I and g(x) is monic.

Theorem V.8 $\Rightarrow$ $\exists$ q(x), r(x) $\in$ F[x] with

$$f(x) \;=\; q(x)\cdot g(x) \;+\; r(x) \qquad \text{and } \deg(r) < \deg(g) = \deg(h).$$

$\Rightarrow$ r(x) $\in$ I

$\Rightarrow$ r(x) = 0, by the assumption about h(x) having least degree,

$\Rightarrow$ I = (g).

To prove that g is unique, suppose $\exists$ g' .$\ni$. I = (g')

$\Rightarrow$ g' $= c_1 \cdot g$, $c_1 \in$ F; also g $= c_2 \cdot g'$, $c_2 \in$ F; $\Rightarrow$ $c_1 \cdot c_2 = 1$.

Since g and g' are monic, $\Rightarrow c_1 = c_2 = 1$.

Q.E.D.

THEOREM V.10 (GREATEST COMMON DIVISOR): Let F be a field. Let f_1, f_2, ..., f_n be polynomials in a polynomial ring F[x], not all zero. Then there exists an unique monic polynomial d(x) $\in$ F[x] with the properties:

1. d(x) | $f_j(x)$, $\qquad$ j = 1, 2, ..., n;

2. any polynomial c(x) $\in$ F[x] dividing each $f_j(x)$ also divides d(x);

3. d can be written $d(x) = b_1 f_1(x) + b_2 f_2(x) + ... + b_n f_n(x)$, b_1, b_2, ..., $b_n \in$ F.

PROOF: PART 1:

$$I = \{\, c_1(x)\cdot f_1(x) + c_2(x)\cdot f_2(x) + ... + c_n(x)\cdot f_n(x) \;|$$
$$c_1(x), c_2(x), ..., c(x)_n \in F[x] \,\}$$

is an ideal.

Not all of the $f_j(x)$ are zero $\Rightarrow$ I $\neq$ 0.

$\therefore$, by theorem V.9, I = (d(x)), where d(x) is a monic polynomial.

$\therefore$, for any $f_j(x) \in$ I, we have d(x) | $f_j(x)$, which proves Part 1.

PART 2: If c(x) divides each $f_j(x)$, then each $f_j(x) \in$ (c(x)).

$\Rightarrow$ $\qquad$ (d) $\subset$ (c)

$\Rightarrow$ $\qquad$ c(x) $= e(x)\cdot d(x)$ $\qquad \Rightarrow$ property 2 holds.

PART 3: (UNIQUENESS OF d(x)). Suppose d'(x) also satisfies the properties. Then (d(x)) = (d'(x)), and by the proof of V.9, d = d'.

Q.E.D.

The polynomial computed in this way is called the **greatest common divisor** of f_1, f_2, ..., f_n; and is written $d(x) = \gcd(f_1(x), f_2(x), ..., f_n(x))$.

If the $\gcd(f_1(x), f_2(x), ..., f_n(x)) = 1$, then the $f_j(x)$ are said to be **relatively prime**.

A repeated application of the division algorithm will give the Euclidean algorithm for the computation of the gcd.

DEFINITION: A polynomial $p(x) \in F[x]$ is **irreducible** over $F \Leftrightarrow$ deg $p(x) > 0$, and $p(x) = a(x) \cdot b(x)$, $\Rightarrow$ either $a(x)$ or $b(x)$ is a constant.

EXAMPLES:

1. $\mathbb{Q}[x]$, the ring of polynomials with rational coefficients. The polynomial $x^2 - 2$ is irreducible.

2. $\mathbb{R}[x]$, the ring of polynomials with real coefficients. The polynomial $x^2 - 2$ is reducible, since it can be written as $x^2 - 2 = (x + \sqrt{2}) \cdot (x - \sqrt{2})$.

3. $\mathbb{Z}_2[x]$, the ring of polynomials with $\mathbb{Z}_2$ - coefficients. The polynomial $x^2 + x + 1$ is irreducible. Since, if $x^2 + x + 1$ were to factor, then we would have

$$(x + a)(x + b) = x^2 + x + 1$$

where $a, b = 0$ or 1. But a direct computation gives:

a	b	$(x + a)(x + b)$	
0	0	$x \cdot x$	$= x^2$
0	1	$x \cdot (x+1)$	$= x^2 + x$
1	0	$(x+1) \cdot x$	$= x^2 + x$
1	1	$(x+1) \cdot (x+1)$	$= x^2 + x + x + 1 = x^2 + 1$

$\therefore$ $x^2 + x + 1$ cannot factor, and is therefore irreducible.

THEOREM V.11: For $f(x) \in F[x]$, for F a field, $F[x]/(f(x))$ is a field $\Leftrightarrow$ $f(x)$ is irreducible over F.

PROOF: (The proof is completely analogous to the proof of theorem V.6.)

$$F[x] / (f(x)) = \{ g(x) + (f(x)) \mid \forall g(x) \in F[x] \}.$$

Each class has a unique representative $r(x)$ with deg $r(x) <$ deg $f(x)$, by the division algorithm.

The distinct residue classes are all classes $r(x) + (f(x))$ where $r(x)$ can be any polynomial with deg $r <$ deg f. Thus, if the field F has q elements, the number of elements of the field $F[x] / (f(x))$ is $q^{\deg f} = q^n$.

Q.E.D.

Field Extensions

«F',+,·» is a **subfield** of a field «F,+,·» if (1) «F',+,·» is a field; and (2) F' is a subset of F. In this case, F is said to be an **extension field** of F'.

A field with no proper subfields is called a **prime field**.

EXAMPLE: «$\mathbb{Z}_p$,+,·», for any prime p, is a prime field.

The prime subfield of any field F is isomorphic to either $\mathbb{Z}_p$ or $\mathbb{Q}$, according as char F = p or 0.

DEFINITION: Let K be a subfield of F, and M a subset of F. Then K(M) = intersection of all subfields of F containing both K and M. K(M) is called the **extension field of K** obtained by adjoining the elements of M.

DEFINITION: Let K be a subfield of F, and $\alpha \in$ F. If there exists an equation

$$c_n\alpha^n + c_{n-1}\alpha^{n-1} + ... + c_1\alpha + c_0 = 0 \qquad c_i \in K, \text{ not all } c_i = 0.$$

then α is **algebraic over K**.

An extension L of K is algebraic over K if every element of L is algebraic over K.

DEFINITION: If $\alpha \in$ F is algebraic over K, then the unique monic polynomial $g \in K[x]$ generating $I = \{ f \in K[x] \mid f(\alpha) = 0 \}$ is called the **minimum polynomial of α over K**.

THEOREM V.12: If $\alpha \in$ F is algebraic over K, then its minimum polynomial g has the properties:

1. g is irreducible in K[x];
2. for $f(x) \in K[x]$, $f(\alpha) = 0 \Leftrightarrow g \mid f$;
3. g is the monic polynomial in K[x] of least degree having α as its root.

PROOF: Parts 1 and 2 follow directly from theorem V.9.

Part 3: Any polynomial in K[x] having α as a root must have be a multiple of g(x), by theorem V.9, therefore such a polynomial is either g or has larger degree than g.

Q.E.D.

If L is an extension field of F, then L can be viewed as a *vector space* over F.

Exercise V.1: Verify that L satisfies the axioms for a vector space.

If L is a finite-dimensional vector space, then write the dimension of this vector space as dim[L:F].

THEOREM V.13: Suppose K, L, and M are all fields. If L is a finite extension of K, and M is a finite extension of L, then

$$\dim [M{:}K] = \dim [M{:}L] \cdot \dim [L{:}K].$$

PROOF : From the theory of vector spaces, if $\{ a_1, a_2, ..., a_n \}$ forms a basis of L over K, and $\{ b_1, b_2, ..., b_m \}$ forms a basis of M over L, then the $m{\cdot}n$ elements $a_i b_j$ form a basis of M over K.

Q.E.D.

THEOREM V.14: Every finite extension of a field K is algebraic.

PROOF: Let L be a finite extension of of K, with $\dim [L{:}K] = n$. For any $\alpha \in L$, the $(n+1)$ elements $1, \alpha, \alpha^2, ..., \alpha^n$ must be linearly dependent.

$$\Rightarrow \exists\ a_0, a_1, ..., a_n\ .\ni.$$

$$a_0 + a_1\alpha + ... + a_n\alpha^n = 0, \qquad a_i \in K, \text{ not all } a_i = 0.$$

$\Rightarrow \alpha$ is algebraic over K.

Q.E.D.

THEOREM V.15: Let $\alpha \in F$ be algebraic of degree n over K, and let g be the minimum polynomial of α over K. Then:

1. $K(\alpha)$ is isomorphic to $K[x]/(g)$;
2. $\dim [K(\alpha){:}K] = n$, and $1, \alpha, \alpha^2, ..., \alpha^{n-1}$ is a basis;
3. every $\beta \in K(\alpha)$ is algebraic over K, and the degree of β over K divides n.

PROOF: Part 1: Consider the ring homomorphism $\pi : K[x] \to K(\alpha)$ given by $\pi(f) = f(\alpha)$.

$\ker \pi = \{ f \in K[x] \mid f(\alpha) = 0 \} = (g)$, by the definition of minimum polynomial.

$$\Rightarrow K[x]/(\ker \pi) \cong K[x]/(g) \cong K(\alpha).$$

Part 2: Any $\beta \in K(\alpha)$ can be written $\beta = f(\alpha)$ for some $f \in K[x]$.

$\therefore$, by the division algorithm, $f = q{\cdot}g + r$, for $q, r \in K[x]$, $\deg r < \deg g = n$.

$\Rightarrow r(\alpha)$ is a linear combination of $1, \alpha, \alpha^2, ..., \alpha^{n-1}$, and

$$h(x) = a_0 + a_1\alpha + ... + a_n\alpha^n = 0$$

only if $h(x)$ has a root and is a multiple of $g(x)$,

$\Rightarrow$ the remainder would be zero $\Rightarrow 1, \alpha, \alpha^2, ..., \alpha^{n-1}$ is a basis.

PART 3: $K(\alpha)$ is a finite extension of K, by part 2.

$\Rightarrow \beta \in K(\alpha)$ is algebraic by theorem V.14.

Also $K(\beta)$ is a subfield of $K(\alpha)$. If d = degree of β over K, then part 2 and theorem V.13

$$\Rightarrow \quad n \quad = \ \dim [K(\alpha):K]$$
$$= \ \dim \ [K(\alpha):K(\beta)] \cdot \dim \ [K(\beta):K]$$
$$= \ d \cdot \dim \ [K(\beta):K]$$
$$\Rightarrow \quad d \mid n.$$

Q.E.D.

Structure Theory of Finite Fields

Now we have developed all of the preliminary material necessary to arrive at the complete description of the structure of finite fields. As we will see, they can all be described by quotients of polynomial rings over some $\mathbb{Z}_p$.

LEMMA V.16: Let F be a finite field, and F' a subfield with q elements. Then F has q^n elements, where m = dim[F : F'].

PROOF: F is a vector space over F'. Since F is finite, F is a *finite-dimensional* vector space over F'. Suppose that dim [F:F'] = m, and let b_1, b_2, ..., b_n be a basis for the vector space over F'.

Then every f $\in$ F can be uniquely written as:

$$f \ = \ a_1b_1 + a_2b_2 + ... + a_nb_n \qquad a_i \in F'$$

Each a_i can have q possible values, $\Rightarrow$ F has q^n elements.

Q.E.D.

THEOREM V.17: Let F be a finite field. Then F has p^n elements, where p is a prime, p = char F, and n = degree of F over its prime subfield.

PROOF: Since F is finite, char F = p (a prime), by corollary V.5. Thus the prime subfield is isomorphic to $\mathbb{Z}_p$. Applying lemma V.16 gives the appropriate result.

Q.E.D.

LEMMA V.18: Let F be a finite field, with q elements. For every a $\in$ F, we have $a^q = a$.

PROOF: The result is trivial for a = 0. Since F is a field, the non-zero elements form a (multiplicative) group of order q-1.

$$\Rightarrow \quad a^{q-1} = 1, \qquad \forall \ a \neq 0$$
$$\Rightarrow \quad a^q \ = a.$$

Q.E.D.

LEMMA V.19: Let F be a finite field, with q elements. Let F' $\subseteq$ F be a subfield. Then $x^q - x$ in F'[x] factors as

$$x^q - x \ = \ \prod_{a \in F} (x\text{-}a).$$

PROOF: The polynomial $x^q - x$ has at most q roots in F. However, by V.18, each element a$\in$ F is a root. Therefore the polynomial splits as desired.

Q.E.D.

THEOREM V.20 (THE EXISTENCE AND UNIQUENESS OF FINITE FIELDS): For every prime p, and every positive integer n, there exists a finite field with p^n elements. Any such field is isomorphic to the splitting field of x^q - x over $\mathbb{Z}_p$.

PROOF: Let q = p^n. Construct x^q - x $\in \mathbb{Z}_p[x]$. Let F be the splitting field of this polynomial over $\mathbb{Z}_p$.

This polynomial has q distinct roots in F. Let S = { a | a $\in$ F, $a^q - a = 0$ }. Then S is a subfield of F, since:

(1) 0, 1 $\in$ S;

(2) a, b $\in$ S $\Rightarrow$ $(a - b)^q = a^q - b^q = a - b$ $\quad \Rightarrow$ a - b $\in$ S.

(3) a, b $\in$ S, b $\neq$ 0 $\Rightarrow$ $(a \cdot b^{-1})^q = a^q \cdot b^{-q} = a \cdot b^{-1}$ $\Rightarrow$ a $\cdot b^{-1} \in$ S.

Also, x^q - x must split in S since S contains all its roots; $\Rightarrow$ F = S.

$\Rightarrow$ F is a finite field with |S| elements.

PROOF OF UNIQUENESS: Let F be a finite field with q = p^n elements.

$\Rightarrow$ char F = p, by theorem V.17;

$\Rightarrow$ F contains $\mathbb{Z}_p$ as a subfield;

$\Rightarrow$ F is a splitting field of x^q - x over $\mathbb{Z}_p$ (by V.19);

$\Rightarrow$ uniqueness by the uniqueness of splitting fields.

Q.E.D.

THEOREM V.21: For every finite field F with q elements, the multiplicative group <F*,·> of (q-1) elements is cyclic.

PROOF: Assume q $\geq$ 3. (The case q = 2 is trivial.)

Let $h = p_1^{r1} \cdot p_2^{r2} \cdot \ldots \cdot p_m^{rm}$ be the prime factor decomposition of the order $h = q-1$ of F^*. We need to find an element of order h in order to prove that F^* is cyclic.

For all i, $1 \le i \le m$, the polynomial $x^{h/p_i} - 1$ has at most h/p_i roots in F.

$\Rightarrow$ there are non-zero elements of F that are *not* roots of this polynomial. Let a_i be such an element, and set $b_i = a_i^{h/p_i^{r_i}}$;

$\Rightarrow$ $b_i^{p_i^{r_i}} = 1$.

$\Rightarrow$ order of $b_i \mid p_i^{r_i}$;

$\Rightarrow$ b_i is of the form $p_i^{s_i}$, $0 \le s_i \le r_i$.

Also, $b_i^{p_i^{r_i-1}} = a_i^{b/p_i} \ne 1$.

$\Rightarrow$ order of $b_i = p_i^{r_i}$.

Construct similarly elements $b_1, b_2, \ldots, b_m$. It is claimed that the element $b = b_1 \cdot b_2 \cdot \ldots \cdot b_m$ has order h. For, suppose that the order of b is a *proper* divisor of h.

$\Rightarrow$ order of b is a divisor of some h/p_i, $1 \le i \le m$.

Then, $1 = b^{h/p1} = b_1^{h/p1} \cdot b_2^{h/p1} \cdot \ldots \cdot b_m^{h/p1}$. If $2 \le i \le m$,

$\Rightarrow$ order of $b_1 \mid h/p_1$, a contradiction.

$\Rightarrow$ $F^* = <b>$, a cyclic group.

Q.E.D.

DEFINITION: A generator of F^* is called a **primitive element** of F.

THEOREM V.22: For every field F with q elements, and every positive integer n, there exists an irreducible polynomial $I(x) \in F_q[x]$ of degree n.

PROOF: Let G be the extension field of F of order q^n, .ə. dim $[G:F] = n$.

Let λ be a primitive element of G. $F[\lambda] \subseteq G$, $F[\lambda]$ contains 0, and all powers of λ, and therefore all elements of G.

$\therefore$ the minimum polynomial of λ over F is an irreducible polynomial of degree n.

Q.E.D.

Conclusions

The conclusions of this introduction into Galois fields or finite fields is that all finite fields can be generated by constructing the ring of polynomials over a prime ground field, and choosing an irreducible polynomial of the appropriate degree.

It can be shown that for a given p and n, the number of irreducible polynomials is $O(p^{n-1})$; consequently there are many choices for irreducible polynomials. This fact alone leads to promising applications of finite fields in cryptology.

Readers may wish to conduct further investigation into the subject of finite fields; for this purpose, there is no better nor more comprehensive treatise than [LIDL 83].

— Appendix VI —
Selected Pascal Programs

This appendix contains the Pascal code for several programs which execute algorithms as described in the book.

As with any set of computer programs written in any computer language, the results are dependent upon on the version of the language used, and often, issues which are outside of the scope of the language, such as the way in which an operating system may interface with the compiler or translator for that language.

The programs contained herein have been written using the Macintosh Pascal interpreter [APPL 84], which is a good approximation of the standard embodied in ANS/IEEE 770X3.97-1983 [ANSI 83], and which itself derives from the original definition of Pascal as found in [JENS 75].

Before giving the listing of these programs, it will be noted that all have been run not only under the Macintosh Pascal interpreter, but also under other compilers, modified where necessary, including the Digital Equipment Corporation DEC/VAX Pascal compiler [DEC 85].

To run under other language translators than the Macintosh's interpreter, a few minor modifications are necessary. The list below will hopefully be complete in terms of such necessary changes:

1. PROGRAM HEADINGS: In many Pascal versions, the first line of a program must explicitly list all files being used in the program, including the files named "input" and "output" for the standard input and output files. Consequently, a Pascal program using external files named "file1" and "file2" will have the program heading:

program ThisProgram(input, output, file1, file2);

The Macintosh Pascal language definition allows the program heading to be simply the name of the program, in other words:

program ThisProgram;

We have tried to be consistent at least in using as the program heading in all cases:

program ThisProgram(input, output);

2. USE OF EXTERNAL FILES: The ANSI standard (and indeed the original Jensen and Wirth definition) have not defined the convention for the introduction of a file created externally to the Pascal language. Apple's convention is not the same as other versions of Pascal for the naming and referencing of external files. For example, in VAX Pascal, the external file must be known to the operating system (VMS) as *<filename>*.dat, where *<filename>* is the name of the external file inside the Pascal program. Furthermore, *<filename>* must also be the variable name of the file inside the program, whereas in the ANSI Standard, the name of the external file is represented by a string, and that string value may appear in an open or close statement as a string expression; in other words, it could be indicated as a literal or as the current value of a string variable.

3. STRINGS: In some Pascal implementations, the data type "string" may not exist. In such a case, create a new type in the type declaration section of the program:

type
     string = **packed array** [1..80] **of** char;

4. A PSEUDO-RANDOM NUMBER GENERATING FUNCTION: There is no definition in the ANSI Standard of Pascal of a random function. As will be noted in the code provided, Macintosh Pascal defines a function with no parameters called "random" which generates a pseudo-random number of data type "integer" in the range [-maxint,maxint]. If another version of Pascal does not include a random number generating function, a simple one which will suffice is a function which takes an integer, multiplies it by some number which is relatively prime to maxint, and reduces modulo maxint, yielding a number in the range [0, maxint-1]. The result of this product is the function value, and also the value of the seed for the next call of the function:

```
function random ( var seed: integer) : integer;
begin
            seed := (seed * 9973) mod maxint;
            random := seed
end;
```

5. THE DATA TYPES DOUBLE AND LONGINT: Macintosh Pascal provides a data type *double* for extended precision reals (similar to DOUBLE PRECISION in FORTRAN). In the one case in which this is used in the accompanying programs, it could be replaced by *real*. Macintosh Pascal also provides a data type *LongInt* as an integer data type occupying a double word in storage. On the Macintosh, an *integer* lies in the range [-32768, 32767], and a *LongInt* in the range [-2 147 483 648, 2 147 483 647]. On many machines, the data type *integer* is represented by a 32-bit word (rather than a 16-bit on the Macintosh). On such machines, all use of *LongInt* here could simply be replaced by *integer*.

The programs provided are in a sequence that follows the appearance of the related material in the book. A list of the programs follows:

Considerable care has been taken by the author to ensure that the program code which follows *actually runs*. The author, as well as many others, has often been victimized by code published in reference works that will not compile, or will not execute, or will not give correct answers. One sacrifice to typography has been made, however. In several cases where procedures or functions are repeated in several programs, the listing is only given the first time the procedure or function appears; on the subsequent appearances, the header is given, along with a backward reference to the page where the procedure is given in its entirety. Furthermore, the claim is only made with this program code that it runs under the Macintosh Pascal interpreter. However, all of the deviations from ANSI Standard Pascal are clearly noted, and the fixes, of course, have been described above.

Finally, the Macintosh Pascal interpreter is an *interpreter;* as such, programs that are heavily compute-bound (in particular, programs P7 and P8) will run very slowly and very inefficiently in this environment.

The publisher of this book will make available to the reader machine-readable copies of the program listings which follow, suitable for execution in the Macintosh environment. Furthermore, modified versions of this code will also be made available by the publisher for MS-DOS computing environments.

program CaesarShift(input, output);

{Program P1: The Caesar Shift   *}*
{This is an implementation, not contemplated by Julius Caesar , of his encryption   *}*
{ algorithm. The algorithm is described in Chapter 1.   *}*

{ MODE OF EXECUTION: This program is designed to be executed interactively.   *}*

{ INPUT: The user is given the option of encrypting or decrypting several messages   *}*
{ or ciphers. If the option is to encrypt (by entering 'E' or 'e'), two other inputs must be   *}*
{supplied: *}*
{   1. A key, being an integer in the range [0,25]. Any larger or smaller integer is   *}*
{   reduced mod 26.   *}*
{   2. Any character string (the message text) of up to 80 characters.   *}*
{ If the option is to decrypt (by entering 'D' or 'd'), one's input, the ciphertext (a character   *}*
{string of up to 80 characters) must be supplied. After each encryption or decryption,   *}*
{the user is prompted for another case ('Y' or 'y' and default) or to quit ('N' or 'n').   *}*

{ OUTPUT: In encrypting, the output is the ciphertext. In decrypting, the output consists   *}*
{the 26 trial decryptions obtained by exhaustive key search.   *}*

{ NOTE: The Caesar shift is only defined for letters. Characters in any message string   *}*
{are not letters or blanks are replaced by blanks. Lower case letters are encrypted as   *}*
{lower case letters; upper case letters as upper case letters; blanks remain unchanged.   *}*

```
   type
     KeySpace = 0..25;                              { Keys can be anywhere from 0 to 25 }
     MessageLength = 1..80;                         Limit our messages to 80 characters }
     TextArray = array[MessageLength] of char;      { Array for message and ciphertext }
     CharSet = set of char;
   var
     MessageText, CipherText : TextArray;                     { Message and cipher  arrays. }
     K : KeySpace;
     j, Last : integer;
     UpperCaseCharacters, LowerCaseCharacters : CharSet;    {Test the character sets }
     chu, chl, ch : char;
     Finished : boolean;
```

*{ *** }*

```
   procedure Encrypt (var MessageText, CipherText : TextArray;
                   UpperCaseCharacters, LowerCaseCharacters : CharSet;
                   Last : integer);
{ The encrypt procedure reads a Message text array, and a key, and produces the         }
{cipher text.                                                                            }
     var
       K : KeySpace;
       j : integer;
   begin
     writeln('Please enter your key:');
     readln(j);
     if (0 <= j) and (j <= 25) then                        {if the key is in the range 0..25}
       K := j
     else                                                  { otherwise reduce mod 25}
       K := j mod 25;
     writeln('Please enter your message:');
     j := 1;
```

```
      while (j <= 80) and not eoln do
        begin
          read(MessageText[j]);
          if MessageText[j] in LowerCaseCharacters then
              { If the message is in lower case characters, produce the cipher in lower case }
              CipherText[j] := chr(ord('a') + ((ord(MessageText[j]) - ord('a') + K) mod 26))
          else if MessageText[j] in UpperCaseCharacters then
                                              { And similarly for Upper Case characters }
              CipherText[j] := chr(ord('A') + ((ord(MessageText[j]) - ord('A') + K) mod 26))
          else
              CipherText[j] := ' ';                          { Otherwise insert a blank }
          j := j + 1
        end;
      Last := j - 1;
      writeln;
      writeln('The cipher text is: ');
      writeln;
      for j := 1 to Last do
        begin
          write(CipherText[j])                              { Write the cipher text }
        end;
      writeln
    end; { procedure Encrypt  }

{  *************************************************************************************  }

    procedure Decrypt (var MessageText, CipherText : TextArray;
                UpperCaseCharacters, LowerCaseCharacters : CharSet;
                Last : integer);
{ The decrypt procedure reads a cipher text array, and                          }
{ produces potential message text by exhaustive key search.                     }
      var
        i, j : integer;
    begin  { procedure Decrypt  }
      writeln('Please enter the cipher text: ');
      i := 1;
      while not eoln do
        begin
          read(CipherText[i]);
          i := i + 1
        end;
      Last := i - 1;
      writeln;
      MessageText := CipherText;                    { Start with a trial message text.}
      writeln;
      writeln('The cipher text as input: ');
      for i := 1 to Last do
        write(CipherText[i]);                            { Write the cipher text. }
      writeln;
      writeln;
      writeln('The 26 trial decryptions are: ');
      writeln;
      for j := 0 to 25 do
        begin
          for i := 1 to Last do
            begin          {Increment the ciphertext by one letter, cyclically, each time.}
              if MessageText[i] = 'z' then
```

```
                  MessageText[i] := 'a'
              else if MessageText[i] = 'Z' then
                  MessageText[i] := 'A'
              else if MessageText[i] in (UpperCaseCharacters +
                  LowerCaseCharacters) then
                  MessageText[i] := succ(MessageText[i])
              else
                  MessageText[i] := ' ';
              write(MessageText[i])
          end;
      writeln
    end
  end; { procedure Decrypt }
```

{ ** }

```
begin { Main program - Caesar Shift }
  UpperCaseCharacters := [];                    {Set the initial values for character sets.}
  LowerCaseCharacters := [];
  chu := 'A';
  chl := 'a';
  for j := 1 to 26 do
    begin
      UpperCaseCharacters := UpperCaseCharacters + [chu];
      LowerCaseCharacters := LowerCaseCharacters + [chl];
      chu := succ(chu);
      chl := succ(chl)
    end;
  Finished := false;
  while not Finished do
    begin
      write('Do you wish to encrypt (enter E)');
      writeln(' or decrypt (enter D)?');
      readln(ch);
      if (ch = 'E') or (ch = 'e') then
        Encrypt(MessageText, CipherText, UpperCaseCharacters,
                        LowerCaseCharacters, Last)
      else
        Decrypt(MessageText, CipherText, UpperCaseCharacters,
                        LowerCaseCharacters, Last);
      writeln;
      writeln('     ***********************     ');
      writeln;
      writeln('Do you want another case? Y for yes, N for no');
      readln;
      readln(ch);
      finished := ((ch = 'N') or (ch = 'n'))
    end
end. { Main program - Caesar Shift }
```

program ComputeFrequencies(input,output);

```
{Program P2: Compute Letter Frequencies in a Text                              }
{The program reads a text file, and computes the frequency distribution of letter }
{occurrences in the file. This method of cryptanalysis is described in Chapter 1.  }

{ MODE OF EXECUTION: This program is designed to be executed in part interactively, }
{ using terminal and data file input.                                           }

{ INPUT: The user is asked to enter the name of a text file to be analyzed.In addition, the }
{ user is asked for the name of an output file to be created. These names must of course }
{ conform to the file-naming conventions of the operating  system being used.In addition, }
{ a header is requested, a string which will be printed at the head of the output file. The }
{ textfile is then read, and a count taken of  the occurrencesof each letter in the text file, }
{ in a non-case sensitive fashion.                                              }

{ OUTPUT: A table of the letters of the alphabet is output, along with the number of }
{ occurrences of that letter, and its frequency of occurrence among all letters. Then the }
{ total  number of letters occurring is printed, and finally  a listing of the letters in }
{ decreasing order of frequency of occurrence. As an example, when this program is }
{ run on the text ofChapter 1, the following is output:                         }
{
Letter Occurrences in Chapter 1
```

Letter	Count	Freq	Letter	Count	Freq	Letter	Count	Freq
a	1592	0.0740	b	375	0.0174	c	837	0.0389
d	642	0.0299	e	2811	0.1307	f	562	0.0261
g	409	0.0190	h	1122	0.0522	i	1396	0.0649
j	61	0.0028	k	226	0.0105	l	744	0.0346
m	611	0.0284	n	1288	0.0599	o	1416	0.0659
p	613	0.0285	q	114	0.0053	r	1318	0.0613
s	1541	0.0717	t	2097	0.0975	u	531	0.0247
v	211	0.0098	w	310	0.0144	x	139	0.0065
y	472	0.0220	z	62	0.0029			

TOTAL   21500

The letters in decreasing frequency of occurrence are:

```
e t a s o i r n h c l d p m f u y g b w k v x q z j
}
  type
    AlphIntArrayType = array['a'..'z'] of integer;
                                              { An integer array type indexed by letters.}
    AlphRealArrayType = array['a'..'z'] of real;    { A real array type indexed by letters.}
  var
    Count : AlphIntArrayType;
    total : integer;                               {Total of all letter occurrences}
    Freq : AlphRealArrayType;                        { An array for frequencies }
    OutputText, Analysis : text;                      { Variable names of files }
    MessageFileName, OutputFileName, Header : string;
          { Literal names of files - follow the operating system's file naming  convention.}
    ch, biggest, ch1 : char;
    i : integer;

{   ************************************************************************************   }
```

```
procedure AnalyzeText (MessageFileName : string;
                          var Count : AlphIntArrayType;
                          var total : integer);
```

{ Procedure AnalyzeText reads the textfile whose name is contained in the value of the *}*
{ string variable MessageFileName, and during the read, collects the number of *}*
{ occurrences of each letter. This value is stored in the array Count and that variable *}*
{ is returned, as is the total count of all letters read. *}*

```
   var
      ch : char;
      MessageText : text;
begin { procedure AnalyzeText }
   open(MessageText, MessageFileName);
   repeat
      while not eoln(MessageText) do
         begin
            read(MessageText, ch);                    { Get a character from the input file.}
            if ('a' <= ch) and (ch <= 'z') then
               begin                                         { if it's a lower case letter }
                  Count[ch] := Count[ch] + 1   {count it}
               end
            else if ('A' <= ch) and (ch <= 'Z') then
               begin                              { or if it's an upper case letter, count it }
                  Count[chr(ord(ch) + ord('a') - ord('A'))]
                        := Count[chr(ord(ch) + ord('a') - ord('A'))] + 1
               end
         end;
      readln(MessageText)
   until eof(MessageText);
   total := 0;
   for ch := 'a' to 'z' do
      total := total + Count[ch]                       { add up all the entries in Count }
end; { procedure AnalyzeText }
```

{ ** *}*

```
procedure GenerateOutputReport (OutputFileName : string;
                                   Header : string;
                                   Count : AlphIntArrayType;
                                   Freq : AlphRealArrayType;
                                   total : integer);
```

{ Procedure Generate Output Report takes the output filename, a header, the Count *}*
{ array, the Freq array, and the total, and prints out a report consisting of a header, each *}*
{ letter, its number of occurrences, and its frequency (printed 3 across); and then the *}*
{ total number of letters read. Finally the letters are given in decreasing frequency order. *}*

```
   var
      OutputText : text;                              { Text file variable for output }
      i : integer;
      ch : char;
      AlreadyCounted : set of char;             { Keep track of letters already listed }
                                                   { in descending order of occurrences. }
begin   { procedure GenerateOutputReport }
   open(OutputText, OutputFileName);
   writeln(OutputText);                            { Print the header, with two lines above }
   writeln(OutputText);                                        { and below. }
   writeln(OutputText, Header);
```

```
        writeln(OutputText);
        writeln(OutputText);
        for ch := 'a' to 'z' do
          Freq[ch] := Count[ch] / total;              { Compute frequencies from Count }
        ch := 'a';
        while ch <= 'z' do                            { Print the results, three across }
          begin
            if ch < 'y' then
              writeln(OutputText, ch : 6, Count[ch] : 8, Freq[ch] : 10 : 4, succ(ch) : 8,
                      Count[succ(ch)] : 8, Freq[succ(ch)] : 10 : 4, succ(succ(ch)) : 8,
                      Count[succ(succ(ch))] : 8,   Freq[succ(succ(ch))] : 10 : 4)
            else
              writeln(OutputText, ch : 6, Count[ch] : 8, Freq[ch] : 10 : 4,
                      succ(ch) : 8, Count[succ(ch)] : 8, Freq[succ(ch)] : 10 : 4);
            ch := succ(succ(succ(ch)))
          end;
        writeln(OutputText);                          { Print the total count. }
        writeln(OutputText, 'TOTAL', total : 8);
        writeln(OutputText);
        AlreadyCounted := [];
        writeln(OutputText);                 { Print a header for decreasing frequency list }
        writeln(OutputText);
        writeln(OutputText, 'The letters in decreasing frequency of occurrence are:');
        writeln(OutputText);
        writeln(OutputText);
        for i := 1 to 26 do
          begin
            ch := 'a';
            while ch in AlreadyCounted do             { Find the letter with the }
              ch := succ(ch);                         { largest number of occurrences. }
            biggest := ch;
            while ch <= 'z' do
              begin
                if (Count[ch] > Count[biggest]) and not (ch in AlreadyCounted) then
                  biggest := ch;
                ch := succ(ch)
              end;
            write(OutputText, biggest : 2);
            AlreadyCounted := AlreadyCounted + [biggest]         { Then eliminate it}
          end;
        writeln(OutputText)
      end;   { procedure GenerateOutputReport }

{  ************************************************************************************  }

begin  { Main program ComputeFrequencies }
  for ch := 'a' to 'z' do
    Count[ch] := 0;                                   { Initialize the count array }
  total := 0;
  writeln('Please enter the file name to analyze:');       {Set up the input and output files.}
  readln(MessageFileName);
  writeln('Please enter the file name for the output file:');
  readln(OutputFileName);
  writeln('Please enter the header for the output file:');
  readln(Header);
  AnalyzeText(MessageFileName, Count, total);
  GenerateOutputReport(OutputFileName, Header, Count, Freq, total)
end.   { Main program ComputeFrequencies }
```

program KeyWordSubstitution(input,output);

```
{ In many  some Pascal implementations, this line could read:                       }
{  program KeyWordSubstitution(input, output,MessageTextFile, CipherTextFile);       }

{Program P3: Key Word Substitution.                                                  }
{The program reads a text file, and a key, and encrypts the text file using Key Word }
{Substitution.This cipher is described in Chapter 1.                                 }

{ MODE OF EXECUTION: This program is designed to be executed in part interactively,  }
{using terminal and data file input.                                                 }

{ INPUT:The user is asked to enter a key for this substitution cipher, namely any string }
{ of letters with the letters non-repeating. Also the user is asked for an input file name }
{  (a file containing the message text). Finally the user is prompted for the name of an   }
{ output file. It should be noted that filenames must conform to the file-naming          }
{conventions of the operating system  being used. The textfile is then read.             }

{ OUTPUT: A textfile,designated by the user, containing the cipher text.              }

{ NOTE: There is an arbitrary limit on the size of a file that can be processed --- 6000 }
{ characters. This can be raised by changing the value of the constant MaxMessage.       }
```

```pascal
  const
    MaxMessage = 6000;
  type
    keystring = packed array[1..26] of char;
    AlphabetSet = set of char;
    TextArrayType = packed array[1..MaxMessage] of char;
  var
    ClearText, CipherText : TextArrayType;
    key : keystring;                                    { keylength - length of key }
    i, k, keylength, CTlen, keynum : integer;           { keynum - how many shifts }
    ch, ch2 : char;
    KeyArray, ReverseKeyArray : array['a'..'z'] of char;
            { Keep the substitution in KeyArray, and its inverse in ReverseKeyArray }
    UsedLetters, UpperCase, LowerCase : AlphabetSet;
            { Sets of letters; UsedLetters is used to ensure no repetition in the key.}
    BadCharFlag : boolean;

{ ********************************************************************************* }

  procedure GetText (var TextArray : TextArrayType;
        var length : integer);
```

```
{ Procedure GetText reads the contents of a text file into an array  of length no greater }
{ than MaxMessage (=6000). The TextArray, together with its length, are returned.         }
```

```pascal
    var
      TextFileName : string;       { NOT ANSI PASCAL:Variable for external file name.}
      MessageTextFile : text;                    { External file variable for input text. }
      i : integer;
  begin     { procedure GetText }
    writeln;
    writeln('Enter the name of the input file:');
    readln(TextFileName);
    open(MessageTextFile, TextFileName);
    i := 1;
    repeat                              { Read raw characters into TextArray }
      while not eoln(MessageTextFile) do
        begin
        read(MessageTextFile, TextArray[i]);
```

```
            i := i + 1
          end;
        readln(MessageTextFile)
      until eof(MessageTextFile);
      length := i                              { The length of the TextArray }
    end;    { procedure GetText }
{  ************************************************************************  }

  procedure PutText (TextArray : TextArrayType;
        CtLen : integer);
```

{ Procedure PutText writes the contents of TextArray into an external file,whose name is }
{provided by the user at a prompt. The line length in the output file will be 66 characters. }
{ Blanks are placed randomly in the output file every 4th to 9th character. This has a }
{cryptographic purpose in that blanks placed in the position they occurred in the input }
{file will provide clues as to potential decryptions.The other required parameter is CTLen, }
{which the length of the data in the TextArray. }

```
    var
      TextFileName : string;        { NOT ANSI PASCAL:Variable for external file name.}
      CipherTextFile : text;                   { External file variable for output text. }
      i, iline, iword, r : integer;   { iline --- position on a line; iword --- position in a word. }
    begin   { procedure PutText }
      writeln;
      writeln('Enter the name of the cipher text file:');
      readln(TextFileName);
      open(CipherTextFile, TextFileName);
      i := 1;
      iline := 1;                                  { Counts characters in a line. }
      iword := 1;                      { Counts characters in a 'word', i.e. is it time for a blank? }
      r := random mod 6 + 3;                        { Get a value at random between 3 and 8 }
      repeat                          { The random function is not ANSI Standard Pascal. }
        write(CipherTextFile, TextArray[i]);
        i := i + 1;
        if iword = r then                           { Insert a blank at this point }
          begin
          write(CipherTextFile, ' ');
          iword := 1;
          r := random mod 6 + 3                      { Get a new random value. }
          end
        else
          iword := iword + 1;
        if iline > 66 then                          { If we have 66 characters, }
          begin
          writeln(CipherTextFile);                      { start a new line. }
          iline := 1
          end
        else
          iline := iline + 1;
      until i = CTLen                               { until we exhaust the TextArray. }
    end;    { procedure PutText }
{  ************************************************************************  }

  procedure CleanText (Intext : TextArrayType;
        ITLength : integer;
        var Outtext : TextArrayType;
        var OTLength : integer;
        LowerCase : AlphabetSet;
        UpperCase : AlphabetSet);
```

```
{ Procedure CleanText takes as an input parameter an array (of up to MaxMessage      }
{ number of characters), and strips this array of everything but lower case letters. The }
{ upper case letters are converted to their lower case counterparts. All other converted }
{ to their lower case counterparts. All other characters are stripped. The contents are  }
{ in the array Outtext. The length of the data in the InText array is given by ITLength.  }
{ The length of the data in OutText is returned in the variable OTLength.                 }
    var
      i, j : integer;
  begin              { procedure CleanText }
    i := 1;
    j := 1;
    while i <= ITLength do
      begin
        if Intext[i] in LowerCase then                          { if a lower case letter, }
        begin                                                   { put it in Outtext }
        Outtext[j] := Intext[i];
        j := j + 1
        end
        else if Intext[i] in UpperCase then                          { if upper case }
        begin                                          { find the lower case counterpart }
        Outtext[j] := chr(ord(Intext[i]) + ord('a') - ord('A'));
        j := j + 1                                               {and  put it in Outtext }
        end;
        i := i + 1
      end;
    OTLength := j - 1                              { set the length of the output array }
  end;               { procedure CleanText }
{  ************************************************************************************  }
begin     { main program KeyWordSubstitution }
  LowerCase := [];                                    { Set up the lower case letters. }
  for ch := 'a' to 'z' do
    LowerCase := LowerCase + [ch];
  UsedLetters := [];                       { Set of letters already used in the mapping. }
  UpperCase := [];                                    { Set up the upper case letters. }
  ch := 'A';
  while ch <= 'Z' do
    begin
      UpperCase := UpperCase + [ch];
      ch := succ(ch)
    end;
  i := 1;
  writeln('Enter a key. If your key contains repeated letters,');
  write('they will be dropped;');
  writeln(' i.e. "tempest" would become "temps":');
  BadCharFlag := false;
  while not eoln do                          { Read the key from the terminal input. }
    begin
      read(ch);
      if (ch in UpperCase) then                     { If it's a capital, make it lower case.}
        ch := chr(ord(ch) + ord('a') - ord('A'));
      if (ch in LowerCase) and not (ch in UsedLetters) then
        begin                          { If it's lower case, and not used yet, put it in key.}
          key[i] := ch;
          UsedLetters := UsedLetters + [ch];                         { Now mark it used. }
          i := i + 1
        end
```

```pascal
        else if not (ch in UsedLetters) then              { If it's an illegal character,}
          BadCharFlag := true                              { flag and ignore it. }
      end;
    readln;
    keylength := i - 1;                                    { Compute the effective keylength. }
    if BadCharFlag then
      write('Your key contained an illegal character.');
      writeln(' It was ignored.');
    writeln;
    writeln('Now enter a shift, a number between 1 and 26:');
    readln(keynum);                                        { Read a shift. }
    writeln;
    writeln;                                  { Write the substitution to the standard output. }
    writeln('Here is the key substitution:');
    writeln;
    for ch := 'a' to 'z' do
      write(ch);
    writeln;                      { Now write the first keylength no. of characters into KeyArray.}
    for ch := 'a' to chr(ord('a') + keylength - 1) do
      KeyArray[ch] := key[ord(ch) - ord('a') + 1];         { Write other letters into KeyArray. }
    for ch := chr(ord('a') + keylength) to 'z' do
      begin
        ch2 := 'a';
        while (ch2 in UsedLetters) do
          ch2 := succ(ch2);
        KeyArray[ch] := ch2;
        UsedLetters := UsedLetters + [ch2]
      end;
    for ch := 'a' to 'z' do          { Now shift all of the letters in KeyArray by keynum places. }
      if (chr(ord(KeyArray[ch]) + keynum) > 'z') then
        KeyArray[ch] := chr(ord(KeyArray[ch]) + keynum - 26)
      else
        KeyArray[ch] := chr(ord(KeyArray[ch]) + keynum);
    for ch := 'a' to 'z' do
      write(KeyArray[ch]);
    writeln;
    for ch := 'a' to 'z' do                                { Now compute the inverse permutation.}
      ReverseKeyArray[KeyArray[ch]] := ch;                  {Set up the inverse substitution }
    writeln;                          { Write the inverse substitution to the standard output. }
    writeln('Here is the inverse key substitution:');
    writeln;
    for ch := 'a' to 'z' do
      write(ch);
    writeln;
    for ch := 'a' to 'z' do
      write(ReverseKeyArray[ch]);
    writeln;
    GetText(ClearText, CTlen);                              { Read the clear text }
    CleanText(ClearText, CTlen, ClearText, CTlen, LowerCase, UpperCase);   { Clean it up }
    i := 1;
    while i < CTlen do
      begin
        CipherText[i] := KeyArray[ClearText[i]];           { Encipher the clear text }
        i := i + 1
      end;
    PutText(CipherText, CTLen)                              { Write the cipher text }
end.     { main program KeyWordSubstitution }
```

```
program Vigenere(input, output);
```

{ *In many Pascal implementations, this line could read:*   }
{ **program** *Vigenere(input, output,MessageTextFile,CipherTextFile);*   }

{*Program P4: The Vigenere cipher.*   }
{*The program reads a text file, and a key, and encrypts the text file using the Vigenere* }
{*cipher.This cipher is described in Chapter 1.*   }

{ *MODE OF EXECUTION: This program is designed to be executed in part interactively,*   }
{*using terminal and data file input.*   }

{ *INPUT:The user is asked to enter a key for this substitution cipher, namely any string* }
{ *of letters with the letters non-repeating. Also the user is asked for an input file name* }
{ *(a file containing the message text). Finally the user is prompted for the name of an* }
{ *output file. It should be noted that filenames must conform to the file-naming*   }
{*conventions of the operating system being used. The textfile is then read.*   }

{ *OUTPUT: A textfile,designated by the user, containing the cipher text.*   }

{ *NOTE: There is an arbitrary limit on the size of a file that can be processed --- 6000* }
{ *characters. This can be raised by changing the value of the constant MaxMessage.*   }

```
   const
     MaxMessage = 6000;                              { Limit on the clear text. }
   type
     keystring = packed array[1..26] of char;
     AlphabetSet = set of char;
     TextArrayType = packed array[1..MaxMessage] of char;
                               { An array type for cleartext and ciphertext. }
   var
     ClearText, CipherText : TextArrayType;          {ClearText and CipherText arrays. }
     key : keystring;                                { An array to hold the key. }
     i, k, keylength, CTlen : integer;               { keylength - length of the key }
                         { CTlen - length of the data in the ClearText/Cipher Text array}
     ch : char;
     RepeatedLetters, UpperCase, LowerCase : AlphabetSet;
```
{ *Sets of letters; RepeatedLetters keeps track of repetitions in the key.*   }
```
     BadCharFlag : boolean;
```

{   **   }

```
   procedure GetText (var TextArray : TextArrayType;
        var length : integer);          { Procedure GetText can be found on page 223. }
```

{   **   }

```
   procedure PutText (TextArray : TextArrayType;
        CtLen : integer);               { Procedure PutText can be found on page 224.}
```

{   **   }

```
   procedure CleanText (Intext : TextArrayType;
        ITLength : integer;
        var Outtext : TextArrayType;
        var OTLength : integer;
        LowerCase : AlphabetSet;
        UpperCase : AlphabetSet)        { Procedure CleanText can be found on page 225.}
```

{   **   }

```
   begin      { main program Vigenere }
     LowerCase := [];                             { Set up the lower case characters }
```

```
for ch := 'a' to 'z' do
  LowerCase := LowerCase + [ch];
UpperCase := [];                              { Set up the upper case characters }
ch := 'A';
while ch <= 'Z' do
  begin
    UpperCase := UpperCase + [ch];
    ch := succ(ch)
  end;
RepeatedLetters := [];
BadCharFlag := false;
i := 1;
writeln('Enter the key for the Vigenere cipher:');
while not eoln do                            { Read the key for the Vigenere cipher }
  begin
    read(ch);
    if (ch >= 'a') and (ch <= 'z') and not (ch in RepeatedLetters)
    then
      key[i] := ch
    else if (ch >= 'A') and (ch <= 'Z') and
        not (chr(ord(ch) + ord('a') - ord('A')) in RepeatedLetters)
    then
      key[i] := chr(ord(ch) + ord('a') - ord('A'))
    else
      BadCharFlag := true;                   { If it's not a letter, flag it and forget it. }
    i := i + 1
  end;
readln;
if BadCharFlag then                          {Tell the user if there was a bad character.}
  begin
    write('Your key contained an illegal character. ');
    writeln(' It was ignored.')
  end;
keylength := i - 1;                          {Establish the key length. }
GetText(ClearText, CTlen);                   { Read the Clear text file. }
CleanText(ClearText, CTlen, ClearText, CTlen, LowerCase, UpperCase);   { Clean it up. }
i := 1;
while i < CTlen do                           { perform the encipherment }
  begin
    k := ord(ClearText[i]) + ord(key[(i - 1) mod keylength + 1]) - ord('a') + 1;
    if k > ord('z') then
      CipherText[i] := chr(k - 26)
    else
      CipherText[i] := chr(k);
    i := i + 1
  end;
PutText(CipherText, CTLen)                   { write the cipher text file }
end.      { main program Vigenere }
```

program Playfair;

{ In many Pascal implementations, this line could read: *}*
{ **program** *Playfair(input, output,MessageTextFile,CipherTextFile);*   *}*

{Program P5: The Playfair cipher.   *}*
{The program reads a text file, and a key, and encrypts the text file using the Playfair   *}*
{square cipher.This cipher is described in Chapter 1.   *}*

{ MODE OF EXECUTION: This program is designed to be executed in part interactively,   *}*
{using terminal and data file input.   *}*

{ INPUT:The user is asked to enter a key for this substitution cipher, namely any string   *}*
{ of letters with the letters non-repeating. Also the user is asked for an input file name *}*
{ (a file containing the message text). Finally the user is prompted for the name of an   *}*
{ output file. It should be noted that filenames must conform to the file-naming   *}*
{conventions of the operating system being used. The textfile is then read.   *}*

{ OUTPUT: A textfile,designated by the user, containing the cipher text.   *}*

{ NOTE: There is an arbitrary limit on the size of a file that can be processed --- 6000   *}*
{ characters. This can be raised by changing the value of the constant MaxMessage.   *}*

```
  const
    MaxMessage = 6000;                                 { Limit on the clear text. }
  type
    message = packed array[1..80] of char;
    keystring = packed array[1..20] of char;
    SquareArray = array[1..5, 1..5] of char;
    AlphabetSet = set of char;
    TextArrayType = packed array[1..MaxMessage] of char;
  var
    ClearText, CipherText : TextArrayType;
    key : keystring;
    Square : SquareArray;                              { keylength - length of key }
    i, j, k, keylength, CTlen, i0, j0 : integer;       { keynum - no. of shifts }
    ch : char;
    Alphabet, UpperCase, LowerCase, UsedLetters : AlphabetSet;
              { Sets of letters; UsedLetters is used to ensure no repetition in the key.}
    SquareIndex : array['a'..'z'] of record
        row, column : integer
      end;
    BadCharFlag : boolean;
```

*{ *** }*

```
  procedure GetText (var TextArray : TextArrayType;
            var length : integer);        { Procedure GetText can be found on page 223. }
```

*{ *** }*

```
  procedure PutText (TextArray : TextArrayType;
            CtLen : integer);             { Procedure PutText can be found on page 224.}
```

*{ *** }*

```
  procedure CleanText (Intext : TextArrayType;
          ITLength : integer;
          var Outtext : TextArrayType;
          var OTLength : integer;
          LowerCase : AlphabetSet;
          UpperCase : AlphabetSet)        { Procedure CleanText can be found on page 225.}
```

*{ *** }*

```
  procedure ReadyForPlayfair (Intext : TextArrayType;
```

```
                    ITLength : integer;
                    var Outtext : TextArrayType;
                    var OTLength : integer);
{ Procedure ReadyForPlayfair performs the additional  pre-processing necessary for      }
{ encipherment: 'j's are converted to 'i's,and double letters have a 'q' between them.   }
     var
        i, j : integer;
  begin           { procedure ReadyForPlayfair }
     j := 1;
     i := 1;
     while i <= ITLength do
        begin
          if InText[i] = 'j' then                            { When a 'j' is read }
             OutText[j] := 'i'                               { Replace with an 'i' }
          else
             OutText[j] := InText[i];               {Otherwise write the character read }
          if InText[i] = InText[i + 1] then
             begin
                OutText[j + 1] := 'q';                { Insert a 'q' between the doubles. }
                i := i + 1
             end
          else
             begin
                if InText[i + 1] = 'j' then
                   OutText[j + 1] := 'i'
                else if InText[i + 1] = InText[i + 2] then
                   begin
                      OutText[j + 1] := InText[i + 1];
                      OutText[j + 2] := 'q';
                      j := j + 1
                   end
                else
                   OutText[j + 1] := InText[i + 1];
                i := i + 2
             end;
          j := j + 2
        end;
{If the total number of letters in the OutText array is odd,pad with another 'q'.The Playfair }
{cipher enciphers digrams,consequently there must be an even  number of characters.    }
     if odd(j) then
        begin
           j := j + 1;
           OutText[j] := 'q'
        end;
     OTLength := j
  end;          { procedure ReadyForPlayfair }
{ ******************************************************************************* }

begin      { Main program Playfair }
  Alphabet := [];                                  { Initialize the Playfair alphabet. }
  UsedLetters := ['j'];                            { Initialize the UsedLetters alphabet. }
  for ch := 'a' to 'z' do
     Alphabet := Alphabet + [ch];
  Alphabet := Alphabet - ['j'];
  LowerCase := Alphabet + ['j'];                   { Initialize the LowerCase alphabet. }
  UpperCase := [];
  ch := 'A';
```

```
      while ch <= 'Z' do                          { Initialize the UpperCase alphabet. }
         begin
            UpperCase := UpperCase + [ch];
            ch := succ(ch)
         end;
      i := 1;
      writeln;
      writeln('Enter a key for the Playfair square cipher.');
      writeln('Characters that are not letters will be ignored.');
      writeln('Letters should not be repeated. ');
      writeln('In other words, "tempest" will become "temps":');
      writeln;
      while not eoln do                           { Read the key from the terminal input. }
         begin
            read(ch);
            if (ch in UpperCase) then              { If it's a capital, make it lower case }
               ch := chr(ord(ch) + ord('a') - ord('A'));
            if (ch in LowerCase) and not (ch in UsedLetters) then
               begin   { If it's lower case, and not used yet, put it in key.}
                  key[i] := ch;
                  UsedLetters := UsedLetters + [ch];              { Now mark it used. }
                  i := i + 1
               end
            else if not (ch in UsedLetters) then    { If it's an illegal character }
               BadCharFlag := true                          { flag and ignore it. }
         end;
      readln;
      keylength := i - 1;                          { Compute the effective keylength. }
      if BadCharFlag then
         writeln('Your key contained an illegal character. It was ignored.');
      k := 1;
      ch := 'a';
      i := 1;
      j := 1;
      while (k <= keylength) do                    { Fill the Playfair square. }
         begin
            Square[i, j] := key[k];                         { Write in the key. }
            k := k + 1;
            if ((j mod 5) <> 0) then
               j := j + 1
            else
               begin
                  j := 1;
                  i := i + 1
               end;
            i0 := i;
            j0 := j
         end;
      while (i0 <= 5) do                           { Then fill in the rest of the alphabet less 'j'. }
         begin
            while (j0 <= 5) do
               begin
                  ch := 'a';
                  while (ch in UsedLetters) do
                     ch := succ(ch);
                  Square[i0, j0] := ch;
                  UsedLetters := UsedLetters + [ch];
```

```
              j0 := j0 + 1
            end;
          j0 := 1;
          i0 := i0 + 1
        end;
  writeln('The Playfair square is:');                          { Display the square }
  writeln;
  for i := 1 to 5 do
    begin
      writeln;
      for j := 1 to 5 do
        write(Square[i, j] : 4)
    end;
  for i := 1 to 5 do                        { Compute indices into the Playfair square }
    for j := 1 to 5 do
      begin
        SquareIndex[Square[i, j]].row := i;
        SquareIndex[Square[i, j]].column := j
      end;
  GetText(ClearText, CTlen);                                   { Read the Clear Text }
  CleanText(ClearText, CTlen, ClearText, CTlen, LowerCase, UpperCase);  { Clean it up. }
  ReadyForPlayfair(ClearText, CTlen, ClearText, CTlen);  { Pre-process it for the cipher. }
  i := 1;
  while i < (CTlen - 1) do
    begin
      if SquareIndex[ClearText[i]].row = SquareIndex[ClearText[i + 1]].row then
        begin
{ If a digram in the cleartext has its letters appearing in the same              }
{ row, encipher as the succeeding pair in the row.                                }
          CipherText[i] := Square[SquareIndex[ClearText[i]].row,
                          SquareIndex[ClearText[i]].column mod 5 + 1];
          CipherText[i + 1] :=  Square[SquareIndex[ClearText[i + 1]].row,
                          SquareIndex[ClearText[i + 1]].column mod 5 + 1]
        end
      else if SquareIndex[ClearText[i]].column
              = SquareIndex[ClearText[i + 1]].column then
{ If a digram in the cleartext has its letters appearing in the same              }
{ column, encipher as the succeeding pair in the column.                          }
        begin
          CipherText[i] := Square[SquareIndex[ClearText[i]].row
                          mod 5 + 1, SquareIndex[ClearText[i]].column];
          CipherText[i + 1] := Square[SquareIndex[ClearText[i + 1]].row  mod 5 + 1,
                          SquareIndex[ClearText[i + 1]].column]
        end
      else
        begin
{ Otherwise choose the opposite diagonal points in the Square as the succeeding pair .  }
          CipherText[i] := Square[SquareIndex[ClearText[i]].row,
                              SquareIndex[ClearText[i + 1]].column];
          CipherText[i + 1] := Square[SquareIndex[ClearText[i + 1]].row,
                              SquareIndex[ClearText[i]].column]
        end;
      i := i + 2
    end;
  PutText(CipherText, CTLen)                                   { Write the Cipher Text }
end.        { Main program Playfair }
```

program DataEncryptionStandard(input, output);

{ *In many Pascal implementations, this line should read:* }
{ **program** *DataEncryptionStandard(input, output, SBoxNumbers);* }

{*Program P6: The Data Encryption Standard.* }
{ *The program reads a message and akey (as 8-byte and 7-byte strings, rather than as* }
{ *64- and 56-bit strings, as defined in the standard), and performs an encryption and a* }
{ *decryption of the message and the resultant cipher. The Data Encryption Standard is* }
{ *described in Chapter 2.* }

{ *MODE OF EXECUTION: This program requests interactive input from the user. In* }
{ *addition, one data file (S-BoxNumbers) must be present.* }

{ *INPUT: The user is asked to enter a plaintext message, namely any 8-byte string.* }
{ *Strictly speaking, the user should be able to enter any 64-bit string; however, for the* }
{ *sake of illustration, the program is designed to be interactive; consequently, it is felt* }
{ *that potential users would be happier keying in 8 bytes of message rather than 64 bits.* }
{ *The user also must furnish a 7-byte key, and here the comment applies as well --- the* }
{ *DES provides for 56-bit keys, but this program is designed for illustration and* }
{ *description rather than practical DES encryption.Users may easily modify the program,* }
{ *however, to have it operate in batch mode with text files and arbitrary 56-bit keys.* }

{ *OUTPUT: A display to the terminal of the (bitwise) message key, and DES cipher; as an* }
{ *option, all internal .computations may be shown, and finally the result of decrypting the* }
{ *cipher is shown.* }

```
   type
      BlockArray = array[0..63] of boolean;
                     { A BlockArray is an array of bits that may be 28, 32, 48, 56, or 64 bits long.}
      Block = record                              { A Block is a record consisting of a }
         body : BlockArray;                       { Block Array, and an integer indicating }
         last : integer                           { the length of the data contained in the block}
        end;
      RoundsOfBits = array[0..16] of Block;                { 0th to 16th rounds of a Block}
      MsgOrKey = record
         body : array[1..8] of char;              { A character array which may }
         last : integer                           { contain eight bytes of.message }
        end;                                       { or seven bytes of key }
      SBoxType = array[0..3, 0..15] of integer;                  {A single S-box}
      SBoxArrayType = array[1..8] of SBoxType;               {The collection of S-boxes}
   var
      Message, Cipher, KeyText : MsgOrKey;
      MString, CString, KString, KTemp : Block;        { KString - the key in binary form}
                  { MString - the message in binary form;CString - the cipher in binary form }
      L, R, K, C, D : RoundsOfBits;
                     { Each of L0 to L16, R0 to R16, K0 to K16, etc. in the Standard. }
      SNumbers : text;
      SB : SBoxArrayType;                                        { The S-box arrays }
      SBoxFileName : string;      { Name for external file. (NOT ANSI STANDARD PASCAL)}
      i, row, col : integer;
      temp : BlockArray;
      ch : char;
```

{ *** }

```
   procedure XOR (W1, W2 : Block;
                  var W3 : Block);
```

```
{ Procedure XOR computes the exclusive-or function of two bitstrings, W1 and W2, and  }
{ places the result in W3. The length of the returned block is that of the  shortest input.  }

    var
       i : integer;
    begin        { Procedure  XOR }
      if W1.last > W2.last then
         W1.last := W2.last;                              { Find the smallest, assign it to W1 }
      for i := 0 to W1.last do                                    { Compute the XOR function }
         W3.body[i] := (W1.body[i] or W2.body[i]) and not (W1.body[i] and W2.body[i]);
      W3.last := W1.last
    end;        { Procedure  XOR }
{  **************************************************************************************  }

    procedure CircLeftShift (W1 : Block;
                         var W2 : Block;
                             shift : integer);

{ Procedure CircLeftShift performs a circular left shift on a block  W1. The result is       }
{ returned in the block W2. Note that those bits shifted are only those up to the length of  }
{ the data in block W1.                                                                      }

    var
       i : integer;
    begin        { Procedure  CircLeftShift }
      for i := 0 to W1.last do                                        { Perform the shift }
         W2.body[i] := W1.body[(i + shift) mod (W1.last + 1)]
    end;           { Procedure  CircLeftShift }
{  **************************************************************************************  }

    procedure GetText (var T : MsgOrKey);

{Procedure GetText is a procedure to read the standard input and to extract either an 8-  }
{ byte message or a 7-byte key and to place this input in the appropriate variable T.      }

    var
       i : integer;
    begin        { Procedure GetText }
      i := 1;
      while not eoln do
        begin
          read(T.body[i]);
          i := i + 1
        end;
      readln;
      T.last := i - 1
    end;        { Procedure GetText }
{  **************************************************************************************  }

    procedure PutText (T : MsgOrKey);

{Procedure PutText is a procedure to write to the standard output either an 8-byte       }
{ message or a 7-byte key according to the value of the appropriate variable T.          }

    var
       i : integer;
```

```
begin        { Procedure PutText }
  for i := 1 to T.last do
    write(T.body[i]);
  writeln
end;          { Procedure PutText }
```

{ ** }

```
procedure TextToBits (T : MsgOrKey;
                      var BT : Block);
```

{ Procedure TextToBits takes as an input parameter a 7- or 8-byte message or key (T), }
{ and converts it to a bit-string of length 56 or 64 bits respectively. The resulting Block }
{ (record including the bit-string and its length) is returned in BT. }

```
  var
    i, j, temp, power : integer;      { power represents a power of 2; used for bit values. }
  begin          { Procedure TextToBits }
    for i := 1 to T.last do
      begin
        temp := ord(T.body[i]);
```
{ Get the integer value corresponding to the character code of the ith byte. This will work }
{ with any character code, i.e. ASCII or EBCDIC, although the resulting values and }
{ therefore the encryptions will be different. }
```
        power := 128;                               { That is, 2**7 = 128. }
        for j := 0 to 7 do
          begin                             { Calculate the jth bit of the (i-1)st byte }
            BT.body[(i - 1) * 8 + j] := (temp div power) = 1;
            temp := temp - power * (temp div power);
            power := power div 2                    { Shift one bit to the right. }
          end;
        BT.last := (T.last * 8) - 1
      end
  end;          { Procedure TextToBits }
```

{ ** }

```
procedure BitsToText (BT : Block;
                      var T : MsgOrKey);
```

{Procedure BitsToText takes as an input parameter a 64-bit string (BT), and converts it }
{ to a string of length 8 bytes. The resulting string is returned in T. }

```
  var
    i, j, temp, power : integer; { power represents a power of 2; used to get bit values. }
  begin          { Procedure BitsToText }
    for i := 1 to 8 do                              { For each character }
      begin
        temp := 0;
        power := 1;
        T.last := 8;
        for j := 7 downto 0 do                      { Add up 1-bit values raised }
          begin                                     { to the appropriate power of 2. }
            if BT.body[8 * (i - 1) + j] then
              temp := temp + power;
            power := power * 2
          end;
        T.body[i] := chr(temp)         { Find the character corresponding to the ordinal }
      end
```

end;   *{ Procedure BitsToText }*

{ *** *}*

procedure PutBlockBits (BT : Block);

{ Procedure PutBlockBits writes a Block's worth of bits to the standard output. The bits }
{ are printed as 0's and 1's, in groups of 8, with a space between. }

```pascal
   var
      i : integer;
   begin         { Procedure  PutBlockBits }
      for i := 0 to BT.last do
        begin
          if BT.body[i] then
            write('1')
          else
            write('0');
          if (i mod 8) = 7 then
            write(' ')
        end;
      writeln
   end;         { Procedure  PutBlockBits }
```

{ *** *}*

procedure IP (var M : Block);

{ Procedure IP performs the Initial Permutation of the message as described by the }
{ function IP in the Data Encryption Standard. The high degree of symmetry in the }
{ definition of IP permits the implementation of this function iteratively rather than }
{ through a table look-up. }

```pascal
   var
      i, j : integer;
      Perm : array[1..64] of integer;
{ An array to hold the values of the permutation, i.e. Perm[1] = 58, Perm[2] = 50, etc.  }
      t : Block;
      Col1 : array[1..8] of integer;
            { An array to hold eight row values from the 1st column of the  permutation. }
   begin         { Procedure IP }
      Col1[1] := 58;                        { The first column will be 58, 60, 62, 64, 57, 59, 61, 63. }
      Col1[5] := 57;
      for i := 2 to 4 do
        begin
          Col1[i] := Col1[i - 1] + 2;
          Col1[i + 4] := Col1[i + 3] + 2
        end;
      for i := 1 to 8 do                    { The value i represents the ith row of IP.}
        begin
          Perm[8 * (i - 1) + 1] := Col1[i];               { Start row i with column 1. }
          for j := 2 to 8 do                              { Fill in the rest of column i. }
            Perm[8 * (i - 1) + j] := Perm[8 * (i - 1) + (j - 1)] - 8
        end;
      for i := 0 to 63 do                    { Perform the permutation }
        t.body[i] := M.body[Perm[i + 1] - 1];
      t.last := M.last;
      M := t
   end;         { Procedure IP }
```

```
{ ******************************************************************************* }
    procedure IPInverse (var M : Block);
```

{ Procedure IPInverse performs the Inverse of the Initial Permutation of the message as }
{ described by the function IP-1 in the Data Encryption Standard. The high degree of   }
{ symmetry in the definition of IP-1 permits the implementation of this function iteratively }
{ rather than through a table look-up.   }

```
    var
      i, j : integer;
      Perm : array[1..64] of integer;
      { An array to hold the values of the permutation, i.e. Perm[1] = 40, Perm[2] = 8, etc. }
      t : Block;
      Row1 : array[1..8] of integer;
              { An array to hold eight column values from the 1st row of the  permutation.}
    begin      { Procedure IPInverse }
      Row1[1] := 40;
      Row1[2] := 8;
      for i := 2 to 4 do                      { The first row will be 40, 8, 48, 16, 56, 24, 64, 32. }
        begin
          Row1[2 * i - 1] := Row1[2 * i - 3] + 8;
          Row1[2 * i] := Row1[2 * (i - 1)] + 8
        end;
      for i := 1 to 8 do                      { The value i represents the ith column of IPInverse. }
        begin
          Perm[i] := Row1[i];                              { Start column i with row 1. }
          for j := 2 to 8 do                               { Fill in the rest of row i. }
            Perm[8 * (j - 1) + i] := Perm[8 * (j - 2) + i] - 1
        end;
      for i := 0 to 63 do                                  { Perform the permutation }
        t.body[i] := M.body[Perm[i + 1] - 1];
      t.last := M.last;
      M := t
    end;      { Procedure IPInverse }
```

```
{ ******************************************************************************* }
    procedure KeyCalcs (KString : Block;
                        var K, C, D : RoundsOfBits);
```

{ Procedure KeyCalcs performs the 16 rounds of Key calculations for the input key now }
{ found in the block KString. The 16 rounds of K, C, and D are returned from this   }
{ procedure KeyCalcs in turn calls the procedures PCOne,PCTwo to accomplish its work }

```
    var
      round : integer;                         { The round number, from 1 to 16. }
      LSSchedule : array[1..16] of integer;    { An array for the schedule of left shifts. }
      ShiftOneSet : set of 1..16; {A set to keep track of which rounds have left shift=1.}
```

```
{ ******************************************************************************* }
    procedure PCOne (KString : Block;
                     var C, D : RoundsOfBits);
```

{ Procedure PCOne implements the DES function PC-1, (for Permuted Choice - 1), which }
{ takes as its input a 56-bit string, permutes it, and writes it into C0 (first 28-bits)   }
{ and D0 (last 28 bits).   }

```
    var
        KStrImbed, T : Block; { KStrImbed is a 64-bit string for the imbedding of KString; }
        i, j, top, index : integer;
    begin        { Procedure PCOne - Permuted Choice 1 }
    index := 0;
    KStrImbed.last := KString.last;
    for i := 0 to 63 do
        if (i mod 8) <> 7 then                    { Imbed KString in 7 of every 8 bits. }
            begin
                KStrImbed.body[i] := KString.body[index];
                index := index + 1
            end
        else
            KStrImbed.body[i] := False;
    top := 56;
    index := top;
{A careful look at PC-1 shows that it is accomplished by writing the bits of its input into   }
{its output, writing row- wise (into an 8 x 7 array), and reading the first column from       }
{ bottom to top, then the second column from bottom  to top, the third from bottom to top,    }
{ and half the fourth from bottom to top. That is accomplished by the following loop.         }
    for j := 0 to 31 do
        if (j mod 8) <> 7 then
            begin
                T.body[j] := KStrImbed.body[index];
                if index >= 8 then
                    index := index - 8
                else
                    begin
                        top := top + 1;
                        index := top
                    end
            end;
{ The last four rows of the output of PC-1 are computed by reading the 7th column bottom }
{ to top, then the 6th, the 5th and the remaining half of the fourth.                    }
    top := 62;
    index := top;
    for j := 32 to 58 do
        if (j mod 8) <> 7 then
            begin
                T.body[j] := KStrImbed.body[index];
                if index >= 8 then
                    index := index - 8
                else
                    begin
                        top := top - 1;
                        index := top
                    end
            end;
    index := 27;
    for j := 59 to 62 do
        begin
            T.body[j] := KStrImbed.body[index];
            index := index - 8
        end;
{ Now the Block T contains the result of PC-1. T is split in  half, the left half (from 0 to 31)   }
{ becoming C0, and the right half (from 32 to 63) becoming D0.                                      }
    index := 0;
```

```
        for i := 0 to 31 do
          if (i mod 8) <> 7 then
            begin
              C[0].body[index] := T.body[i];
              D[0].body[index] := T.body[i + 32];
              index := index + 1
            end;
          C[0].last := 27;                    { Last values of data are established for C0, D0 }
          D[0].last := 27
        end;          { Procedure PCOne - Permuted Choice 1 }
```

{ *** }

```
        procedure PCTwo (round : integer;
                         C, D : RoundsOfBits;
                         var K : RoundsOfBits);
```

{ *Procedure PCTwo computes the function PC-2, or Permuted Choice 2 for each round of* }
{ *encryption algorithm. The input consists of the round number i, the values of Ci and Di,* }
{ *and the resulting output is the derived key Ki.* }

```
          begin          { Procedure PCTwo - Permuted Choice 2 }
```
{ *This procedure could be executed in other ways, but this will be as efficient as any,* }
{ *although the code may look rather silly. There is no apparent symmetry in PC-2 that* }
{ *would make this procedure more subject to being computed by some iterative function.* }
```
            K[round].body[0] := C[round].body[13];   K[round].body[1] := C[round].body[16];
            K[round].body[2] := C[round].body[10];   K[round].body[3] := C[round].body[23];
            K[round].body[4] := C[round].body[0];    K[round].body[5] := C[round].body[4];
            K[round].body[5] := C[round].body[4];    K[round].body[6] := C[round].body[2];
            K[round].body[7] := C[round].body[27];   K[round].body[8] := C[round].body[14];
            K[round].body[9] := C[round].body[5];    K[round].body[10] := C[round].body[20];
            K[round].body[11] := C[round].body[9];   K[round].body[12] := C[round].body[22];
            K[round].body[13] := C[round].body[18];  K[round].body[14] := C[round].body[11];
            K[round].body[15] := C[round].body[3];   K[round].body[16] := C[round].body[25];
            K[round].body[17] := C[round].body[7];   K[round].body[18] := C[round].body[15];
            K[round].body[19] := C[round].body[6];   K[round].body[20] := C[round].body[26];
            K[round].body[21] := C[round].body[19];  K[round].body[22] := C[round].body[12];
            K[round].body[23] := C[round].body[1];   K[round].body[24] := D[round].body[12];
            K[round].body[25] := D[round].body[23];  K[round].body[26] := D[round].body[2];
            K[round].body[27] := D[round].body[8];   K[round].body[28] := D[round].body[18];
            K[round].body[29] := D[round].body[26];  K[round].body[30] := D[round].body[1];
            K[round].body[31] := D[round].body[11];  K[round].body[32] := D[round].body[22];
            K[round].body[33] := D[round].body[16];  K[round].body[34] := D[round].body[4];
            K[round].body[35] := D[round].body[19];  K[round].body[36] := D[round].body[15];
            K[round].body[37] := D[round].body[20];  K[round].body[38] := D[round].body[10];
            K[round].body[39] := D[round].body[27];  K[round].body[40] := D[round].body[5];
            K[round].body[41] := D[round].body[24];  K[round].body[42] := D[round].body[17];
            K[round].body[43] := D[round].body[13];  K[round].body[44] := D[round].body[21];
            K[round].body[45] := D[round].body[7];   K[round].body[46] := D[round].body[0];
            K[round].body[47] := D[round].body[3];
            K[0].last := 47
          end;          { Procedure PCTwo - Permuted Choice 2 }
```

{ *** }

```
        begin          { Procedure Key Calculations }
          PCOne(KString, C, D);                       { Perform the permutation PC-1 }
          ShiftOneSet := [1, 2, 9, 16];
```
{ *On the first, second, ninth, and sixteenth rounds there is a left shift of one position. All* }

```
{ other rounds have shifts of two positions.                                              }
      for round := 1 to 16 do                               { Cycle through 16 rounds }
        begin
          if round in ShiftOneSet then                      { Compute the value of LS }
            LSSchedule[round] := 1                          { according to LS, the key }
          else                                              { schedule of left shifts. }
            LSSchedule[round] := 2;  { Perform the appropriate left shift on both Ci and Di. }
          CircLeftShift(C[round - 1], C[round], LSSchedule[round]);
          CircLeftShift(D[round - 1], D[round], LSSchedule[round]);
          PCTwo(round, C, D, K)                              { Execute PC-2 }
        end
    end;           { Procedure Key Calculations }
{  ************************************************************************************  }

    procedure T (i : integer;
                 SB : SBoxArrayType;
                 var L, R, K : RoundsOfBits);

{ Procedure T computes one entire round of the DES transformation. In turn, T calls F.   }

      var
        FRK : Block;                      { A block to contain the function f(R(i-1),Ki) }
        j : integer;
{  ************************************************************************************  }

      procedure F (round : integer;
                   R, K : RoundsOfBits;
                   SB : SBoxArrayType;
                   var FRK : Block);

{ Procedure F reads R(i-1) and Ki, and computes the DES function  f(R(i-1),Ki) =         }
{ P(S(E(R(i-1)) XOR Ki )). F calls in the functions E, SBoxes, XOR, and P (and XOR is    }
{ already  defined above.                                                                }

        var
          ER, ERK, SE : Block;
{  ************************************************************************************  }

        procedure E (R : Block;
                     var ER : Block);

{ Procedure E imbeds the block R (of length 32 bits) in a block of length 48 bits, called }
{ E(R). This represents  the DES function E.                                             }

          var
            i, index : integer;
          begin              {Procedure E}
          ER.last := 47;
{The DES function E imbeds every four bits of R in a 6-bit block,where the 1st bit of the }
{ 6-bit block is the last bit of the preceding 4-bit block, and the 6th bit of the 6-bit block }
{ is the 1st bit of the following 4-bit block. Note that "preceding" and "following" are  }
{ thought of cyclically: the  first 4-bit block follows the last, etc.                    }
          ER.body[0] := R.body[31];
          ER.body[47] := R.body[0];
          for i := 0 to 31 do                          { Place the 32 bits of E appropriately. }
            ER.body[i + (2 * (i div 4)) + 1] := R.body[i];
          for i := 1 to 7 do           { Compute the other 16 bits from their neighbors in E. }
```

```
        begin
          ER.body[6 * (i - 1) + 5] := ER.body[6 * i + 1];
          ER.body[6 * i] := ER.body[6 * i - 2]
        end
    end;                    {Procedure E}
```

{ ** }

```
    procedure SBoxes (E : Block;
                      SB : SBoxArrayType;
                      var SE : Block);
```

{ *Procedure SBoxes computes the S-Box functions on its input block E, returning the* }
{ *block SE. To accomplish this, SBoxes computes the eight 6-bit blocks of E, and calls* }
{ *ComputeSBox to shrink the 6-bit blocks to 4-bits.* }

```
    type
      Block6 = array[0..5] of boolean;                    { A 6-bit array }
      Block4 = array[0..3] of boolean;                    { A 4-bit array }
    var
      B : array[1..8] of Block6;                      { B - 8 arrays of 6-bits }
      ShrunkenB : array[1..8] of Block4;                { 8 arrays of 4 bits }
      i, j : integer;
```

{ ** }

```
    procedure ComputeSBox (S : SBoxType;
                           B : Block6;
                           var ShrunkenB : Block4);
```

{ *Procedure ComputeSBox performs the individual computation of S-Box values on the* }
{ *block B, returning the block ShrunkenB. To do this, it uses the values contained in the* }
{ *input array S, which contains all of the values of the 8 S-Boxes.* }

```
        var
          i, row, col, power : integer;
        begin          {Procedure ComputeSBox}
          row := 0;
```
{ *The values in B must be converted from 6-bit strings to pairs of integers. This is* }
{ *accomplished here. The first and last bit of B yield a row number, in the range 0..3,* }
{ *for the index into the appropriate S-box.* }
```
          if B[0] then
            row := row + 2;
          if B[5] then
            row := row + 1;
          col := 0;
          power := 1;
```
{ *The middle four bits of B are converted to an integer in order to give a column number,* }
{ *in the range 0..15, as an index into the column of the appropriate S-Box.* }
```
          for i := 4 downto 1 do
            begin
              if B[i] then
                col := col + power;
              power := power * 2
            end;
          power := 8;
          i := 0;
```
{ *Now compute the shrunken 4-bit string according to the value found in the S-Box.* }
{ *Convert this value, which is in the range 0..15, into a 4-bit string.* }

```
          while i <= 3 do
            begin
              ShrunkenB[i] := (S[row, col] >= power);
              if ShrunkenB[i] then
                S[row, col] := S[row, col] - power;
              i := i + 1;
              power := power div 2
            end
        end;        {Procedure ComputeSBox}
```

{ *** }

```
        begin      {Procedure SBoxes}
          for i := 1 to 8 do                          { Compute the 8 S-Box functions. }
            begin
              for j := 0 to 5 do
                B[i, j] := E.body[6 * (i - 1) + j];
                                        { Assign the appropriate 6-bit block of E to B[i]}
              ComputeSBox(SB[i], B[i], ShrunkenB[i])
                                        { Submit B[i] to the appropriate S-Box }
            end;            { Reconvert the 8 ShrunkenB 4-bit arrays to the 32-bit block SE. }
          for i := 1 to 8 do
            for j := 0 to 3 do
              SE.body[4 * (i - 1) + j] := ShrunkenB[i, j];
          SE.last := 31
        end;        {Procedure SBoxes}
```

{ *** }

```
        procedure P (SE : Block;
                        var FRK : Block);
```

{ Procedure P performs the permutation P on 32-bit strings.   }

```
        begin      { Procedure P }
```
{ This procedure could be executed in other ways, but this will be as efficient as any,   }
{ although the code may look rather silly. There is no apparent symmetry in P that   }
{ would make this procedure more subject to being computed by some iterative function. }
```
          FRK.last := 31;
          FRK.body[0] := SE.body[15];          FRK.body[1] := SE.body[6];
          FRK.body[2] := SE.body[19];          FRK.body[3] := SE.body[20];
          FRK.body[4] := SE.body[28];          FRK.body[5] := SE.body[11];
          FRK.body[6] := SE.body[27];          FRK.body[7] := SE.body[16];
          FRK.body[8] := SE.body[0];           FRK.body[9] := SE.body[14];
          FRK.body[10] := SE.body[22];         FRK.body[11] := SE.body[25];
          FRK.body[12] := SE.body[4];          FRK.body[13] := SE.body[17];
          FRK.body[14] := SE.body[30];         FRK.body[15] := SE.body[9];
          FRK.body[16] := SE.body[1];          FRK.body[17] := SE.body[7];
          FRK.body[18] := SE.body[23];         FRK.body[19] := SE.body[13];
          FRK.body[20] := SE.body[31];         FRK.body[21] := SE.body[26];
          FRK.body[22] := SE.body[2];          FRK.body[23] := SE.body[8];
          FRK.body[24] := SE.body[18];         FRK.body[25] := SE.body[12];
          FRK.body[26] := SE.body[29];         FRK.body[27] := SE.body[5];
          FRK.body[28] := SE.body[21];         FRK.body[29] := SE.body[10];
          FRK.body[30] := SE.body[3];          FRK.body[31] := SE.body[24]
        end;        { Procedure P }
```

{ *** }

```
        begin      { Procedure F }
```

```
        E(R[round], ER);              { Get the appropriate value of Ri, imbed it in ER = E(Ri). }
        XOR(ER, K[round + 1], ERK);  { Get the XOR of ER = E(Ri) with K(i+1), giving ERK. }
                    { Submit ERK to the S-Boxes, yielding SE = S(ERK) = S(E(Ri) XOR K(i+1)). }
        SBoxes(ERK, SB, SE);
        { Compute the permutation P on SE, yielding FRK = P(SE) = P( S(E(Ri) XOR K(i+1)) ) }
                                                                            { = f(Ri, K(i+1)). }
        P(SE, FRK)
      end;      { Procedure F }
```

{ *** }

```
      begin        { Procedure T }
        L[i + 1] := R[i];                                  { Compute the new L(i+1) (= Ri ) }
        F(i, R, K, SB, FRK);                                              { Compute f. }
        XOR(L[i], FRK, R[i + 1])              { XOR the results of f with Li, yielding R(i+1). }
      end;      { Procedure T }
```

{ *** }

```
  begin         { Main Program  DataEncryption Standard }
    SBoxFileName := 'SBoxNumbers';
                  { Open the external file SBoxNumbers which contains the S-Box Numbers. }
    Open(SNumbers, SBoxFileName);         { Read the S-Box Numbers into the array SB. }
    for i := 1 to 8 do
       for row := 0 to 3 do
          for col := 0 to 15 do
             read(SNumbers, SB[i, row, col]);
    for i := 0 to 16 do                    { Initialize the lengths of L,R,K,C,D blocks. }
       begin
          L[i].last := 31;
          R[i].last := 31;
          K[i].last := 47;
          C[i].last := 27;
          D[i].last := 27
       end;
    writeln('Please enter your 8-byte message:');
    GetText(Message);                                                       { Echo it back. }
    writeln('The message in character form is: ');
    PutText(Message);
    writeln;
    writeln('And in bit form is : ');
    TextToBits(Message, MString);
    PutBlockBits(MString);
    IP(MString);                                              {Perform the initial permutation. }
    for i := 0 to 31 do  { Assign to L0 and R0 }
       begin
          L[0].body[i] := MString.body[i];
          R[0].body[i] := MString.body[32 + i]
       end;
    writeln;
    writeln('Please enter your 7-byte key:');
    GetText(KeyText;                                                         { Echo it back. }
    writeln('The key in character form is: ');
    PutText(KeyText);
    writeln;
    writeln('And in bit form is : ');
    TextToBits(KeyText, KString);
    PutBlockBits(KString);
    writeln;
```

```
KeyCalcs(KString, K, C, D);                    { Perform the key calculations. }
for i := 0 to 15 do                            { Perform the 16 rounds of DES. }
  T(i, SB, L, R, K);
{ Note that on the 16th round of DES, the left and right halves  are not switched. This    }
{ algorithm has switched them (above)  and now switches them right back:                    }
temp := R[16].body;
R[16].body := L[16].body;
L[16].body := temp;
CString.last := 63;                            { Initialize the length of the Cipher string. }
for i := 0 to 31 do                            { Assign L16 and R16 to the Cipher string. }
  CString.body[i] := L[16].body[i];
for i := 32 to 63 do
  CString.body[i] := R[16].body[i - 32];
           { Finally, perform the inverse permutation IP-1, giving the  cipher text CString. }
IPInverse(CString);
writeln;
writeln('The ciphertext is: ');
writeln;
PutBlockBits(CString);
writeln;
writeln;          { There is an option for the listing of all details of the DES transformation.   }
                  { This is presented interactively. }
writeln('If you want to see the details of the DES calculation,');
writeln('in other words, the values of Ci, Di, Ki, Li, and Ri, ');
writeln('please indicate so by typing "y" for yes (or "n" for no. ');
writeln('("n" is the default): ');
readln(ch);
if (ch = 'y') or (ch = 'Y') then
  begin
    writeln;
    writeln('********************');
    writeln;
    writeln('Ci, i = 0 to 16: ');
    writeln;
    for i := 0 to 16 do
      PutBlockBits(C[i]);
    writeln;
    writeln('********************');
    writeln;
    writeln('Di, i = 0 to 16: ');
    writeln;
    for i := 0 to 16 do
      PutBlockBits(D[i]);
    writeln;
    writeln('********************');
    writeln;
    writeln('Ki, i = 0 to 16: ');
    writeln;
    for i := 0 to 16 do
      PutBlockBits(K[i]);
    writeln;
    writeln('********************');
    writeln;
    writeln('Li, i = 0 to 16: ');
    writeln;
    for i := 0 to 16 do
      PutBlockBits(L[i]);
```

```
        writeln;
        writeln('********************');
        writeln;
        writeln('Ri, i = 0 to 16: ');
        writeln;
        for i := 0 to 16 do
           PutBlockBits(R[i])
      end;
```

{   **   }

{ Now for the decryption process. We have to re-run the 16 rounds, but we will   }
{ invert the Ki's, exchanging 1 for 16, 2 for 15, etc.   }

```
      writeln;
      writeln('DECRYPTION PROCESS: ');
      writeln;
      writeln('The ciphertext is:');
      PutBlockBits(CString);
      KTemp.last := K[1].last;
      IP(CString);                              { Perform IP on the cipher text. }
      for i := 0 to 31 do                       { Start up again with the cipher text }
        begin          { as the initial text }
           L[0].body[i] := CString.body[i];
           R[0].body[i] := CString.body[32 + i]
        end;
      for i := 1 to 8 do                         { Reverse the order of the derived keys Ki. }
        begin
           KTemp := K[i];
           K[i] := K[17 - i];
           K[17 - i] := KTemp
        end;
      for i := 0 to 15 do                         { Perform the 16 DES rounds. }
        T(i, SB, L, R, K);
      temp := R[16].body;                      { Undo the switch of the halves on round 16.}
      R[16].body := L[16].body;
      L[16].body := temp;
      MString.last := 63;            { Compute the new value of MString from L16 and R16. }
      for i := 0 to 31 do
        MString.body[i] := L[16].body[i];
      for i := 32 to 63 do
        MString.body[i] := R[16].body[i - 32];
      IPInverse(MString);                                      { Finally apply IPInverse }
      writeln;
      writeln('The original text is:  ');
      writeln;
      PutBlockBits(MString);
      BitsToText(MString, Message);
      writeln;
      PutText(Message)
   end.          { Main Program  DataEncryption Standard }
```

```
program LargePrime(INPUT, OUTPUT);
```

{ Program P7: The Lehmann and Peralta Primality Test.   }

{Clara Jaramillo   July 14,1986 Csci 4990 - 001 / Dr. Patterson   }
{TASK: The purpose of this program is to determine whether a 100 digit integer is }
{prime or not prime. The method used is the primality test due to Lehmann & Peralta. }

{INPUT:The input file will consist of any number of lines. Each line will consist of }
{ one 100 digit integer.   }

{OUTPUT: The output file will tell for each large integer, whether the large   }
{ digit integer is prime or not. If there was an error in the input file , then an error }
{ message will be displayed.   }

{ NOTE: Although this program is written for large integers of up to 200 digits, running }
{ this program under interpreted Macintosh Pascal will result in extremely long }
{runs, unless the size of the integers and the number of primality tests performed }
{(100 in this program) are reduced significantly.Otherwise, this program could be }
{more reasonably run in a compiled version.   }

```
   const
     max = 100;                              { max value for a large integer }
     limit = 200;                            { limit on index of large integer array }
   type
     digits = 0..9;                                          { digits are 0..9 }
     largetype = array[1..limit] of digits;     { holds digits of a large integer }
     largeint = record
         number : largetype;                            { digits of the integer }
         last : 0..limit;                       { index of first digit of integer }
       end;
   var
     Candat : largeint;              { large integer that will be tested for primality }
     Numberprimecandat,
             { true if the number is not factorable by a small prime number, otherwise false }
     Prime,                             { true if the number is prime,otherwise false }
     Errormessage : boolean;               { true if error in input,otherwise false }
{   ********************************************************************************* }
   procedure Lettermessage;
```

{TASK: The task of this procedure is to give an error message because the digits }
{entered did not produce an integer.   }
{INPUT: none.   }
{OUTPUT: The output will consist of several lines explaining the error.   }

```
   begin        { begin procedure lettermessage }
     writeln('   ***** ERROR *****');
     writeln('The digits that have been entered');
     writeln(' include a character that is not');
     writeln('  a number between 0 and 9.');
     writeln(' Operation will not proceed.');
     writeln('   Please check input.');
     writeln('   ***** ERROR *****');
     writeln
   end;        { end procedure lettermessage }
{   ********************************************************************************* }
   procedure Digiterrormessage;
```

{TASK: The task of this procedure is to give an error message because the total }
{ number of the digits was more than 100.   }

```
{INPUT: none.                                                                              }
{OUTPUT: The output will consist of several lines explaining the error.                    }

   begin        { begin digiterrormessage }
     writeln('     ***** ERROR *****');
     writeln('The number that has been entered');
     writeln(' is larger than 100 digits.');
     writeln(' Operation will not proceed.');
     writeln('   Please check input.');
     writeln('     ***** ERROR *****');
     writeln
   end;         { end procedure digiterrormessage }
{   ********************************************************************************* }

   procedure JUSTIFY (var candat : largeint);

{TASK:   The task of this procedure is to justify to the right the large integer.        }
{ INPUT:  The input will be: candat - the large integer.                                 }
{OUTPUT: The output will be:candat - the right justified large integer.                  }

   var
     tempint : largetype;                          {temporary storage for an integer }
     X,                                            {used as index for array}
     INDEX : integer;                              {used as index for loop}
   begin        { begin procedure justify }
     X := limit;                                              {initialize to limit}
     for INDEX := candat.last downto 1 do        { right justify the integer in the array }
       begin
         tempint[X] := candat.number[INDEX];                          {transfer digits}
         X := X - 1
       end;
     candat.last := X + 1;
     while (X > 0) do            { add leading zeros to fill up the integer in the array }
       begin
         tempint[X] := 0;
         X := X - 1
       end;
     candat.number := tempint                     { candat is right justified }
   end;         { end procedure justify }
{   ********************************************************************************* }

   procedure Readin (var candat : largeint;
                     var Ermessage : boolean);

{TASK: The task of this procedure is to read in the digits of the large integer. The      }
{ procedure will also write an error message if the digits being read is more than        }
{ 100 digits or if the digits entered have a digit that is not an integer.                }
{INPUT: The input will be: Nextint-the digit that is entered.                             }
{ OUTPUT: The output will be: Candat  - the large integer.                                }
{                      Ermessage-true if error in input,false if no error.                }

   var
     Bad : boolean;                          { true if error in input, otherwise false }
     Nextint : char;                         { a digit of the large integer }
     index : integer;
   begin        { begin procedure readin }
     Bad := false;                                    {initialize bad to false}
     candat.last := 0;                                {initialize  to 0 }
     while (not Bad) and (not eoln) do
       begin
```

```
            read(NEXTINT);                              {see if digit is not an integer}
            if (ord(nextint) < ord('0')) or (ord(nextint) > ord('9')) then
              begin                                     {digit is not an integer}
                ERMESSAGE := true;
                LETTERMESSAGE;
                Bad := true
              end                    {see if large number exceeds more than 100 digits }
            else if (candat.last >= MAX) then
              begin                                {more than 100 digits were entered}
                Bad := true;
                ERMESSAGE := true;
                DIGITERRORMESSAGE
              end
            else                                         { large integer is valid }
              begin
                candat.last := candat.last + 1;
                candat.number[candat.last] := ord(NEXTiNT) - ord('0')
              end
          end;
        if not eof then                                  { point to next line of input }
          readln;
        writeln('The prime candat: ');
        for index := 1 to candat.last do
          write(candat.number[index] : 1);
        writeln;
        if not bad then
          justify(candat);                               { right justify the large integer }
        writeln;
      end;        { end procedure readin }
{   ********************************************************************************* }

    procedure clearnumber (var number : largeint);

{ TASK:   The task of this procedure is to initialize number to zero.               }
{INPUT:  The input will be: number - the number to be initialized to zero.          }
{OUTPUT: The output will be: number - the number initialized to zero.               }

      var
        i : integer; { index for loop }
      begin          { begin procedure clearnumber }
        for i := 1 to limit do
          number.number[i] := 0;
        number.last := limit;
      end;        { end procedure clearnumber }
{   ********************************************************************************* }

    procedure Add (number1, number2 : largeint;
                   var answer : largeint);

{TASK:   The task of this procedure is to add the two large integers.               }
{INPUT:  The input will be:   number1 - first number to be added.                   }
{                             number2 - second number to be added.                  }
{OUTPUT: The output will be: answer - equals first number + second number           }

      var
        found : boolean;                                 { flag for loop }
        i,                                               { index for loop }
        Carry,                                           { used to carry in addition }
        F,                                               { index of the bigger integer }
        Index,                                           { holds position in the array }
```

```
      Sum : integer;                          { sum of the value in the index of both arrays }
begin      { begin procedure add }
   clearnumber(answer);                                           { answer := 0 }
   Carry := 0;                                         { initialize CARRY }
   if (Number1.last < Number2.last) then
      F := Number1.last                                { first number is bigger }
   else
      F := Number2.last;                               { second number is bigger }
   for INDEX := limit downto F do                      { add number1 and number2 }
      begin
         SUM := Number1.number[INDEX] + Number2.number[INDEX];   { add two digits }
         Answer.number[Answer.Last] := (SUM + CARRY) mod 10;   { add with the carry }
         Answer.Last := Answer.Last - 1;
         if ((SUM + CARRY) div 10 = 1) then                    { see if you have to carry }
            CARRY := 1                                          { carry 1 }
         else
            CARRY := 0                                          { no carry }
      end;
   Answer.Last := Answer.Last + 1;
   if (CARRY = 1) then                               { add the carry if necessary }
      begin
         Answer.Last := Answer.Last - 1;
         Answer.number[Answer.Last] := 1
      end;
   found := false;            { have the index of answer point to the first non-zero digit }
   i := 1;
   while (not found) and (i <= limit) do
      if answer.number[i] <> 0 then
         found := true
      else
         i := i + 1;
   if i = (limit + 1) then
      answer.last := limit
   else
      answer.last := i
end;      { end procedure add }
```

{ *** }

```
   procedure Subtraction (first, second : largeint;
                   var answer : largeint);
```

{TASK: The task of this procedure is to subtract the second integer from the first   }
{INPUT: The input will be: First- the number to be subtracted from.   }
{   Second- the number that will be subtracted.   }
{OUTPUT: The output will be: Answer - equals first - second   }

```
   var
      Found : boolean;                                     { flag for loop }
      Temp,                                                { index }
      I : integer;                                         { index }
begin      { begin procedure subtraction }
   clearnumber(answer);                                    { answer := 0 }
   for I := limit downto first.last do              { subtract second from first }
      begin
         if FIRST.number[I] < SECOND.number[I] then    { see if you have to borrow }
            begin                                          {have to borrow}
               ANSWER.number[Answer.last]
                        := FIRST.number[I] + 10 - SECOND.number[I];
               TEMP := I - 1;
```

```
            while (first.number[TEMP] = 0) do                        {find the num <> 0}
               begin
                  first.number[TEMP] := 9;
                  TEMP := TEMP - 1
               end;
               first.number[temp] := first.number[temp] - 1
            end
          else                                                {don't have to borrow}
             ANSWER.number[Answer.last] := FIRST.number[I] - SECOND.number[I];
          Answer.last := Answer.last - 1
       end;
     found := false;                  { have the index of answer point to the first non-zero digit }
     i := 1;
     while (not found) and (i <= limit) do
        if answer.number[i] <> 0 then
           found := true
        else
           i := i + 1;
     if i = (limit + 1) then
        answer.last := limit
     else
        answer.last := i
  end;        { end procedure subtraction }
```
{ *** }
```
  function equal (number1, number2 : largeint) : boolean;
```
{TASK: The task of this function is to see if two numbers are equal.   }
{INPUT: The input will be: number1 - the first number, number2 - the second number.   }
{OUTPUT: The output will be: boolean true if number1 = number2 , otherwise false.   }
```
     var
        first : integer;
     begin        { begin function equal }
        if not (number1.last = number2.last) then              { see if the numbers are equal }
           equal := false                        { numbers are of different length so not equal }
        else                                                    { see if the digits are equal }
           begin
              first := number1.last;
              while ((number1.number[first] = number2.number[first]) and (first < limit)) do
                 first := first + 1;
              if number1.number[first] = number2.number[first] then
                 equal := true                                          { numbers are equal }
              else
                 equal := false                                     { numbers are not equal }
           end
     end;        { end function equal }
```
{ *** }
```
  function lessthan (number1, number2 : largeint) : boolean;
```
{TASK: The task of this function is to see if number1 is less than number2.   }
{ INPUT: The input will be: number1 - the number to be tested against number2.   }
{   number2 - the number to be tested against number1.   }
{ OUTPUT: The output will be boolean true if number1 < number2 , otherwise false.   }
```
     var
        first : integer;   { index for large integer }
     begin        { begin function lessthan }
        if number1.last < number2.last then
```

```
        lessthan := false
      else if number1.last > number2.last then
        lessthan := true
      else
        begin
          first := number1.last;              { check the digits to see if number1 < number2 }
          while ((number1.number[first] = number2.number[first]) and (first < limit)) do
            first := first + 1;
          if number1.number[first] < number2.number[first] then
            lessthan := true
          else
            lessthan := false
        end
    end;      { end function lessthan }
```

{ *** }

```
    procedure Subtract (Number1, number2 : largeint;
                        var answer : largeint;
                        var negative : boolean);
```

{TASK: The task of this procedure is to determine the largest of the two input numbers, }
{ then to perform the subtraction of the smaller in magnitude from the larger.   }
{INPUT: The input will be: number1 - number to subtract from.   }
{   number2 - the number to be subtracted.   }
{OUTPUT: The output will be: negative - true if the result will be a negative number.   }
{   Answer - equals abs(number1 - number2)   }

```
      var
        FIRST,                                              {index of first number }
        SECOND : integer;                                   {index of second number}
      begin       { begin procedure subtract }
        negative := false;                               { difference starts off as positive }
                                          { subtract the smaller number from the larger number }
        if (lessthan(number2, number1)) then                {first number is larger}
          SUBTRACTION(number1, number2, answer)
        else if (lessthan(number1, number2)) then           {second number is larger}
          begin
            SUBTRACTION(number2, number1, answer);
            negative := true                                {answer is negative}
          end
        else                                               { numbers are equal }
          SUBTRACTION(number1, number2, answer)
      end;      { end procedure subtract }
```

{ *** }

```
    function notmodded (number1, modsys : largeint) : boolean;
```

{TASK: The task of this function is to see if you still have to mod number1 by modsys.   }
{INPUT: The input will be: number1-the number to be tested to see if it has to be modded. }
{   modsys - the mod system.   }
{OUTPUT: The output will be boolean true if the number has not been modded, else false. }

```
      begin       { begin function notmodded }
        if lessthan(number1, modsys) then                { notmodded is true if number1 is }
          notmodded := false                             { larger than or equal to modsys }
        else if lessthan(modsys, number1) then
          notmodded := true
        else
          notmodded := true
      end;        { end function notmodded }
```

```
{ ***************************************************************************** }
   procedure transfer (var number1 : largeint;
                number2 : largeint);

{ TASK:  The task of this procedure is to assign the number2 to number1.       }
{ INPUT:  The input will be: number1 - the number that will be assigned to.     }
{                     number2 - the number that will transfer to number1.       }
{ OUTPUT: The output will be : number1 := number2.                             }

   begin        { begin procedure transfer }
      number1.last := number2.last;
      number1.number := number2.number
   end;         { end procedure transfer }
{ ***************************************************************************** }
   procedure Multiply (First, Second : largeint;
                var answer : largeint);

{TASK:  The task of this procedure is to multiply the two integers.            }
{INPUT:  The input will be: first, second - two numbers that will be multiplied. }
{OUTPUT: The output  will be: answer = equals first * second.                  }

   var
      found : boolean;                              { flag for loop }
      tempanswer : largeint;                { temporary storage location }
      INDEX,                                             { index}
      CARRY,                           { used to carry in multiplication}
      I,                                                 { index}
      RESULT,                          { result of the multiplication}
      TEMP : integer;                            { temporary answer}
   begin        { begin procedure multiply }
      clearnumber(answer);       { answer := 0. Now use normal multiplication algorithm}
      for INDEX := limit downto second.last do         {sum the partial products}
         begin
            CARRY := 0;
            Answer.last := index;
            for I := limit downto first.last do                    {compute partial products}
               begin
                  RESULT := SECOND.number[INDEX] * FIRST.number[I];
                  TEMP := RESULT + CARRY + Answer.number[Answer.last];
                  Answer.number[Answer.last] := TEMP mod 10;
                  CARRY := TEMP div 10;
                  Answer.last := Answer.last - 1
               end;
            if (CARRY > 0) then
               begin
                  Answer.number[Answer.last] := CARRY;
                  Answer.last := Answer.last
               end
            else
               Answer.last := Answer.last + 1
         end;
      found := false;           { have the index of answer point to the first non-zero digit }
      i := 1;
      while (not found) and (i <= limit) do
         if answer.number[i] <> 0 then
            found := true
         else
            i := i + 1;
```

```
     if i = (limit + 1) then
        answer.last := limit
     else
        answer.last := i
     end;        { end procedure multiply }
{    ************************************************************************************* }

     procedure division (var number1, number2 : largeint;
                         var answer, remainder : largeint;
                         var negative : boolean);
```

{TASK: The task of this procedure is to divide number1 by number2.   }
{INPUT: The input will be: number1 - the dividend; number2 - the divisor.   }
{OUTPUT: The output will be: answer - equals number1 div number2.   }
{   remainder- the remainder from number1 div number2   }

```
     var
        first,count, i : integer;                                        { indexes }
        sum,                                                  { holds sum to be divided }
        largecount,                                                      { counter }
        temp,                                                    { temporary location }
        tempanswer,                                              { temporary location }
        one,                                                       { the number one }
        ten : largeint;                                            { the number 10 }
        firstnumbergotten,              { boolean true if firstnumber was gotten to divide }
        found,                                                      { flag for loop }
        done : boolean;              { boolean true if done dividing,otherwise false }
     begin        { begin procedure divide }
        clearnumber(largecount);                         { initialization :  largecount := 0 }
        clearnumber(ten);                                             { ten := 0 }
        clearnumber(answer);                                       { answer := 0 }
        clearnumber(remainder);                                  { remainder := 0 }
        clearnumber(one);                                             { one := 0 }
        clearnumber(sum);                                             { sum := 0 }
        done := false;                                       { start off as not done }
        ten.last := limit - 1;                                        { ten := 10 }
        ten.number[ten.last] := 1;
        one.number[one.last] := 1;                                    { one := 1 }
        first := number1.last;
           { answer := number1 div number 2; remainder - remainder of number1 div number2 }
        while not done do                                       { divide longhand }
           begin
              firstnumbergotten := false;
              while (lessthan(sum, number2)) and (first <= limit) do
                 begin
                    clearnumber(tempanswer);
                    multiply(sum, ten, tempanswer);
                    transfer(sum, tempanswer);
                    if firstnumbergotten then
                       begin
                          clearnumber(temp);
                          multiply(answer, ten, temp);
                          transfer(answer, temp)
                       end;
                    clearnumber(temp);
                    temp.number[temp.last] := number1.number[first];
                    clearnumber(tempanswer);
                    add(sum, temp, tempanswer);
                    transfer(sum, tempanswer);
```

```
                    first := first + 1;
                    firstnumbergotten := true
                 end;
              if lessthan(sum, number2) then
                 begin                                            { have a remainder }
                    clearnumber(tempanswer);
                    multiply(answer, ten, tempanswer);
                    transfer(answer, tempanswer);
                    transfer(remainder, sum);
                    done := true
                 end
              else                                                { here to divide }
                 begin
                    count := 0;
                    while (lessthan(number2, sum)) or (equal(number2, sum)) do
                       begin
                          count := count + 1;
                          clearnumber(tempanswer);
                          subtract(sum, number2, tempanswer, negative);
                          transfer(sum, tempanswer)
                       end;
                    largecount.number[limit] := count;
                    clearnumber(tempanswer);
                    multiply(answer, ten, tempanswer);
                    transfer(answer, tempanswer);
                    clearnumber(tempanswer);
                    add(answer, largecount, tempanswer);
                    transfer(answer, tempanswer);
                    found := false;
                    i := 1;
                    while (not found) and (i <= limit) do
                       if answer.number[i] <> 0 then
                          found := true
                       else
                          i := i + 1;
                    if i = (limit + 1) then
                       answer.last := limit
                    else
                       answer.last := i;
                    if (lessthan(sum, number2) and (first > limit)) then
                       begin                                       { have a remainder }
                          transfer(remainder, sum);
                          done := true
                       end
                 end
           end
     end;        { end procedure divide }
{ ************************************************************************************** }
     procedure Multmod (First, Second, modsys : largeint;
                        var answer : largeint;
                        var negative : boolean);

{TASK:   The task of this procedure is to multiply the two integers.              }
{INPUT:  The input will be: first, second - the two numbers to be multiplied mod modsys.  }
{OUTPUT: The output will be: answer - equals (first * second) mod modsys         }

     var
        found : boolean;                                          { flag for loop }
```

```
        one,                                                    { number 1 }
        modsysminusone,                                         { number = modsys - 1 }
        remainder,                                              { remainder when dividing }
        tempanswer : largeint;                                  { answer from multiplying }
        INDEX,                                                           {index}
        CARRY,                                          {used to carry in multiplication}
        I,                                                              {index}
        RESULT,                                         {result of the multiplication}
        TEMP : integer;                                         {temporary answer}
    begin       { begin procedure multmod }
      clearnumber(answer);                                      { answer := 0 }
      for INDEX := limit downto second.last do
        begin
          CARRY := 0;
          Answer.last := index;
          for I := limit downto first.last do
            begin
              RESULT := SECOND.number[INDEX] * FIRST.number[I];
              TEMP := RESULT + CARRY + Answer.number[Answer.last];
              Answer.number[Answer.last] := TEMP mod 10;
              CARRY := TEMP div 10;
              Answer.last := Answer.last - 1
            end;
          if (CARRY > 0) then
            begin
              Answer.number[Answer.last] := CARRY;
              Answer.last := Answer.last
            end
          else
            Answer.last := Answer.last + 1
        end;
      found := false;              { have the index of last point to the first non-zero digit }
      i := 1;
      while (not found) and (i <= limit) do
        if answer.number[i] <> 0 then
          found := true
        else
          i := i + 1;
      if i = (limit + 1) then
        answer.last := limit
      else
        answer.last := i;                  { make sure answer has been modded by modsys }
      if notmodded(answer, modsys) then
        begin                                             { here to mod answer }
          clearnumber(remainder);
          clearnumber(tempanswer);
          division(answer, modsys, tempanswer, remainder, negative);
          transfer(answer, remainder)
        end;                               { make sure the number has been modded }
      clearnumber(modsysminusone);                            { if answer = modsys - 1 then }
      clearnumber(one);                             {mod one more time to get answer as -1 }
      one.number[one.last] := 1;
      subtract(modsys, one, modsysminusone, negative);
      if (equal(answer, modsysminusone)) then
        begin
          clearnumber(tempanswer);
          subtract(answer, modsys, tempanswer, negative);
```

```
                transfer(answer, tempanswer);
          end
     end;        { end procedure multmod }
{    ********************************************************************************* }

     function even (number : largeint) : boolean;

{ TASK:  The task of this function is to see if the number is an even number.        }
{ INPUT:  The input will be: number - the number to be tested.                       }
{ OUTPUT:  The output will be boolean true if the number is even , otherwise false.  }

     begin        { begin function even }
          if (number.number[limit] mod 2) = 0 then    { the number is even if number mod 2 = 0 }
             even := true
          else
             even := false
     end;         { end function even }
{    ********************************************************************************* }

     function divBy3 (number : largeint) : boolean;

{TASK:  The task of this function is to see if the number is divisible by 3.         }
{INPUT:  The input will be: number - the number to be tested.                        }
{OUTPUT: The output will be boolean true if the number is divisible by three.        }

     var
        sum,                                        { sum of the digits of the number }
        count : integer;                                            { index for loop }
     begin        { begin function divby3 }
        sum := 0; { the number is divisible by three if the sum of the digits is divisible by three}
        for count := number.last to limit do
          sum := sum + number.number[count];
        if (sum mod 3) = 0 then
          divBy3 := true
        else
          divBy3 := false
     end;         { end function divby3 }
{    ********************************************************************************* }

     function lastDigit5 (number : largeint) : boolean;

{TASK:   The task of this function is to see if the last digit of the number is a 5.   }
{INPUT:  The input will be: number - the number to be tested.                          }
{OUTPUT: The output will be boolean true if the last digit of the number is a 5.       }

     begin        { begin function lastdigit5 }
        if (number.number[limit] = 5) then
          lastDigit5 := true
        else
          lastDigit5 := false
     end;         { end function lastdigit5 }
{    ********************************************************************************* }

     function divBy11 (number : largeint) : boolean;

{TASK:   The task of this function is to see if the number is divisible by 11.         }
{INPUT:  The input will be: number - the number to be tested.                          }
{OUTPUT: The output will be boolean true if the number is divisible by 11.             }

     var
        sum1,                   { sum of digits of the even digit positions of the number }
        sum2,                                            { sum of every other digit }
```

```
            count : integer;                                        { index for loop }
      begin        { begin function divisibleby11 }
{ A number is divisible by 11 if the sum of its digits in the even positions is equal to the    }
{sum  of its digits in the odd positions, mod 11.                                               }
         sum1 := 0;                                        { start off with sums = 0 }
         sum2 := 0;
         for count := number.last to limit do
           begin
             if (count mod 2) = 0 then
                sum1 := sum1 + number.number[count]
             else
                sum2 := sum2 + number.number[count]
           end;
         if sum1 = sum2 then
            divBy11 := true
         else if (abs(sum1 - sum2) mod 11) = 0 then
            divBy11 := true
         else
            divBy11 := false
      end;        { end function divisibleby11 }
{    ************************************************************************************    }

      function notZero (number : largeint) : boolean;

{TASK:  The task of this function is to see if the number is zero.                    }
{INPUT:  The input will be : number - the number to be tested.                        }
{OUTPUT:  The output will be boolean true if the number is not zero, otherwise false. }

      begin        { begin function notzero }
         if (number.last = limit) and (number.number[number.last] = 0) then
            notzero := false
         else
            notzero := true
      end;        { end function notzero }
{    ************************************************************************************    }

      procedure getaNumber (var seed : integer;
                            var number : largeint;
                            modsys : largeint);

{ TASK:  The task of this proc is to generate a random number in the range (1, modsys). }
{ INPUT:  The input will be: seed - the generator for random numbers.                   }
{                            modsys - number the random number cannot exceed.           }
{ OUTPUT:  The output will be: number - the randomly generated number.                  }

      var
         throw,                                             { random number }
         i : integer;                                       { index for loop }
         found : boolean;                                   { flag for loop }
      begin        { begin function getanumber }
         clearnumber(number);                               { number := 0 }
         if notzero(modsys) then
           begin                                            { get a random large number }
             for i := limit downto (modsys.last) do
               begin
                 throw := random mod 10;
                 number.number[i] := throw;
               end;
             i := 1;
             while (number.number[i] <> 0) and (i < 200) do  { point to the first non-zero digit }
```

```
         i := i + 1;
       number.last := i;
       found := false;
       i := 1;
       while (not found) and (i <= limit) do
         if number.number[i] <> 0 then
           found := true
         else
           i := i + 1;
       if i = (limit + 1) then
         number.last := limit
       else
         number.last := i;                        { make sure the number is < modsys}
       if (number.last = modsys.last) and (number.number[number.last]
                                      >= modsys.number[modsys.last]) then
         begin
           number.number[number.last] := 0;
           number.last := number.last + 1
         end;                                 { make sure the number is > 0 }
       if (number.last = limit) and (number.number[number.last] = 0) then
         number.number[number.last] := 1;
     end
   end;      { end procedure getanumber }
{  ********************************************************************************  }

   procedure fastex (base, exponent, modsys : largeint;
                 var result : largeint;
                 var negative : boolean);

{ TASK: The task of this procedure is to exponentiate a number ( base) to the (exponent) }
{ INPUT:  The input will be:  base - the number to be exponentiated.                      }
{exponent-what the number will be exponentiated to;modsys-the mod system  used.          }
{ OUTPUT:The output will be:result - equals abs((base)**exponent).                        }
{                             negative - boolean true if result is negative.              }
{NOTE: this procedure uses the so-called "fast exponentiation" algorithm.                 }

     var
       base1,                                                      { base }
       exponent1,                                                  { exponent }
       tempanswer,                                        { temporary storage location }
       remainder,                                         { remainder from division }
       one,                                                        { the number one }
       two : largeint;                                             { the number two }
       i : integer;                                                { index }
     begin       { begin procedure fastex }
       clearnumber(result);                                        { result := 0 }
       clearnumber(one);                                           { one := 0 }
       clearnumber(two);                                           { two := 0 }
       one.number[one.last] := 1;                                  { one := 1 }
       two.number[two.last] := 2;                                  { two := 2 }
       transfer(base1, base);                                      { base1 := base }
       transfer(exponent1, exponent);                           {exponent1 := exponent }
       result.number[limit] := 1;       { result := 1 ( value for the exponential expression ) }
       result.last := limit;
       while (notzero(exponent1)) do
         begin
           while even(exponent1) do                { whether the current bit is 0 or 1 }
             begin                                 { exponent1 := exponent div 2 }
               clearnumber(tempanswer);
```

```
                division(exponent1, two, tempanswer, remainder, negative);
                transfer(exponent1, tempanswer);  { base1 := (base1 * base1) mod modsys }
                clearnumber(tempanswer);
                 multmod(base1, base1, modsys, tempanswer, negative);
                 transfer(base1, tempanswer);
              end;
          clearnumber(tempanswer);                              { base1 := base1 - 1 }
          subtract(exponent1, one, tempanswer, negative);
          transfer(exponent1, tempanswer);
          clearnumber(tempanswer);            { result := (result * base1) mod modsys }
          multmod(result, base1, modsys, tempanswer, negative);
          transfer(result, tempanswer);
        end;                                                  {result is the answer}
    end;        { end procedure fastex }
{    ************************************************************************************* }

    procedure PeraltaTest (candat : largeint;
                   var prime : boolean);
```

{TASK: The task of this procedure is to test a number for primality by using the   }
{ Peralta test algorithm.   }
{INPUT: The input will be: candat - the number to be tested for primality.   }
{ OUTPUT: The output will be: prime - boolean true if the number is prime,otherwise false. }
{ NOTE: The Peralta test is described in Chapter 5.   }

```
     var
        EqualNeg1,                           { counts number of times result equal -1 }
        count : integer;                                        { counter for loop }
        aNumber,                                     { number to be exponentiated }
        Exponent,                                                     { (p-1)/2 }
        result,                                          { result of exponentiation }
        one,                                                       { the number 1 }
        two,                                                       { the number 2 }
        modsys,                                             { the modsystem = p  }
        tempanswer,                                     { temporary storage location }
        remainder : largeint;                               { remainder from division }
        Negative,                         { true if result is negative ,otherwise false }
        good : boolean;                                      { boolean flag for loop }
     begin        { begin procedure Peralta Test }
        clearnumber(modsys);                          { Initialization: modsys = 0 }
        clearnumber(remainder);                                  { remainder = 0 }
        clearnumber(two);                                            { two := 0 }
        two.number[two.last] := 2;                                   { two := 2 }
        equalneg1 := 0;
        prime := false;                          { start off as number not prime }
        good := true;                                    { start off as good }
        count := 0;
        clearnumber(one);                                            { one := 0 }
        one.number[limit] := 1;                                      { one := 1 }
        transfer(exponent, candat);                              { exponent := p }
        clearnumber(tempanswer);       { exponent := exponent - 1;  modsys := p - 1 }
        subtract(exponent, one, tempanswer, negative);
        transfer(modsys, tempanswer);
        transfer(exponent, tempanswer);
        clearnumber(tempanswer);                        { exponent := exponent div 2 }
        division(exponent, two, tempanswer, remainder, negative);
        transfer(exponent, tempanswer);
        while good and (count < max) do        { process tests until test count = 100 }
          begin                                { or a result is neither 1 nor -1 }
```

```
            count := count + 1;
            GetaNumber(seed, aNumber, modsys);
            clearnumber(result);                        { fast exponentiate the number }
            fastex(aNumber, exponent, candat, result, negative);
            if (result.last = limit) and (result.number[result.last] = 1) then
                if negative then
                    equalNeg1 := equalNeg1 + 1
                else
                else                                    { result is neither 1 nor -1 }
                    good := false
            end;                                        { end while loop }
        if good and (equalNeg1 > 0) then
            prime := true;
    end;        { end procedure Peralta Test }
{   **************************************************************************** }
begin       { begin main }
    while not eof do        { keep processing while still more large numbers to be tested. }
        begin
            readin(candat, errormessage);
            if not errormessage then
                begin
                    numberprimecandat := false;    { see if candat is divisible by a small prime. }
                    if not (even(candat)) and not (divby3(candat)) and not (lastdigit5(candat))
                                        and not (divby11(candat)) then
                        numberprimecandat := true;
                    prime := false;
                    if numberprimecandat then
                        PeraltaTest(candat, prime); { the number is prime if prime is true , else false }
                    if prime then
                        writeln(' is prime.')
                    else
                        writeln(' is not prime.')
                end
        end
end.        { end main }
```

```
program RSACryption(input, output);

{ In many  Pascal implementations, this line could read:                }
{ program RSACryption(input, output,PrimeFile,MessageFile, CipherOut);   }

{ Program P8: The RSA Encryption and Decryption Algorithm.               }
{The program reads a file of two secret primes, and a textfile, generates the RSA   }
{public keys, and encrypts (and decrypts) the given textfile.This public key        }
{ cryptosystem is described in Chapter 5.                                }

{ MODE OF EXECUTION: This program is designed to be executed in part interactively, }
{using terminal and data file input.                                     }

{ INPUT:The user must create a file of two large primes,under the external name 'Primes'. }
{ This file is read, together with an input message file, whose name is to be provided     }
{ by the user after the appropriate prompt.  The primes may be generated by program P7.    }

{ OUTPUT: The cipher text may either be displayed at the terminal or directed to a file.   }

{ NOTE: Although this program is written for large integers of up to 200 digits, running   }
{ this program under interpreted Macintosh Pascal will result in extremely long            }
{runs, unless the size of the integers and the amount of cleartext to be encrypted         }
{(up to 6000 characters) are reduced significantly.Otherwise, this program could be        }
{more reasonably run in a compiled version.                              }

  const
    max = 201;                              { max value for a large integer }
    limit = 402;                            { limit on index of large integer array }
  type
    digits = 0..9;                                    { digits are 0..9 }
    largetype = array[1..limit] of digits;    { holds digits of a large integer }
    largeint = record
        number : largetype;                       { digits of the integer }
        last : 0..limit;                     { index of first digit of integer }
      end;
    TextArrayType = array[1..6000] of char;            {holds the message text}
  var
    p, q, n, e, d, m, EulerFnOfN, EM, DM : largeint;    { p, q - secret primes; n = p*q; }
{ e - encrypting key;  d = decrypting key = e**(-1) mod PHI(n); EulerFnOfN = Euler or  }
{ totient function of n;  EM - encrypted message; DM - decrypted message.              }
    MoreMessage, WriteToDisk : boolean;
         {MoreMessage true if more to encrypt;WriteToDisk true if encryption to be stored}
    blksize, blkstart, length, i : integer;
                              { blkstart, blkstart: encryption block size and starting value}
    Message : TextArrayType;
    ch : char;

{ *********************************************************************************** }

  procedure clearnumber (var number : largeint);
                              {procedure clearnumber can be found on page 247.}

{ *********************************************************************************** }

  procedure GetLargePrimes (var p, q : LargeInt);

  { Procedure GetLargePrimes reads a textfile containing the secret primes, one line each.}

    var
      PrimeFile : text;                       { the internal name of the text file}
      i, j : integer;
      ch : char;
```

```
        temp : array[0..max] of char;              {storage for digits before conversion}
  begin        {procedure GetLargePrimes}
    clearnumber(p);
    clearnumber(q);
    open(PrimeFile, 'Primes');                     {The file must be externally named 'Primes'.}
    i := 0;
    while not eoln(PrimeFile) do
      begin                                        {get the first prime}
        read(PrimeFile, ch);
        if (ch >= '0') and (ch <= '9') then        {only store digit characters}
          begin
            temp[i] := ch;
            i := i + 1
          end
      end;
    for j := 0 to (i - 1) do
      p.number[limit - (i - 1) + j] := ord(temp[j]) - ord('0');        {convert to digits}
    p.last := limit - (i - 1);
    i := 0;
    readln(PrimeFile);
    while not eof(PrimeFile) do                     {get the second prime}
      begin
        read(PrimeFile, ch);
        if (ch >= '0') and (ch <= '9') then         {only store digit characters}
          begin
            temp[i] := ch;
            i := i + 1
          end
      end;
    for j := 0 to (i - 1) do
      q.number[limit - (i - 1) + j] := ord(temp[j]) - ord('0');        {convert to digits}
    q.last := limit - (i - 1)
  end;        {procedure GetLargePrimes}
```

{ ** }

```
  procedure GetText (var TextArray : TextArrayType;
        var length : integer);          { Procedure GetText can be found on page 223. }
```

{ ** }

```
  procedure WriteOutFile (Cipher : LargeInt);
```

{Procedure WriteOutFile writes the cipher, a LargeInt, to an output file named 'Cipher File'.}

```
    var
      i : integer;
      CipherOut : text;
    begin        {procedure WriteOutFile}
      open(CipherOut, 'Cipher');
      for i := Cipher.last to limit do
        write(CipherOut, Cipher.number[i] : 1);
      writeln(CipherOut)
    end;        {procedure WriteOutFile}
```

{ ** }

```
  procedure WriteStdOut (number : LargeInt);
```

{Procedure WriteOutFile writes a LargeInt (large integer) to the standard output file.   }

```
    var
      i : integer;
   begin         {procedure WriteStdOut}
     for i := number.last to limit do
       write(number.number[i] : 1);
     writeln
   end;          {procedure WriteStdOut}
```

{ *** }

```
   function notZero (number : LargeInt) : boolean;
                              { function notZero can be found on page 256. }
```

{ *** }

```
   procedure Add (number1, number2 : largeint;
                 var answer : largeint);    { Procedure Add can be found on page 247. }
```

{ *** }

```
   procedure Subtraction (first, second : largeint;
                 var answer : largeint);
                              { Procedure Subtraction can be found on page 248. }
```

{ *** }

```
   function equal (number1, number2 : largeint) : boolean;
                              { function equal can be found on page 249. }
```

{ *** }

```
   function lessthan (number1, number2 : largeint) : boolean;
                              { function lessthan can be found on page 249. }
```

{ *** }

```
   procedure Subtract (Number1, number2 : largeint;
                 var answer : largeint; {Procedure subtract can be found on page 250}
                 var negative : boolean);
```

{ *** }

```
   function notmodded (number1, modsys : largeint) : boolean;
                              { Function notmodded can be found on page 250}
```

{ *** }

```
   procedure transfer (var number1 : largeint;
                 number2 : largeint);    { Procedure transfer can be found on page 251}
```

{ *** }

```
   procedure Multiply (First, Second : largeint;
                 var answer : largeint); {Procedure Multiply can be found on page 251}
```

{ *** }

```
   procedure DivisionByTwo (number : largeint;
                 var answer: largeint);
```

{Procedure DivisionByTwo divides a large integer by 2, digit by digit (short division). Any }
{ remainder is discarded.   }

```
    var
      carry, i : integer;
   begin         { procedure divisionbyTwo}
```

```
      clearnumber(answer);
      answer.last := number.last;
      carry := 0;
      for i := number.last to limit do
        begin                                                 {divide by two}
          answer.number[i] := (carry + number.number[i]) div 2;
          carry := 10 * ((carry + number.number[i]) mod 2)
        end;                           {add to the next digit if there's a remainder}
      if answer.number[answer.last] = 0 then              {If the highest digit is zero, }
        answer.last := answer.last + 1                    { make the next digit the highest}
    end;       { procedure divisionbyTwo}
```

{ *** }

```
    procedure division (var number1, number2 : largeint;
                  var answer, remainder : largeint;
                  var negative: boolean);
```
                                      {Procedure division can be found on page 252}

{ *** }

```
    function even(number : Largeint) : boolean; {function even can be found on page 255}
```

{ *** }

```
    procedure Multmod (First, Second, modsys : largeint;
                  var answer : largeint; {Procedure MultMod can be found on page 253}
                  var negative : boolean);
```

{ *** }

```
    procedure fastex (base, exponent, modsys : largeint;
                  var result : largeint;    {Procedure fastex can be found on page 257}
                  var negative : boolean);
```

{ *** }

```
    procedure FormModulus (p, q : Largeint;
                  var n : Largeint);
```

{Procedure FormModulus multiplies two large primes,p and q,to get part of the public
{ key, n.

```
    begin       { procedure FormModulus }
      Multiply(p, q, n)
    end;       { procedure FormModulus }
```

{ *** }

```
    procedure GetBlockSize (n : Largeint;
                  var blk : integer);
```

{Procedure GetBlockSize determines how many bytes can be encrypted in a block by
{calculating the largest multiple of 8 bits which will give a number less than n.Generally,
{the blocksize doesn't need to be byte-oriented if the cleartext is given as a bitstring.

```
      const
        Log2ToTheBase10 = 3.3219281;
        LogEToTheBase2 = 1.442695;
      begin         { procedure GetBlockSize}
      blk := trunc(Log2ToTheBase10 * (limit + 1 - n.last)
                    + LogEToTheBase2 * ln(n.number[n.last])) div 8
```

```
   end;          { procedure GetBlockSize}
{  ************************************************************************  }

   procedure GetEuler (p, q : LargeInt;
                       var phi : LargeInt);

{Procedure GetEuler computes the Euler function of n = (p-1) * (q-1).          }

      var
         one, temp1, temp2 : LargeInt;
      begin     {procedure GetEuler }
      clearnumber(temp1);
      clearnumber(temp2);
      clearnumber(one);
      clearnumber(phi);
      one.number[one.last] := 1;
      subtraction(p, one, temp1);                        { compute (p-1) }
      subtraction(q, one, temp2);                        { compute (q-1) }
      multiply(temp1, temp2, phi)                  { compute (p-1) * (q-1) }
   end;          {procedure GetEuler }

{  ************************************************************************  }

   procedure GenerateEncryptionKey (n : Largeint;
                       var e : LargeInt);

{Procedure GenerateEncryptionKey  gets a number at random less than the modulus, n, }
{ and relatively prime to it.                                                }

      var
         i : integer;
         gcd, one : largeint;

{  ************************************************************************  }

   procedure ComputeGCD (a, b : LargeInt;
                       var g : LargeInt);

{Procedure ComputeGCD finds the greatest common divisor of two large integers. The    }
{value is returned in g. The algorithm used for computing GCD is described in Appendix III }

      var
         a0, b0, temp1, temp2 : LargeInt;
         negative : boolean;                  { tests the sign of a subtraction }
      begin     { procedure Compute GCD }
      clearnumber(a0);
      clearnumber(b0);
      transfer(a0, a);
      transfer(b0, b);
      clearnumber(temp1);
      clearnumber(temp2);
      while notzero(a0) do     { repeat  until the value of a0 is zero. When it is, GCD = b0}
         begin
         negative := false;
         transfer(temp2, b0);
         while not negative do          {while temp1 - a0 is positive, keep subtracting}
            begin
            transfer(temp1, temp2);
            subtract(temp1, a0, temp2, negative)
            end;
         transfer(b0, a0);                                {make the new b0 the old a0}
```

```
        transfer(a0, temp1)                    {make the new a0 the old b0 - k*a0  ( < b0 ) }
      end;
    transfer(g, b0)
  end;        { procedure Compute GCD }
{ **************************************************************************** }

  begin        { procedure GenerateEncryptionKey }
    clearnumber(gcd);
    clearnumber(one);
    one.number[limit] := 1;
    while not (equal(gcd, one)) do        { repeat until a key e with GCD(e,n) = 1 is found}
      begin
        e.last := n.last;
        for i := (e.last + 1) to limit do
          e.number[i] := random mod 10;                { NOT ANSI STANDARD PASCAL }
        e.number[e.last] := random mod n.number[n.last];
        i := e.last;        {choose the highest digit to be less than the highest digit of n}
        while (e.number[i] = 0) do
          i := i + 1;
        e.last := i;                {if the highest digit is zero, find the highest non-zero digit}
        ComputeGCD(e, n, gcd)
      end
  end;        { procedure GenerateEncryptionKey }

{ **************************************************************************** }

  procedure GenerateDecryptionKey (phi, e : LargeInt;
                  var d : LargeInt);

{Procedure GenerateDecryptionKey  finds the secret decryption key, d, by finding the   }
{inverse of e mod phi, the Euler function of n. The inversion algorithm is the 3x2 algorithm }
{described in Chapter 5.                                                              }

  var
    a : array[1..3, 1..2] of LargeInt;                        {the 3 x 2 array }
    one, zero,  mult, rem, temp1, temp2 : LargeInt;           {one = 1; zero = 0; }
      { mult = the  multiplier in the 3x2 algorithm; rem , temp1, temp2 are temporaries.}
    neg : boolean;                                {the sign after a subtraction}
  begin        { procedure GenerateDecryptionKey}
    clearnumber(one);
    clearnumber(zero);
    clearnumber(d);
    one.number[one.last] := 1;
    transfer(a[1, 1], phi);                        {set up the 3x2 array}
    transfer(a[2, 1], one);
    transfer(a[3, 1], zero);
    transfer(a[1, 2], e);
    transfer(a[2, 2], zero);
    transfer(a[3, 2], one);
    transfer(mult, one);
    while notzero(a[1, 2]) do
      begin
        division(a[1, 1], a[1, 2], mult, rem, neg);        {find a value for the multiplier}
        if neg then
          subtract(phi, mult, mult, neg);                {change sign if necessary}
        multmod(mult, a[1, 2], phi, temp1, neg);          {update the first row}
        if neg then
          subtract(phi, temp1, temp1, neg);
        subtract(a[1, 1], temp1, temp2, neg);
```

```
        if neg then
          subtract(phi, temp2, temp2, neg);
        transfer(a[1, 1], a[1, 2]);
        transfer(a[1, 2], temp2);
        multmod(mult, a[2, 2], phi, temp1, neg);              {update the second row}
        if neg then
          subtract(phi, temp1, temp1, neg);
        subtract(a[2, 1], temp1, temp2, neg);
        if neg then
          subtract(phi, temp2, temp2, neg);
        transfer(a[2, 1], a[2, 2]);
        transfer(a[2, 2], temp2);
        multmod(mult, a[3, 2], phi, temp1, neg);              {update the third row}
        if neg then
          subtract(phi, temp1, temp1, neg);
        subtract(a[3, 1], temp1, temp2, neg);
        if neg then
          subtract(phi, temp2, temp2, neg);
        transfer(a[3, 1], a[3, 2]);
        transfer(a[3, 2], temp2)
      end;                                      { When the value in position [1,2] is zero, }
    transfer(d, a[3, 1])                        { the inverse is found in position [3,1] .}
  end;          { procedure GenerateDecryptionKey}

{  ********************************************************************************* }

  procedure FormMessageBlock (MessageText : TextArrayType;
                  var blockstart : integer;
                  var MessageInt : LargeInt;
                  blk : integer);

{Procedure FormMessageBlock converts one block's worth of message text to          }
{large integer form, and returns the value in MessageInt.                          }

  var
    one, two, PowerOfTwo : LargeInt;    {PowerOfTwo will contains successive 2**n's.}
    i, j, temp : integer;
  begin
    clearnumber(MessageInt);
    clearnumber(PowerOfTwo);
    clearnumber(one);
    clearnumber(two);
    one.number[one.last] := 1;
    two.number[two.last] := 2;
    PowerOfTwo := one;                                        {Start with 2**0 = 1.}
    for i := (blockstart + blk - 1) downto blockstart do
                            {leftmost byte becomes the high part of the large integer}
      begin  {the block interval of MessageText goes from blockstart to blockstart+blk-1}
        temp := ord(MessageText[i]);                  {convert one byte to integer form}
        for j := 1 to 8 do
          begin
            if (odd(temp)) then                              {if the current bit is 1,}
              add(MessageInt,PowerOfTwo,MessageInt); {add the corresponding 2**j}
            multiply(PowerOfTwo, two, PowerOfTwo);              {update to 2**(j+1)}
            temp := temp div 2
          end
      end;
    blockstart := blockstart + blk              {also return the start value for the next block}
  end;
```

```
{ ******************************************************************************* }

    procedure Cryption (m, e, n : LargeInt;
                    var CryptMessage : LargeInt);

{Procedure cryption computes m**e mod n, and can be used either                  }
{for RSA encryption or decryption                                                }

    var
      neg : boolean;
    begin        {procedure Cryption }
      fastex(m, e, n, CryptMessage, neg);
      if neg then
        Subtraction(n, CryptMessage, CryptMessage)
    end;          {procedure Cryption }

{ ******************************************************************************* }

begin     { Main program RSAEncryptionDecryption }
    writeln('If the encryption is to be stored in an output file named "Cipher", enter "y":');
    readln(ch);
    WriteToDisk := (ch = 'y') or (ch = 'Y');
    MoreMessage := true;                    {while there's still some cleartext left to encrypt}
    GetLargePrimes(p, q);                              {read in the secret primes}
    FormModulus(p, q, n);                                    {compute p*q = n}
    writeln('The modulus, n, is:');                             {write it out}
    WriteStdOut(n);
    GetBlockSize(n, blksize);                       {find the appropriate blocksize}
    GetEuler(p, q, EulerFnOfN);                         {compute (p-1) *(q-1)}
    WriteStdOut(EulerFnOfN);                                     {write it out}
    GenerateEncryptionKey(EulerFnOfN, e);       {generate a random encryption key, e.}
    writeln('The encryption key, e, is:');                        {write it out}
    WriteStdOut(e);
    GenerateDecryptionKey(EulerFnOfN, e, d);   {compute the decryption key, d = e**(-1).}
    writeln('The decryption key, d (which of course remains secret), is:');   {write it out}
    WriteStdOut(d);
    GetText(Message, length);                              {read the cleartext file}
    blkstart := 1;
    while MoreMessage do                         {until all the cleartext is encrypted}
      begin
        if (blkstart + blksize - 1 > length) then
          begin          {pad the cleartext with blanks when the end of the file is reached}
          for i := (length + 1) to (blkstart + blksize - 1) do
            Message[i] := ' ';
          length := blkstart + blksize - 1
          end;
        FormMessageBlock(Message, blkstart,m, blksize); {convert some clear to integer}
        Cryption(m, e, n, EM);                                  {then encrypt it}
        writeln('Encrypted output:');                      {display the encryption}
        WriteStdOut(EM);
        if WriteTodDisk then                        {save it in 'Cipher' if desired}
          WriteOutFile(EM);
        Cryption(EM, d, n, DM);                               {and decrypt it .}
        writeln('And its decryption:');                     {display the decryption}
        WriteStdOut(DM);
        MoreMessage := (length >= blkstart);       {is there any cleartext left to encrypt?}
      end
end.    { Main program RSAEncryptionDecryption }
```

```
program Sawtooths(input, output);

{ In many  Pascal implementations, this line could read:                          }
{ program Sawtooths(input, output, Outfile);                                       }

{Program P9: Generate Sawtooth Curves.                                             }
{ This program computes a number of test intervals for which the two sawtooth curves }
{ may intersect the x-axis in the corresponding public knapsack set 467, 355, 131, 318, }
{ etc.as in the Chapter 4 example.The algorithm is straightforward:For each consecutive }
{pair of the knapsack numbers,the intersections of the intervals[w'k,w'k+ r/(2**(n-k))] }
{ and [w'(k+1),w'(k+1) + s/(2**(n-k-1))] are computed. The consecutive intervals are }
{ printed. This intersection is used to give a necessary condition for the location of }
{ knapsack pairs.                                                                  }

{ MODE OF EXECUTION: This program is designed to be executed without input.        }

{ INPUT: None.                                                                     }

{ OUTPUT: A textfile, named Outfile, containing a list of intervals.               }

{ NOTE: It is a simple matter to adapt this program to any other knapsack set rising from }
{ a Merkle-Hellman PKC, assuming that the values in the public set are small enough. }

  var
    w1, w2, oldw1, oldw2 : double;      { double-precision reals NOT STANDARD PASCAL}
    nums : array[1..5] of integer;                    {an array for 5 knapsack numbers}
    w1left, w2left : boolean;
    OutFile : text;                                              {the output file}
    LP : (w1l, w1r, w2l, w2r);     {is LP a left interval of the first knapsack number{w1l), }
                                   { a right interval of the first knapsack number (w1r), etc.}
    i, exp : integer;
begin      { Main program Sawtooths }
  nums[1] := 467;                                  {enter the five knapsack numbers}
  nums[2] := 355;
  nums[3] := 131;
  nums[4] := 318;
  nums[5] := 113;
  open(OutFile, 'Sawtooth Output');                        {open the output file}
  exp := 256;
  i := 1;
  while i < 5 do              { for pairs (nums[1], nums[2]); (nums[2], nums[3]) etc.}
    begin
      writeln(OutFile);                                         {output a header}
      writeln(OutFile, 'Comparison Number ', i : 3,
                   ' of Public Knapsack Numbers');
      writeln(OutFile);
      writeln(OutFile);
      exp := exp div 2;
      w1 := 1 / nums[i];                        { set the left interval points for the }
      w1left := true;                                   { two knapsack numbers }
      w2 := 1 / nums[i + 1];
      w2left := true;
      LP := w2r;
      while (w1 < 1) and (w2 < 1) do
        begin                                       { find overlapping intervals }
          if w1 < w2 then
            if w1left then                        { if we're at a left endpoint for w1 }
              begin
                if (LP = w1l) or (LP = w2l) then                        { overlap }
                  writeln(OutFile, 'W1 LEFT  = ', w1 : 20 : 12);
```

```
                  LP := w1l;
                  oldw1 := w1;
                  w1 := w1 + 1 / (nums[i] * exp);                    { increment for w1 }
                  w1left := false
                end
              else                                   { if we're at a right endpoint for w1 }
                begin
                  if LP <> w1l then
                    writeln(OutFile, 'W1  RIGHT =', w1 : 20 : 12);
                  w1 := oldw1 + (1 / nums[i]);                       { go to next multiple of 1/w1}
                  LP := w1r;
                  w1left := true
                end
            else if w2left then                          { at a left endpoint for w2 }
              begin
                if (LP = w1l) or (LP = w2l) then
                  writeln(OutFile, 'W2 LEFT  = ', w2 : 20 : 12);
                oldw2 := w2;
                w2 := w2 + 1 / (nums[i + 1] * (exp div 2));          { increment for w2 }
                LP := w2l;
                w2left := false
              end
            else
              begin
                if LP <> w2l then
                  writeln(OutFile, 'W2  RIGHT =', w2 : 20 : 12);
                w2 := oldw2 + (1 / nums[i + 1]);                     { go to next multiple of 1/w2}
                LP := w2r;
                w2left := true
              end
          end;
        page(OutFile);
        i := i + 1
      end
end.          { Main program Sawtooths }
```

(Reformatted) output of program P9:

Comparison Number 1 of Public Knapsack
Numbers

W1 LEFT =	0.053533190578
W2 RIGHT =	0.053565140845
W1 LEFT =	0.107066381156
W2 RIGHT =	0.107086267606
W1 LEFT =	0.160599571734
W2 RIGHT =	0.160607394366
W1 RIGHT =	0.160616300857
W2 LEFT =	0.473239436620
W1 RIGHT =	0.473250133833
W2 RIGHT =	0.473283450704
W1 LEFT =	0.526766595289
W2 RIGHT =	0.526804577465
W1 LEFT =	0.580299785867
W2 RIGHT =	0.580325704225
W1 LEFT =	0.633832976445
W2 RIGHT =	0.633846830986
W1 RIGHT =	0.633849705567
W1 LEFT =	0.687366167024
W2 RIGHT =	0.687367957746
W1 RIGHT =	0.687382896146
W2 LEFT =	0.946478873239
W1 RIGHT =	0.946483538544
W2 RIGHT =	0.946522887324

Comparison Number 2 of Public Knapsack
Numbers

W1 LEFT =	0.053521126761
W2 RIGHT =	0.053673664122
W1 LEFT =	0.107042253521
W2 RIGHT =	0.107108778626
W2 LEFT =	0.236641221374
W1 RIGHT =	0.236663732394
W2 RIGHT =	0.236879770992
W1 LEFT =	0.290140845070
W2 RIGHT =	0.290314885496
W1 LEFT =	0.343661971831
W2 RIGHT =	0.343750000000
W1 LEFT =	0.397183098592
W2 RIGHT =	0.397185114504
W1 RIGHT =	0.397227112676
W2 LEFT =	0.473282442748
W1 RIGHT =	0.473283450704
W2 RIGHT =	0.473520992366
W1 LEFT =	0.526760563380
W2 RIGHT =	0.526956106870
W1 LEFT =	0.580281690141
W2 RIGHT =	0.580391221374
W1 LEFT =	0.633802816901
W2 RIGHT =	0.633826335878
W1 RIGHT =	0.633846830986
W1 LEFT =	0.763380281690

W2 RIGHT =	0.763597328244
W1 LEFT =	0.816901408451
W2 RIGHT =	0.817032442748
W1 LEFT =	0.870422535211
W2 RIGHT =	0.870467557252

Comparison Number 3 of Public Knapsack
Numbers

W2 LEFT =	0.053459119497
W1 RIGHT =	0.053673664122
W2 LEFT =	0.106918238994
W1 RIGHT =	0.107108778626
W2 RIGHT =	0.107114779874
W2 LEFT =	0.160377358491
W1 RIGHT =	0.160543893130
W2 RIGHT =	0.160573899371
W2 LEFT =	0.213836477987
W1 RIGHT =	0.213979007634
W2 RIGHT =	0.214033018868
W2 LEFT =	0.267295597484
W1 RIGHT =	0.267414122137
W2 RIGHT =	0.267492138365
W2 LEFT =	0.320754716981
W1 RIGHT =	0.320849236641
W2 RIGHT =	0.320951257862
W2 LEFT =	0.374213836478
W1 RIGHT =	0.374284351145
W2 RIGHT =	0.374410377358
W2 LEFT =	0.427672955975
W1 RIGHT =	0.427719465649
W2 RIGHT =	0.427869496855
W2 LEFT =	0.481132075472
W1 RIGHT =	0.481154580153
W2 RIGHT =	0.481328616352
W1 LEFT =	0.572519083969
W2 RIGHT =	0.572523584906
W1 RIGHT =	0.572757633588
W1 LEFT =	0.625954198473
W2 RIGHT =	0.625982704403
W1 RIGHT =	0.626192748092
W1 LEFT =	0.679389312977
W2 RIGHT =	0.679441823899
W1 RIGHT =	0.679627862595
W1 LEFT =	0.732824427481
W2 RIGHT =	0.732900943396
W1 RIGHT =	0.733062977099
W1 LEFT =	0.786259541985
W2 RIGHT =	0.786360062893
W1 RIGHT =	0.786498091603
W1 LEFT =	0.839694656489
W2 RIGHT =	0.839819182390
W1 RIGHT =	0.839933206107
W1 LEFT =	0.893129770992
W2 RIGHT =	0.893278301887
W1 RIGHT =	0.893368320611
W1 LEFT =	0.946564885496
W2 RIGHT =	0.946737421384

W1 RIGHT = 0.946803435115

Comparison Number 4 of Public Knapsack Numbers

W1 LEFT =	0.009433962264
W2 RIGHT =	0.009955752212
W1 LEFT =	0.053459119497
W2 RIGHT =	0.054203539823
W1 LEFT =	0.062893081761
W2 RIGHT =	0.063053097345
W1 RIGHT =	0.063089622642
W1 LEFT =	0.097484276730
W2 RIGHT =	0.098451327434
W1 LEFT =	0.106918238994
W2 RIGHT =	0.107300884956
W2 LEFT =	0.141592920354
W1 RIGHT =	0.141705974843
W2 RIGHT =	0.142699115044
W1 LEFT =	0.150943396226
W2 RIGHT =	0.151548672566
W1 LEFT =	0.160377358491
W2 RIGHT =	0.160398230088
W1 RIGHT =	0.160573899371
W1 LEFT =	0.194968553459
W2 RIGHT =	0.195796460177
W1 LEFT =	0.204402515723
W2 RIGHT =	0.204646017699
W1 LEFT =	0.238993710692
W2 RIGHT =	0.240044247788
W1 LEFT =	0.248427672956
W2 RIGHT =	0.248893805310
W2 LEFT =	0.283185840708
W1 RIGHT =	0.283215408805
W2 RIGHT =	0.284292035398
W1 LEFT =	0.292452830189
W2 RIGHT =	0.293141592920
W1 LEFT =	0.301886792453
W2 RIGHT =	0.301991150442
W1 RIGHT =	0.302083333333
W1 LEFT =	0.336477987421
W2 RIGHT =	0.337389380531
W1 LEFT =	0.345911949686
W2 RIGHT =	0.346238938053
W2 LEFT =	0.380530973451
W1 RIGHT =	0.380699685535
W2 RIGHT =	0.381637168142
W1 LEFT =	0.389937106918
W2 RIGHT =	0.390486725664
W1 LEFT =	0.433962264151
W2 RIGHT =	0.434734513274
W1 LEFT =	0.443396226415
W2 RIGHT =	0.443584070796
W1 RIGHT =	0.443592767296
W1 LEFT =	0.477987421384
W2 RIGHT =	0.478982300885
W1 LEFT =	0.487421383648
W2 RIGHT =	0.487831858407

W2 LEFT =	0.522123893805
W1 RIGHT =	0.522209119497
W2 RIGHT =	0.523230088496
W1 LEFT =	0.531446540881
W2 RIGHT =	0.532079646018
W1 LEFT =	0.540880503145
W2 RIGHT =	0.540929203540
W1 RIGHT =	0.541077044025
W1 LEFT =	0.575471698113
W2 RIGHT =	0.576327433628
W1 LEFT =	0.584905660377
W2 RIGHT =	0.585176991150
W1 LEFT =	0.619496855346
W2 RIGHT =	0.620575221239
W1 LEFT =	0.628930817610
W2 RIGHT =	0.629424778761
W2 LEFT =	0.663716814159
W1 RIGHT =	0.663718553459
W2 RIGHT =	0.664823008850
W1 LEFT =	0.672955974843
W2 RIGHT =	0.673672566372
W1 LEFT =	0.682389937107
W2 RIGHT =	0.682522123894
W1 RIGHT =	0.682586477987
W1 LEFT =	0.716981132075
W2 RIGHT =	0.717920353982
W1 LEFT =	0.726415094340
W2 RIGHT =	0.726769911504
W2 LEFT =	0.761061946903
W1 RIGHT =	0.761202830189
W2 RIGHT =	0.762168141593
W1 LEFT =	0.770440251572
W2 RIGHT =	0.771017699115
W1 LEFT =	0.814465408805
W2 RIGHT =	0.815265486726
W1 LEFT =	0.823899371069
W2 RIGHT =	0.824115044248
W1 LEFT =	0.858490566038
W2 RIGHT =	0.859513274336
W1 LEFT =	0.867924528302
W2 RIGHT =	0.868362831858
W2 LEFT =	0.902654867257
W1 RIGHT =	0.902712264151
W2 RIGHT =	0.903761061947
W1 LEFT =	0.911949685535
W2 RIGHT =	0.912610619469
W1 LEFT =	0.921383647799
W2 RIGHT =	0.921460176991
W1 RIGHT =	0.921580188679
W1 LEFT =	0.955974842767
W2 RIGHT =	0.956858407080
W1 LEFT =	0.965408805031
W2 RIGHT =	0.965707964602

program FindKnapsackPairs(input, output);

{ In many Pascal implementations, this line could read: }
*{ **program** FindKnapsackPairs(input, output, Outfile);   }*

{Program P10: Find Knapsack Pairs.   }
{ This program computes a number of possible easy knapsack pairs arising from the   }
{ condition that such a pair (M,P) must lie in either the interval [L1,R1] or [L2,R2]. These }
{ intervals were found by comparing the intersections of the intervals produced by the }
{ program P9, Generate Sawtooth Curves. Furthermore, since the given knapsack set }
{has no number larger than 500, we can assume that the desired value for p will be<1000. }

{ MODE OF EXECUTION: This program is designed to be executed without input.   }

{ INPUT: None.   }

{OUTPUT:A textfile,internally named Outfile,and externally named 'Trial Knapsack Sets'. }

{ NOTE: It is a simple matter to adapt this program to any other knapsack set rising from }
{ a Merkle-Hellman PKC, assuming that the values in the public set are small enough.   }

```
const
  L1 = 0.053533190578;                          { the intervals produced by P9 }
  L2 = 0.107066381156;
  R1 = 0.053565140845;
  R2 = 0.107086267606;
type
  KnapsackSet = array[1..8] of integer;
var
  wprime, w : KnapsackSet;  {wprime = the public knapsack set; w = the trial 'easy' set }
  num, denom, i : integer;
  { num, denom: the numerator and denominator of trial fractions.If a pair (num, denom)}
           { satisfies a quotient test, they become a candidate for a knapsack pair (M,P). }
  OutFile : text;
```

{ •• }

procedure Sort (**var** w : KnapsackSet);

{ Sort is a simple bubble sort used to rearrange eight knapsack numbers.   }

```
  var
    i, j, temp : integer;
    done : boolean;
  begin       { procedure Sort }
    done := false;
    i := 8;
    while i >= 2 do
      begin
        done := true;
        for j := 1 to 7 do
          if w[j] > w[j + 1] then
            begin
              temp := w[j];
              w[j] := w[j + 1];
              w[j + 1] := temp;
              done := false;
            end;
        i := i - 1
      end
  end;      { procedure Sort }
```

```
{ ************************************************************************ }
begin     { main program FindKnapsackPairs }
  wprime[1] := 467;     {Initialize the given public knapsack set 467, 355, 131, 318, etc. }
  wprime[2] := 355;
  wprime[3] := 131;
  wprime[4] := 318;
  wprime[5] := 113;
  wprime[6] := 21;
  wprime[7] := 135;
  wprime[8] := 215;
  open(OutFile, 'Trial Knapsack Sets');                    { create the output file }
  for denom := 2 to 1000 do                    { test all denominators up to 1000}
    begin
      num := trunc(R1 * denom);                { find the closest possible numerator }
      if (num / denom >= L1) and (num / denom <= R1) then
        begin                  { if the trial fraction falls in the first interval, write it out }
          writeln(OutFile,'Solution for interval 1:     ', num, denom, num / denom : 20:12);
          for i := 1 to 8 do                    { also compute the resulting knapsack set }
            w[i] := (wprime[i] * num) mod denom;
          Sort(w);                              { wi's probably not sorted, so sort them }
          writeln(OutFile, 'The trial knapsack set is: '); { write out the trial knapsack set }
          for i := 1 to 8 do
            write(OutFile, w[i] : 6);
          writeln(OutFile);
          writeln(OutFile, ' ********************** ');
          writeln(OutFile)
        end;
      num := trunc(R2 * denom);
      if (num / denom >= L2) and (num / denom <= R2) then
        begin                  { if the trial fraction falls in the second interval, write it out }
          writeln(OutFile, 'Solution for interval 2:     ', num, denom, num / denom :20:12);
          for i := 1 to 8 do                    { again compute the resulting knapsack set }
            w[i] := (wprime[i] * num) mod denom;
          Sort(w);                              { wi's probably not sorted, so sort them }
          writeln(OutFile, 'The trial knapsack set is: '); { write out the trial knapsack set }
          for i := 1 to 8 do
            write(OutFile, w[i] : 6);
          writeln(OutFile);
          writeln(OutFile, ' ********************** ');
          writeln(OutFile)
        end;
    end
end.     { main program FindKnapsackPairs }
```

The following is the (reformatted) output of Program P10:

```
Solution for interval 1:      25   467    0.053533190578
The trial knapsack set is:         0   2   6  11  23  58  106  238
**********************
Solution for interval 2:      50   467    0.107066381156
The trial knapsack set is:         0   4   9  12  22  46  116  212
**********************
Solution for interval 2:      53   495    0.107070707071
The trial knapsack set is:         1   5  10  13  24  49  123  225
**********************
Solution for interval 1:      28   523    0.053537284895
```

The trial knapsack set is:	1	3	7	13	26	65	119	267

Solution for interval 2:   56   523   0.107074569790

The trial knapsack set is:	2	6	11	14	26	52	130	238

Solution for interval 2:   59   551   0.107078039927

The trial knapsack set is:	3	7	12	15	28	55	137	251

Solution for interval 1:   31   579   0.053540587219

The trial knapsack set is:	2	4	8	15	29	72	132	296

Solution for interval 2:   62   579   0.107081174439

The trial knapsack set is:	4	8	13	16	30	58	144	264

Solution for interval 2:   65   607   0.107084019769

The trial knapsack set is:	5	9	14	17	32	61	151	277

Solution for interval 1:   34   635   0.053543307087

The trial knapsack set is:	3	5	9	17	32	79	145	325

Solution for interval 1:   37   691   0.053545586107

The trial knapsack set is:	4	6	10	19	35	86	158	354

Solution for interval 1:   40   747   0.053547523427

The trial knapsack set is:	5	7	11	21	38	93	171	383

Solution for interval 1:   43   803   0.053549190535

The trial knapsack set is:	6	8	12	23	41	100	184	412

Solution for interval 1:   46   859   0.053550640279

The trial knapsack set is:	7	9	13	25	44	107	197	441

Solution for interval 1:   49   915   0.053551912568

The trial knapsack set is:	8	10	14	27	47	114	210	470

Solution for interval 1:   50   934   0.053533190578

The trial knapsack set is:	0	4	12	22	46	116	212	476

Solution for interval 2:   100   934   0.107066381156

The trial knapsack set is:	0	8	18	24	44	92	232	424

Solution for interval 2:   103   962   0.107068607069

The trial knapsack set is:	1	9	19	25	46	95	239	437

Solution for interval 1:   52   971   0.053553038105

The trial knapsack set is:	9	11	15	29	50	121	223	499

Solution for interval 1:   53   990   0.053535353535

The trial knapsack set is:	1	5	13	24	49	123	225	505

Solution for interval 2:   106   990   0.107070707071

The trial knapsack set is:	2	10	20	26	48	98	246	450

program BasisReduction(input, output);

{Program P11: The Lenstra-Lenstra-Lovacz Basis Reduction Algorithm }
{This program computes, for any lattice which forms a basis of an n-dimensional vector }
{space (n<=20),a reduced basis in the sense of Lenstra-Lenstra-Lovasz.The algorithm }
{ is described in detail in Chapter 6. In essence, the Gram-Schmidt orthonormalization }
{procedure is applied to find an orthonormal basis, and then these basis vectors are }
{transformed to satisfy the criteria of being a reduced basis.The value of this "L-cubed" }
{algorithm is that it can be applied to many other combinatorially hard problems, in }
{particular to the problem of the cryptanalysis of most knapsack PKCs. }

{ MODE OF EXECUTION: This program is designed to be executed interactively. }

{ INPUT: The input consists of the choice of dimension for a set of basis vectors over }
{R**n, where n <= 20, and then the entry of the n components of the n basis vectors. }

{ OUTPUT: The output is directed to the standard output, and it consists of: a) the }
{components of the reduced basis; b)the Mu-coefficients developed in the algorithm;and }
{c) the comparison of the 2n expressions B(i) + Mu(i,i-1)*B(i-1) and (3/4) B(i-1), showing }
{that for each value of i, the first of these expressions is greater than the second. }

{NOTE:It is possible that certain choices of basis vectors may cause overflow in the }
{ calculations; also there is no guarantee of the result if the n vectors entered do not }
{form a basis of n-space. }

```
   type
      BVector = array[1..20, 1..20] of real;   { This type will hold all the components of all }
                                               { basis vectors up to 20 x 20 }

      BL = array[1..20] of real;
   var
      I, J, K, L, M, N : integer;
      Mu1, B1, Temp : real;
      B, Mu : BVector;       {B is the initial basis. The Mu's are the Gram-Schmidt coefficients}
      BLength : BL;                    { BLength is the square of the length of a basis vector }
      Finished : boolean;
      ch : char;

{      ************************************************************************************* }

   procedure GetVectors (var N : integer;
                 var B : BVector);

{The procedure GetVectors gets a set of basis vectors, either by generating a test }
{ case, or by requesting user input. }

   var
      I, J : integer;
   begin       {procedure GetVectors}
      writeln('Test input?');                    { If the user selects Test Input mode,}
      writeln('Enter y or Y for YES:');          { a sample 8 x 8 basis is generated. }
      readln(ch);
      if (ch = 'y') or (ch = 'Y') then
         begin
            N := 8;
            for I := 1 to 5 do
               for J := 1 to N do
                  B[I, J] := (i + J) mod 5;
            for I := 5 to N do
               for J := 1 to N do
                  B[I, J] := (i + J) mod 6
         end
```

```
   else
     begin        { Enter the size of the basis and the components of the basis vectors }
       writeln('Choose the size of the basis: ');
       readln(N);
       for I := 1 to N do
         begin
           writeln('Enter the components of the ', I : 4, 'th basis vector');
           for J := 1 to N do
             read(B[I, J]);
           readln
         end
     end;
   writeln('Echoing the basis vectors.');
   for I := 1 to N do
     begin
       for J := 1 to N do
         write(B[I, J] : 6 : 1);
       writeln
     end
 end;        {procedure GetVectors}

{  *********************************************************************************  }

 procedure InitBLengths (N : integer;
                  B : BVector;
                var Mu : BVector;
                var BLength : BL);

{ Procedure InitBlengths computes the initial values of the lengths of N vectors BStar,  }
{ obtained by the Gram-Schmidt process.                                                  }

   var
     BStar : BVector;
     I, J, K : integer;
   begin        { procedure InitBLengths }
     for I := 1 to N do                                    { Compute a Gram-Schmidt basis BStar }
       begin
         for K := 1 to N do
           BStar[I, K] := B[I, K];
         for J := 1 to (I - 1) do
           begin
             Mu[I, J] := 0;
             for K := 1 to N do
               Mu[I, J] := Mu[I, J] + B[I, K] * BStar[J, K];
             Mu[I, J] := Mu[I, J] / BLength[J];
             for K := 1 to N do
               BStar[I, K] := BStar[I, K] - Mu[I, J] * BStar[J, K];
           end;
         BLength[I] := 0;
         for K := 1 to N do
           BLength[I] := BLength[I] + BStar[I, K] * BStar[I, K]
                                              { It is no longer necessary to keep }
       end        { track of the BStar's, only the length BLength generated by the BStar's }
     end;        { procedure InitBLengths }

{  *********************************************************************************  }

 procedure MuAdjust (var Mu : BVector;
                 var B : BVector;
                 K, L, N : integer);
```

```
{ The procedure MuAdjust is invoked when values in the  basis must be changed to      }
{ reduce  the size of values of Mu                                                     }
      var
        I, J, R : integer;
      begin         { Procedure MuAdjust }
      if Abs(Mu[K, L]) > 0.5 then
        begin
          R := round(Mu[K, L]);
          for I := 1 to N do
            B[K, I] := B[K, I] - R * B[L, I];              { Replace  B vectors by B - R*B(I) }
          for J := 1 to (L - 1) do
            Mu[K, J] := Mu[K, J] - R * Mu[L, J];              { Adjust corresponding Mu's }
          Mu[K, L] := Mu[K, L] - R
        end
      end;        { Procedure MuAdjust }
{     ***************************************************************************     }

    procedure WriteResults (N : integer;
                  B, Mu : BVector;
                  BLength:BL);

{ This procedure WriteResults simply prints out the final reduced basis, the values of     }
{ Mu, and the inequalities required in the definition of a reduced basis                   }

      var
        I, J : integer;
        LHS, RHS : real;
      begin          { procedure WriteResults }
      writeln;
      writeln('*****************************');   writeln;
      for I := 1 to N do
        begin
          writeln('Here are the components of the ', I : 3, 'th reduced basis vector');
          for J := 1 to N do
            begin
              write(B[I, J] : 10 : 6, '   ');
              if ((J mod 4) = 0) then
                writeln
            end;
          writeln
        end;
      writeln;
      writeln('*****************************');   writeln;
      for I := 2 to N do
        begin
          writeln('The Mu coefficients for Mu( ', I : 3, ', J ) are : ');   writeln;
          for j := 1 to (I - 1) do
            write(Mu[I, J] : 10 : 6);
          writeln; writeln
        end;          { Print out the comparisons of the lengths of B(i) + Mu(i,i-1) * B(i-1) }
      writeln;                 { with (3/4) B(i-1), the other requirement for a reduced basis  }
      LHS := 0;
      RHS := 0;
      for I := 2 to N do
        begin
          LHS := BLength[I] + Mu[I, I - 1] * Mu[I, I - 1] * BLength[I - 1];
          RHS := 0.75 * BLength[I - 1];
```

```
              writeln;
              writeln('*******************************');   writeln;
              writeln('For i = ', I : 3, ', the comparison of LHS and RHS is: ');  writeln;
              writeln(LHS : 15 : 8, '    ', RHS : 15 : 8)
         end
  end;              { procedure WriteResults }

{      *********************************************************************************      }

begin        { Main Program BasisReduction }
  GetVectors(N, B);
  InitBLengths(N, B, Mu, BLength);
  K := 2;
  Finished := False;
  repeat
    MuAdjust(Mu, B, K, K - 1, N);
    if (BLength[K]<(0.75 - Mu[K, K - 1] * Mu[K, K - 1]) * BLength[K - 1]) and (K >= 2) then
       begin      { Case One: Swap last two basis vectors, make corresponding changes }
         Mu1 := Mu[K, K - 1];
         B1 := BLength[K] + Mu1 * Mu1 * BLength[K - 1];
         Mu[K, K - 1] := Mu1 * BLength[K - 1] / B1;
         BLength[K] := BLength[K - 1] * BLength[K] / B1;
         BLength[K - 1] := B1;
         for M := 1 to N do
           begin
             Temp := B[K - 1, M];
             B[K - 1, M] := B[K, M];
             B[K, M] := Temp
           end;
         for J := 1 to (K - 2) do
           begin
             Temp := Mu[K - 1, J];
             Mu[K - 1, J] := Mu[K, J];
             Mu[K, J] := Temp
           end;
         for I := (K + 1) to N do
           begin
             Mu[I, K - 1] := Mu[K, K-1] * Mu[I, K-1] + Mu[I, K] - Mu1 * Mu[I, K] * Mu[I, K-1];
             Mu[I, K] := Mu[I, K - 1] - Mu1 * Mu[I, K]
           end;
         if K > 2 then
           K := K - 1
      end
    else
       begin              { Case Two : Find the Mu's that have to be adjusted from K-2 down }
         if K = 1 then
           K := 2
         else
           begin
         for L := (K - 2) downto 1 do
           MuAdjust(Mu, B, K, L, N);
         Finished := (K = N);
         K := K + 1
           end
      end
  until Finished;
  WriteResults(N, B, Mu, BLength)
end.      { Main Program BasisReduction }
```

program ComputePowersInAGaloisField(input, output);
{ *In many Pascal implementations, this line could read:* }
{ **program** *ComputePowersInAGaloisField (input, output, OutputFile);* }

{*Program P12: Galois Field Table* }
{*This program computes a table of the values for x**j in a Galois field GF(p,n) generated* }
{*by some irreducible polynomial x**n + an* x**(n-1) + a1*x + a0. The only bound of the* }
{*program is that n must be <= 16.Since the program produces approximately p**n-1 lines* }
{*of output,the user should be prudent in the choice of p and n.If the polynomial selected* }
{*is not only an irreducible polynomial but an indexing polynomial as well, the powers of x* }
{*will generate the entire Galois field (except for the zero element, and the table for the* }
{*entire field will be written out.* }

{*MODE OF EXECUTION:This program is designed to be executed in an interactive mode.* }

{ *INPUT: The user is prompted to enter the prime, p and then the exponent, n, for the* }
{*Galois field. Next, the irreducible polynomial is entered, term by term, beginning with* }
{*the (n-1)st term and going down to zero.* }

{ *OUTPUT: A textfile, internally named OutputFile, and externally named 'Galois Field* }
{ *Table'. Each line of the output file gives the value for a power of x, written in* }
{ *increasing order, beginning with x to the first power.* }

{*NOTE:This method is only useful for small values of p and n,at least small enough so* }
{ *that p**n - 1 is representable as an integer. As a side benefit, this program can also* }
{ *determine whether or not an irreducible polynomial is an indexing polynomial (which will* }
{*be the case if no polynomial in the table is repeated), or to determine if an arbitrary* }
{*polynomial is irreducible(if the polynomial with all zero coefficients is found in the table).* }

```
  type
    Coeffs = array[0..15] of integer;                    { An array for polynomials }
    CompMat = array[0..15, 0..15] of integer;  {Companion matrix of the irreducible poly}
  var
    Poly : Coeffs;                              { Polynomial for various powers of x}
    A : CompMat;                                     { The (nxn) companion matrix }
    i, j, p, n, size : integer;                 { p is the prime; n, the exponent }
    OutputFile : text;
{   ************************************************************************************   }

    procedure GetNewPoly (var Poly : Coeffs;
                              A : CompMat;
                              p, n : integer);
```

{*Procedure GetNewPoly left-multiplies the companion matrix, A by the current ,* }
{ *polynomial thought of as an (nx1) column matrix, producing another column matrix* }
{ *which is the new polynomial representing one higher power of x.* }

```
    var
      i, j : integer;
      temp : Coeffs;
    begin      { procedure GetNewPoly }
      for i := 0 to (n - 1) do                       { initialize a temporary polynomial}
        begin
          temp[i] := 0;
          for j := 0 to (n - 1) do  { perform the array multiplication;all multiplication is mod p}
            temp[i] := (temp[i] + A[i, j] * Poly[j]) mod p
        end;
      Poly := temp
    end;       { procedure GetNewPoly }
{   ************************************************************************************   }

    procedure PrintPoly (var Poly : Coeffs;
                             j : integer;
```

```
                          var OutputFile : text;
                          n : integer);

{Procedure PrintPoly writes the polynomial,Poly,in the form x**j=a(n-1)*x**(n-1)+a(n-2)*  }
{x**(n-2)+ ...+ a1*x + a0. The value j represents the power  of x in the above expression.  }

      var
         i : integer;
      begin      { procedure PrintPoly }
         if (j mod 10 = 1) then                              { Write a blank line every tenth }
            writeln(OutputFile);
         write(OutputFile, 'X** ', j : 3, ' = ');                        { Polynomial for x**j }
         for i := (n - 1) downto 2 do
            write(OutputFile, Poly[i] : 2, ' x**', i : 2, ' + ');
         write(OutputFile, Poly[1] : 2, ' x + ');
         write(OutputFile, Poly[0] : 2);
         writeln(OutputFile)
      end;      { procedure PrintPoly }
{  ************************************************************************************  }
begin      {Main program ComputePowersInAGaloisField}
   open(OutputFile, 'Galois Field Table');                       { Get the Galois field data. }
   writeln('This program generates the Galois Field table for the powers of X where the ');
   writeln('user supplies the prime, p, the exponent, n, and the irreducible polynomial.');
   writeln;
   writeln('Enter the prime, p:');
   readln(p);
   writeln('Enter the exponent, n:');
   readln(n);
   writeln(OutputFile, 'The Galois Field Table for GF( ', p : 2, ',', n : 2, ' )');
   writeln(OutputFile);
   for i := 0 to (n - 1) do                                  { initialize the companion matrix }
      for j := 0 to (n - 1) do
         A[i, j] := 0;
   for i := 0 to (n - 2) do
      A[i + 1, i] := 1;
   writeln('Now enter the irreducible polynomial.');
   writeln(' It is assumed that the polynomial is monic,so that the coefficient ');
   writeln(' of x**', n : 2, ' is 1.You will be prompted for each other coefficient:');
   for i := (n - 1) downto 0 do
      begin
         writeln;  writeln('Enter the coefficient of x**', i : 2, ' :');
         readln(j);
         A[i, n - 1] := (p - j) mod p      { Assign the negatives of the polynomial coefficients }
      end;                        { to the last column of the companion matrix, in ascending order }
   size := p;                            { Compute the overall size of the multiplicative group }
   for i := 1 to (n - 1) do                                        {of the Galois field, p**n - 1. }
      size := size * p;
   size := size - 1;              { Initialize the polynomial to 0x**(n-1) + ... + 0x**2 + 1x + 0. }
   for i := 0 to (n - 1) do
      Poly[i] := 0;
   Poly[1] := 1;                 { For all the other powers of x, write x**i and compute x**(i+1).}
   for i := 2 to size do
      begin
         PrintPoly(Poly, i - 1, OutputFile, n);
         GetNewPoly(Poly, A, p, n)
      end
end.      {Main program ComputePowersInAGaloisField}
```

The following output resulted from
entering the Galois field GF(3,4) with
irreducible polynomial $x^4 + x^3 + 2$.

The Galois Field Table for GF(3, 4)

X**   1 = 0 x**3 + 0 x**2 + 1 x + 0
X**   2 = 0 x**3 + 1 x**2 + 0 x + 0
X**   3 = 1 x**3 + 0 x**2 + 0 x + 0
X**   4 = 2 x**3 + 0 x**2 + 0 x + 1
X**   5 = 1 x**3 + 0 x**2 + 1 x + 2
X**   6 = 2 x**3 + 1 x**2 + 2 x + 1
X**   7 = 2 x**3 + 2 x**2 + 1 x + 2
X**   8 = 0 x**3 + 1 x**2 + 2 x + 2
X**   9 = 1 x**3 + 2 x**2 + 2 x + 0
X** 10 = 1 x**3 + 2 x**2 + 0 x + 1

X** 11 = 1 x**3 + 0 x**2 + 1 x + 1
X** 12 = 2 x**3 + 1 x**2 + 1 x + 1
X** 13 = 2 x**3 + 1 x**2 + 1 x + 2
X** 14 = 2 x**3 + 1 x**2 + 2 x + 2
X** 15 = 2 x**3 + 2 x**2 + 2 x + 2
X** 16 = 0 x**3 + 2 x**2 + 2 x + 2
X** 17 = 2 x**3 + 2 x**2 + 2 x + 0
X** 18 = 0 x**3 + 2 x**2 + 0 x + 2
X** 19 = 2 x**3 + 0 x**2 + 2 x + 0
X** 20 = 1 x**3 + 2 x**2 + 0 x + 2

X** 21 = 1 x**3 + 0 x**2 + 2 x + 1
X** 22 = 2 x**3 + 2 x**2 + 1 x + 1
X** 23 = 0 x**3 + 1 x**2 + 1 x + 2
X** 24 = 1 x**3 + 1 x**2 + 2 x + 0
X** 25 = 0 x**3 + 2 x**2 + 0 x + 1
X** 26 = 2 x**3 + 0 x**2 + 1 x + 0
X** 27 = 1 x**3 + 1 x**2 + 0 x + 2
X** 28 = 0 x**3 + 0 x**2 + 2 x + 1
X** 29 = 0 x**3 + 2 x**2 + 1 x + 0
X** 30 = 2 x**3 + 1 x**2 + 0 x + 0

X** 31 = 2 x**3 + 0 x**2 + 0 x + 2
X** 32 = 1 x**3 + 0 x**2 + 2 x + 2
X** 33 = 2 x**3 + 2 x**2 + 2 x + 1
X** 34 = 0 x**3 + 2 x**2 + 1 x + 2
X** 35 = 2 x**3 + 1 x**2 + 2 x + 0
X** 36 = 2 x**3 + 2 x**2 + 0 x + 2
X** 37 = 0 x**3 + 0 x**2 + 2 x + 2
X** 38 = 0 x**3 + 2 x**2 + 2 x + 0
X** 39 = 2 x**3 + 2 x**2 + 0 x + 0
X** 40 = 0 x**3 + 0 x**2 + 0 x + 2

X** 41 = 0 x**3 + 0 x**2 + 2 x + 0
X** 42 = 0 x**3 + 2 x**2 + 0 x + 0
X** 43 = 2 x**3 + 0 x**2 + 0 x + 0
X** 44 = 1 x**3 + 0 x**2 + 0 x + 2
X** 45 = 2 x**3 + 0 x**2 + 2 x + 1
X** 46 = 1 x**3 + 2 x**2 + 1 x + 2
X** 47 = 1 x**3 + 1 x**2 + 2 x + 1

X** 48 = 0 x**3 + 2 x**2 + 1 x + 1
X** 49 = 2 x**3 + 1 x**2 + 1 x + 0
X** 50 = 2 x**3 + 1 x**2 + 0 x + 2

X** 51 = 2 x**3 + 0 x**2 + 2 x + 2
X** 52 = 1 x**3 + 2 x**2 + 2 x + 2
X** 53 = 1 x**3 + 2 x**2 + 2 x + 1
X** 54 = 1 x**3 + 2 x**2 + 1 x + 1
X** 55 = 1 x**3 + 1 x**2 + 1 x + 1
X** 56 = 0 x**3 + 1 x**2 + 1 x + 1
X** 57 = 1 x**3 + 1 x**2 + 1 x + 0
X** 58 = 0 x**3 + 1 x**2 + 0 x + 1
X** 59 = 1 x**3 + 0 x**2 + 1 x + 0
X** 60 = 2 x**3 + 1 x**2 + 0 x + 1

X** 61 = 2 x**3 + 0 x**2 + 1 x + 2
X** 62 = 1 x**3 + 1 x**2 + 2 x + 2
X** 63 = 0 x**3 + 2 x**2 + 2 x + 1
X** 64 = 2 x**3 + 2 x**2 + 1 x + 0
X** 65 = 0 x**3 + 1 x**2 + 2 x + 0
X** 66 = 1 x**3 + 0 x**2 + 2 x + 0
X** 67 = 2 x**3 + 2 x**2 + 0 x + 1
X** 68 = 0 x**3 + 0 x**2 + 1 x + 2
X** 69 = 0 x**3 + 1 x**2 + 2 x + 0
X** 70 = 1 x**3 + 2 x**2 + 0 x + 0

X** 71 = 1 x**3 + 0 x**2 + 0 x + 1
X** 72 = 2 x**3 + 0 x**2 + 1 x + 1
X** 73 = 1 x**3 + 1 x**2 + 1 x + 2
X** 74 = 0 x**3 + 1 x**2 + 2 x + 1
X** 75 = 1 x**3 + 2 x**2 + 1 x + 0
X** 76 = 1 x**3 + 1 x**2 + 0 x + 1
X** 77 = 0 x**3 + 0 x**2 + 1 x + 1
X** 78 = 0 x**3 + 1 x**2 + 1 x + 0
X** 79 = 1 x**3 + 1 x**2 + 0 x + 0

program TransformToString (input, output);

```
{Program P13: Transform to String of Fixed Weight                               }
{The purpose of this program is to perform the standard mapping from the interval }
{[1,C(p,n)] (in Z)where this notation signifies the number of combinations of p things }
{ taken n at a time -- and  the set of bit-strings of length p and weight n. The program is }
{ meant to be demonstrative rather than practical. For a practical version of the program, }
{ a data structure called LargeInt should be created that will handle numbers of, say, 200 }
{ digits,rather than the type LongInt used here, which is not ANSI Standard Pascal data }
{ type,but in this implementation allows values of up to 2**32 - 1= 2, 147, 483, 647.This }
{ program presents two options--namely(1)to demonstrate the entire mapping and print it }
{ out, or (2) to compute the result of the mapping on a single integer in the interval. }

{ MODE OF EXECUTION: This program is designed to be executed interactively.       }

{INPUT: The user is prompted for a number p which will be the length of the output string, }
{and a number n which will be the weight of the output string(s).Then the user is prompted }
{to indicate whether the entire mapping of the interval [1,C(p,n)] to strings of length p, }
{ weight n is to be  produced, or the conversion of one or more integers in the  domain. }

{ OUTPUT: A listing is sent to the standard output, showing the  requested mappings. }

{ NOTE: A limitation of this program is that the string length must be no greater than 12. }
{  ******************************************************************************** }
    type
       StringStruct = record
           arr : packed array[1..50] of char;
           Len : integer
         end;                    { will store the string that we generate along  with its length }
       FractionPart = (top, bottom);
                                 { numerator and denominators  of combinatorial expressions }
       FactStructure = record
           arr : array[1..50, top..bottom] of LongInt;
           p : integer;                                  { array for precomputing }
           n : integer;                                  { factorials, also p and n }
           Len : integer
         end;
    var
       Fact : FactStructure;                                      { factorial array }
       s : StringStruct;                                          { target string }
       IntGiven : LongInt;                               { integer in the domain }
       i, j, k : integer;
       ch : char;
{  ******************************************************************************** }
    procedure PreComputeFactorials (var Fact : FactStructure);

{Procedure PreComputeFactorials:In order not to recompute,compute p(p-1)...(p-k+1), }
{ 1 <= k <= p Store these in Factorial array [k,top]. Also store j!,1<=j<= n in Fact[j,bottom] }

    var
       i : integer;
    begin        {procedure PreComputeFactorials}
    Fact.arr[1, top] := Fact.p;
    Fact.arr[1, bottom] := 1;
    for i := 2 to (2 + Fact.n) do
      begin
        Fact.arr[i, top] := Fact.arr[i - 1, top] * (Fact.p - i + 1);
        Fact.arr[i, bottom] := Fact.arr[i - 1, bottom] * i
      end;
```

```
    for i := (Fact.n + 2 + 1) to Fact.p do
        Fact.arr[i, top] := Fact.arr[i - 1, top] * (Fact.p - i + 1)
    end;          {procedure PreComputeFactorials}
{  ******************************************************************************  }

    function Combination (p, n : integer;
                    Fact : FactStructure) : integer;

{Function Combination finds C(p,n),using the pre-computed values in the structure Fact  }

    begin       {function Combination}
        Combination := Fact.arr[n, top] div Fact.arr[n, bottom]
    end;        {function Combination}
{  ******************************************************************************  }

    procedure ProduceString (Fact : FactStructure;
                    IntGiven : integer;
                    var s : StringStruct);

{The procedure ProduceString takes a value k in [1,C(p,n)], and walks a path in     }
{ directed graph representing the Pascal triangle as described in Figure 7.2. If, at any  }
{node representing C(p',n'),the remaining value of k is less than  or equal to C( p'-1,n'-1 ), }
{ then a 1 - bit  is adjoined to the string, k is replaced by  k - C(p'-1,n'-1), and the next  }
{ step in the path is upward and to the left . If k is greater than C(p'-1,n'-1), then a 0-bit  }
{ is adjoined,  k is not changed, and the next step in the path is upward and to the right.  }

    var
        i, j, p0, n0, temp : integer;
        C : array[0..50, 0..50] of LongInt;                 { to store values of  C(p,n) }
    begin            {procedure ProduceString}
        p0 := Fact.p;
        n0 := Fact.n;
        temp := IntGiven;
        C[p0, n0] := Combination(p0, n0, Fact);              { start with C(p0, n0) }
        j := 1;
        while (p0 > n0) and (n0 > 0) do                      { end loop with p0=n0 or n0=0 }
            begin
                C[p0 - 1, n0] := C[p0, n0] * (p0 - n0) div p0;       { C(p0-1,n0) from C(p0,n0) }
                if n0 >= 1 then
                    C[p0 - 1, n0 - 1] := C[p0, n0] * n0 div p0;      { C(p0-1,n0-1) from C(p0,n0) }
                if temp <= C[p0 - 1, n0 - 1] then
                    begin
                        s.arr[j] := '1';
                        n0 := n0 - 1
                    end
                else
                    begin
                        s.arr[j] := '0';
                        temp := temp - C[p0 - 1, n0 - 1]
                    end;
                j := j + 1;
                p0 := p0 - 1
            end;
        if p0 = n0 then                                     { if all the rest of the steps are }
            for i := j to Fact.p do                         { up and left, pad with 1-bits }
                s.arr[i] := '1'
        else
            for i := j to Fact.p do                         { if all the rest of the steps are }
                s.arr[i] := '0';                            { up and right, pad with 0-bits }
        s.Len := Fact.p
```

```
   end;      {procedure ProduceString}
{  *********************************************************************************  }
begin       {Main program TransformToString}
  writeln('Please enter the number p, corresponding to');
  writeln('to the string length. p should be <= 12:');
  readln(Fact.p);
  while (Fact.p < 1) or (Fact.p > 12) do
    begin
      writeln('Your choice of prime p is outside of the range 1..12.');
      writeln('Please re - enter. ');
      readln(Fact.p)
    end;
  writeln('Please enter n, the weight of the string:');
  readln(Fact.n);
  while (Fact.n < 0) or (Fact.n > Fact.p) do
    begin
      writeln('Your choice of weight n is outside of the range 0..', Fact.p : 3, ' . ');
      writeln('Please re - enter. ');
      readln(Fact.n)
    end;
  PreComputeFactorials(Fact);
  writeln;
  writeln;
  writeln('Now you have two options. Entering B for batch will ');
  writeln('print a table of all values from 1 to C(p,n) ');
  writeln('showing the complete mapping for');
  writeln('for these choices of p and n.');
  writeln;
  writeln('Entering I for interactive will allow ');
  writeln('you to perform one conversion ');
  writeln('at a time. You will have the ');
  writeln('opportunity of selecting several cases until');
  writeln('you terminate input with a zero.');
  writeln;
  writeln;
  writeln('****************************************************');
  writeln;
  writeln;
  writeln('Please choose B for batch or I for interactive: ');
  readln(ch);
  if (ch = 'B') or (ch = 'b') then
    begin
      writeln;
      writeln;
      writeln('*************************************');
      writeln;
      writeln;
      writeln('Given integer                 String');
      writeln('=============                 ======');
      writeln;
      writeln;
      for k := 1 to Combination(Fact.p, Fact.n, Fact) do
        begin
          ProduceString(Fact, k, s);
          writeln(k : 6, '                    ', s.arr)
        end
    end
```

```
else
  begin
    writeln('Please enter the integer to convert:');
    readln(IntGiven);
    while IntGiven <> 0 do
      begin
        if (IntGiven > 0)
          and (IntGiven <= Combination(Fact.p, Fact.n, Fact)) then
          begin
            ProduceString(Fact, IntGiven, s);
            writeln;
            writeln;
            writeln('**************************************');
            writeln;
            writeln;
            writeln('The given integer is:   ', IntGiven);
            writeln('The string is        :   ', s.arr);
            writeln;
            writeln
          end
        else
          begin
            writeln('Your choice of ', IntGiven, ' is not in the range:');
            writeln('        [ 1 , C ( ', Fact.p : 2, ', ', Fact.n : 2, ' ) ]');
            writeln('Please try again.');
            writeln
          end;
        write('Please enter the next integer to convert,');
        writeln(' or zero (0) to terminate:');
        readln(IntGiven);
        writeln
      end
  end
end.       {Main program TransformToString}
```

```
program FastExponentiation(input, output);

{This is an implementation of the so-called  FastExponentiation Algorithm, to     }
{ calculate a**m (mod n) in O(log m) time.                                        }

{Program P14:  Fast Exponentiation                                                }
{This program computes the value of a**m (mod n) by analyzing the bit string or binary }
{ representation of m.  The algorithm, described in Appendix III, computes an interim }
{ product, beginning with a = atemp, and either squaring atemp or squaring atemp and }
{ multiplying it by a, depending on whether the current bit being examined in the binary }
{ representation of m is 0 or 1. The bits of m are examined beginning with the second }
{highest bit and going down (the high bit is ignored).                            }

{ MODE OF EXECUTION: This program is designed to be executed interactively.       }

{ INPUT: The user is prompted for a integers a, m, and n  for which the expression a**m }
{ (mod n) will  be output.                                                        }

{ OUTPUT: The result is sent to the standard output.                              }

{ NOTE: A limitation of this program is that the values of a, m ,n  must be of integer data }
{ type, i.e.  <= 32,767.                                                          }
{  ***************************************************************************************** }
    var
      a, m, n, atemp, mtemp, x : integer;
                                  { a is the base; m the exponent; and n defines the modulo }
    begin        { Main program FastExponentiation }
      writeln('Please enter, in this order, the base a,');
      writeln('the exponent m, and the modulo n,');
      writeln('for the computation of a**m (mod n):');
      readln(a, m, n);
      atemp := a;
      mtemp := m;
      x := 1;                                      { value for the exponential expression }
      while mtemp <> 0 do
        begin
          while mtemp mod 2 = 0 do                  { whether the current bit is 0 or 1 }
            begin
              mtemp := mtemp div 2;                 { look at next significant bit of m }
              atemp := (atemp * atemp) mod n                              { square }
            end;
          mtemp := mtemp - 1;
          x := (x * atemp) mod n                    {  and multiply if the bit was 1 }
        end;
      writeln('The result of ', a : 5, ' ** ', m : 5, ' mod ', n : 5, ' is : ', x)
    end.        { Main program FastExponentiation }
```

Bibliography

[ANSI 84]   *ANSI National Standard Pascal Computer Programming Language*, ANS/IEEE 770X3.97–1983, Wiley-Interscience, New York, 1983.

[APPL 84]   *Macintosh Pascal Reference Manual*, Apple Computer Company, Cupertino, Calif., 1984.

[ASMU 83]   C. Asmuth and J. Bloom, "A Modular Approach to Key Safeguarding," *IEEE Trans. on Information Theory*, Vol. IT-30, 1983, pp. 208-210.

[BERL 68]   E. Berlekamp, *Algebraic Coding Theory*, McGraw-Hill, New York, 1968.

[BIRK 53]   G. D. Birkhoff and S. MacLane, *A Survey of Modern Algebra*, Macmillan, New York, 1953.

[BLAK 79]   G. R. Blakley, "Safeguarding Cryptographic Keys," *Proceedings of the National Computer Conference, 1979*, American Federation of Information Processing Societies -- Conference Proceedings, Vol. 48, 1979, pp. 313-317.

[BLAK 85]   G. R. Blakley and Catherine Meadows, "Security of Ramp Schemes," *Advances in Cryptology: Proceedings of Crypto 84*, Springer-Verlag, Berlin, 1985, pp. 242-268.

[BOON 59]   W. W. Boone, "The Word Problem," *Annals of Math.* Vol. 70, 1959, pp.207-265.

[BOSE 62]   R.C. Bose and S. Chowla, "Theorems in the Additive Theory of Numbers," *Comment. Math. Helvet.*, Vol. 37, 1962, pp. 141-147.

[BRIC 83]   Ernest Brickell, "Are Most Low Density Polynomial Knapsacks Solvable in Polynomial Time?" *Proc. 14th Southeastern Conference on Combinatorics, Graph Theory, and Computing*, 1983.

[CHOR 85]   Benny Chor and Ronald L. Rivest, "A Knapsack Type Public Key Cryptosystem Based on Arithmetic in Finite Fields," *Advances in Cryptology: Proceedings of Crypto 84*, Springer-Verlag, Berlin, 1985, pp. 54-65.

[COOK 71]   Stephen Cook, "The Complexity of Theorem-Proving Procedures," *Proc. 3rd Ann. ACM Symp. on the Theory of Computing*, Association for Computing Machinery, pp. 151-158.

[COOP 80]   R.H. Cooper, "Linear Transformaions in Galois Fields and Their Application to Cryptography," *Cryptologia* , Vol. 4, 1980, pp.184-188.

[COOP 84a]   R.H. Cooper and Wayne Patterson, "A Generalization of the Knapsack Method Using Galois Fields," *Cryptologia*, Vol. 8(4), 1984, pp. 343-347.

[COOP 84b]   R.H. Cooper, William Hyslop, and Wayne Patterson, "An Application of the Chinese Remainder Theorem to Multiple-Key Encryption in Data Base Systems," *Computer Security: A Global Challenge, Proc. of the 2nd IFIP International Conference on Computer Security, IFIP/Sec '84,* 1984, pp. 553-556.

[COPP 75]   D. Coppersmith, unpublished.

[COPP 84]   D. Coppersmith, "Fast Evaluation of Logarithms in Fields of Characteristic Two," *IEEE Trans. on Information Theory*, Vol. IT-30, 1984, pp. 587-594.

[COPP 86]   D. Coppersmith, A. M. Odlyzko, and R.Schroeppel, "Discrete Logarithms in GF(p)," *Algorithmica* Vol. 1, 1986, pp. 1-15.

[DATE 82]   C. J. Date, *An Introduction to Database Systems*, Volumes I and II, 3rd edition, Addison-Wesley, Reading, Mass., 1982.

[DEAV 80] C. A. Deavours, "How the British Broke Enigma," *Cryptologia,* Vol. 4(3), 1980, pp. 129-132.

[DEC 84] *VAX-11 Pascal Language Reference Manual,* Digital Equipment Corporation, Maynard, Mass., 1982.

[DENN 82] Dorothy E.R. Denning, *Cryptography and Data Security,* Addison-Wesley, Reading, Mass., 1982.

[DES 77] "Data Encryption Standard," FIPS PUB 46, National Bureau of Standards, Washington, January 1977.

[DESM 84] Y. Desmedt, J.-J. Quisquater, and M. Davio, "Dependance of output on input in DES: small avalanche characteristics," *Advances in Cryptology: Proceedings of Crypto 84,* Springer-Verlag, Berlin, 1985, pp. 359-376.

[DIFF 76] W. Diffie and M. E. Hellman, "New Directions in Cryptography," *IEEE Trans. on Information Theory,* Vol. IT-22, 1976, pp. 644-654.

[DIFF 77] W. Diffie and M. E. Hellman, "Exhaustive Cryptanalysis of the NBS Data Encryption Standard," *Computer* Vol. 10, 1977, pp. 74-84.

[DIFF 79] W. Diffie and M. E. Hellman, "Privacy and Authentication: An Introduction to Cryptography," *Proceedings of the IEEE,* Vol. 67, March 1979, pp. 397-427.

[ELGA 85] Taher ElGamal, "A Public Key Cryptosystem and a Signature Scheme Based on Discrete Logarithms," *Advances in Cryptology: Proceedings of Crypto 84,* Springer-Verlag, Berlin, 1985, pp.10-18.

[FEIS 73] H. Feistel, "Cryptography and Computer Privacy," *Scientific American,* Vol. 228(5), May 1973, pp. 15-23.

[FORT 85] Steven Fortune and Michael Merritt, "Poker Protocols," *Advances in Cryptology: Proceedings of Crypto 84,* Springer-Verlag, Berlin, 1985, pp.454-464.

[GARE 76] M.R. Garey and D.S. Johnson, *Computers and Intractability: A Guide to the Theory of NP-Completeness,* W.H. Freeman & Co., San Francisco, 1976.

[GIFF 85] David Gifford and Alfred Spector, "Case Study: An Electronic Banking Network," *CACM* Vol. 28(8), August 1985, pp. 797-807.

[GOLD 82] S. Goldwasser and S. Micali, "Probabilistic Encryption and How to Play Mental Poker Keeping Secret All Partial Information," *Proceedings of the 14th Symp. on the Theory of Computing*, 1982, pp. 365-377.

[HODG 83] Andrew Hodges, *Alan Turing: The Enigma*, Simon and Schuster, 1983.

[HORO 83] E. Horowitz, *Fundamentals of Programming Languages*, Computer Science Press, Rockville, Md, 1983.

[HSIA 79] David K. Hsiao, Douglas S. Kerr, and Stuart E. Madnick, *Computer Security*, Academic Press, New York, 1979.

[ISO 85] "Annual Report 1984," ISO/TC 97/SC 20/WG 2, International Standards Organization, 1985.

[JENS 75] K. Jensen and N. Wirth, *Pascal Users Manual and Report*, Springer-Verlag, Berlin, 1974.

[KAHN 67] David Kahn, *The Codebreakers*, Macmillan, New York, 1967.

[KALI 85a] Burt S. Kaliski, Ronald L. Rivest, and Alan T. Sherman, "Is the Data Encryption Standard a Group?" *Proceedings of Eurocrypt '85*, to appear.

[KALI 85b] Burt S. Kaliski, Ronald L. Rivest, and Alan T. Sherman, "Is the DES a Pure Cipher?" *Proceedings of Crypto '85*, Springer-Verlag, Berlin, 1986, pp. 212-227.

[KARN 83] E. D. Karnin, J. W. Greene and M. E. Hellman, "On Sharing Secret Systems," *IEEE Trans. on Information Theory*, Vol. IT-29, 1983, pp. 35-41.

[KNUT 69] Donald Knuth, *The Art of Computer Programming: Seminumerical Algorithms*, Volume II, Addison-Wesley, Reading, Mass., 1969.

[KONH 81] Alan Konheim, *Cryptography: A Primer*, Wiley, 1981.

[KOTH 85]   S.C. Kothari, "Generalized Linear Threshold Scheme," *Advances in Cryptology: Proceedings of Crypto 84*, Springer-Verlag, Berlin, 1985, pp. 231-241.

[LAGA 85]   J.C. Lagarias and A.M. Odlyzko, "Solving Low-Density Subset Sum Problems," *Journal of the Association for Computing Machinery*, January 1985.

[LEHM 82]   D. J. Lehmann, "On Primality Tests," *SIAM J. of Computing*, Vol. 11(2), May 1982, pp. 374-375.

[LENS 83]   A.K. Lenstra, H.W. Lenstra, Jr., and L. Lovász, "Factoring Polynomials with Rational Coefficients," *Mathematische Annalen* Vol. 261, 1982, pp. 515-534.

[LENS 85]   H.W. Lenstra, Jr., "Elliptic Curve Factorization," to appear.

[LEVE 56]   W. J. LeVeque, *Topics in Number Theory*, Volume 1, Addison-Wesley, Reading, Mass., 1956.

[LIDL 83]   Rudolf Lidl and Harald Niederreiter, "Finite Fields," *Encyclopedia of Mathematics*, Volume 20, Addison-Wesley, Reading, Mass., 1983.

[LIPT 81]   R. Lipton, "How to cheat at mental poker," *Proceedings of the AMS Short Course in Cryptography,* 1981.

[LYND 83]   R.C. Lyndon and P.E. Schupp, "Combinatorial Group Theory," Springer-Verlag, Berlin, 1983.

[MacW 78]   F.J. MacWilliams and N.J.A. Sloane, *The Theory of Error-Correcting Codes*, North Holland, Amsterdam, 1978.

[McCO 75]   N. H. McCoy, *Introduction to Modern Algebra*, Allyn and Bacon, Boston, 1975.

[McEL 83]   R.J. McEliece, "A Public Key Cryptosystem Based on Algebraic Coding Theory," *DSN Progress Report 42-44,* Jet Propulsion Laboratory, 1978, pp. 114-116.

[MERK 78]   R.C. Merkle and M.E. Hellman, "Hiding Information and Signatures in Trap-Door Knapsacks," *IEEE Transactions on Information Theory,* IT-24 (1978), 525-530.

[MEYE 82]   C. H. Meyer and S. M. Matyas, *Cryptography: A New Dimension in Computer Data Security*, Wiley, 1982.

[MORR 75]   M. A. Morrison and J. Brillhart, "A Method of Factoring and the Factorization of F_7," *Math. Comp.* Vol. 29, 1975, pp. 183-205.

[NOVI 55]   P.S. Novikov, "On the Algorithmic Unsolvability of the Word Problem in Group Theory," *Trudy Mat. Inst. Steklov* Vol. 44(143), 1955.

[ONG 84]   H. Ong, C. P. Schnorr, and A. Shamir, "An Efficient Signature Scheme Based on Quadratic Equations," *Proc. of the 16th Ann. ACM Symp. on the Theory of Computing,* ACM 1984, pp. 208-216.

[ONG 85]   H. Ong, C. P. Schnorr, and A. Shamir, "Efficient Signature Scheme Based on Polynomial Equations," *Advances in Cryptology: Proceedings of Crypto 84*, Springer-Verlag, Berlin, 1985, pp.37-46.

[PATT 75]   N. J. Patterson, "The Algebraic Decoding of Goppa Codes," *IEEE Trans. on Information Theory* , Vol. IT-21, 1975, pp. 203-207.

[PERA 85]   Rene Peralta, private communication.

[PETE 61]   W. W. Peterson, *Error-Correcting Codes*, MIT Press, Cambridge, Mass., 1961.

[POHL 78]   S. C. Pohlig and M. E. Hellman, "An Improved Algorithm for Computing Logarithms over GF(p) and Its Cryptographic Significance," *IEEE Trans. on Information Theory*, Vol. IT-24, 1978, pp. 106-110.

[POLL 84]   J. M. Pollard and C. P. Schnorr, "Solution of $x^2 + ky^2 \equiv m$ (mod n)," to appear.

[POME 85]   C. Pomerance, "The Quadratic Sieve Algorithm," *Advances in Cryptology: Proceedings of Crypto 84*, Springer-Verlag, Berlin, 1985, pp. 169-182.

[PRIC 86]   W. Price, "Progress in Security Standards," *IACR Newsletter*, Vol. 3 No. 1, January 1986, pp. 5-6.

[PURD 74]   G.B. Purdy, "A High-Security Log-in Procedure," *CACM* Vol. 18, No. 8, August 1974, pp. 442-445.

[RABI 79]   M.O. Rabin, "Digitalized Signatures and Public-Key Functions as Intractable as Factorization," *Tech. Report No. TR-212,* MIT Lab. for Computer Science, 1979.

[RIVE 78]   R.L. Rivest, A. Shamir, and L. Adelman, "A Method for Obtaining Digital Signatures and Public-Key Cryptosystems," *Communications of the Association for Computing Machinery,* Vol. 21, February, 1978, pp. 120-126.

[SCHN 84]   C. P. Schnorr and H.W. Lenstra, Jr., "A Monte Carlo Factoring Algorithm with Linear Storage," *Math. Comp.* Vol. 43, 1984, pp. 289-311.

[SHAM 80]   Adi Shamir and R. E. Zippel, "On the Security of the Merkle-Hellman Cryptographic Scheme," *IEEE Trans. on Information Theory,* Vol. IT-26(3), 1980, pp. 339-40.

[SHAM 82]   Adi Shamir, "A Polynomial Time Algorithm for Breaking the Basic Merkle-Hellman Cryptosystem," *Proceedings of the 23rd Annual Symposium on the Foundations of Computer Science (IEEE),* 145-152, 1982.

[SHAM 85]   Adi Shamir, "On the Security of DES," *Proceedings of Crypto 85,* Springer-Verlag, Berlin, 1986, pp. 280-282.

[SHAN 49]   Claude Shannon, "Communication Theory of Secrecy Systems," *Bell System Technical Journal,* Vol. 28, October 1949, pp. 656-715.

[SOLO 77]   R. Solovay and V. Strassen, "Fast Monte-Carlo Tests for Primality," *SIAM Journal on Computing,* 1977, pp. 84-85.

[TUCH 78]   W. L. Tuchman, talk presented at the National Computer Conference, June 1978.

[WAGN 85]   Neal R. Wagner and Marianne R. Magyarik, "A Public Key Cryptosystem Based on the Word Problem," *Advances in Cryptology: Proceedings of Crypto 84,* Springer-Verlag, Berlin, 1985, pp.19-36.

[WELC 82]   Gordon Welchman, *The Hut Six Story: Breaking the Enigma Codes,* McGraw-Hill, New York, 1982.

[WILL 85]   H.C. Williams, "Some Public-Key Crypto-Functions as Intractable as Factorization," *Advances in Cryptology: Proceedings of Crypto 84*, Springer-Verlag, Berlin, 1985, pp. 66-70.

Index